ULTIMATE COLLEGE SHOPPER'S GUIDE

THE ULTIMATE COLLEGE SHOPPER'S GUIDE

COMPILED BY
HEATHER EVANS AND DEIDRE SULLIVAN

CADER BOOKS

ADDISON-WESLEY PUBLISHING COMPANY, INC.

Reading, Massachusetts Menlo Park, California New York
Don Mills, Ontario Wokingham, England Amsterdam Bonn
Sydney Singapore Tokyo Madrid San Juan
Paris Seoul Milan Mexico City Taipei

We gratefully acknowledge permission to reprint material from the following:

Public Accounting Report, © 1991 Strafford Publications, Inc.;

1991 NACUBO Endowment Study: Prepared by Cambridge Associates, Inc. ©1992, National Associations of College and University Business Officers;

© September 30, 1991, *U.S. News & World Report.*

The Gourman Report, © 1989 by Dr. Jack Gourman.

Many of the designations used by manufacturers and sellers to distinguish their products are claimed as trademarks. Where those designations appear in this book and Addison-Wesley was aware of a trademark claim, the designations have been printed in initial capital letters.

Produced by Cader Books
24 W. 10th Street
New York, N.Y. 10011

Library of Congress Cataloging-in-Publication Data

Evans, Heather.
   The ultimate college shopper's guide / Heather Evans,
 Deidre Sullivan.
       p.   cm.
   Includes index.
   ISBN 0-201-60894-4
   1. Universities and colleges--United States--Evaluation--Handbooks, manuals, etc. 2. College, Choice of--United States--Handbooks, manuals, etc. I. Sullivan, Deidre A. II. Title.
LB 2331.63.E93   1992
378.73--dc20   92-450
                                                                               CIP

Copyright © 1992 by Heather Evans, Deidre Sullivan, and Cader Company Inc.

All rights reserved. No part of this publication may be reproduced, stored in a retrieval system, or transmitted, in any form or by any means, electronic, mechanical, photocopying, recording, or otherwise, without the prior written permission of the publisher. Printed in the United States of America.

Cover design by Stephen Gleason
Text design by Cader Books
Set in 12 point Times by Cader Books

1 2 3 4 5 6 7 8 9—MW—95949392
First printing, July 1992

CONTENTS

INTRODUCTION IX

ADMISSIONS 1
    SAT CHART—VERBAL   34
    SAT CHART—MATH   46
    ACT CHART   58

FINANCES 65
    BEST BUYS   34
    NUMERICAL COST CHART   46

ACADEMICS 101
    ACADEMIC STRUCTURE   103
    DEPARTMENT RANKINGS   121
        AGRICULTURE   122
        ALLIED HEALTH   124
        ARCHITECTURE AND PLANNING   130
        ART AND DESIGN   133
        BUSINESS AND MANAGEMENT   142
        COMMUNICATION   146
        EDUCATION AND SOCIAL WORK   148
        ENGINEERING AND COMPUTER   151
            SCIENCE
        HUMANITIES   157
        NATURAL SCIENCES   164
        SOCIAL SCIENCES   179
    SELECTED RANKINGS   196

STUDENT LIFE 213

DEMOGRAPHICS	215
POLITICS	227
MEDIA	242
ACTIVITIES	248
SPIRITUAL LIFE	255
CAMPUS LIFE	266
A WHEELCHAIR GUIDE	279
GAY LIFE ON CAMPUS	285

ATHLETICS 293

CAREERS 361

INDEX OF SCHOOLS 375

THE ULTIMATE COLLEGE SHOPPER'S GUIDE

INTRODUCTION

Shopping for a college is complicated business, particularly since college is major investment in your future and a major investment of any family's resources. THE ULTIMATE COLLEGE SHOPPER'S GUIDE changes the college shopping process, by revealing which schools specialize in the areas that interest you. With this book in hand, you can get a clear and objective sense of the schools that will appeal to you most—and know which schools you need to investigate more thoroughly.

Because college shopping is an important process for the whole family, this book is compiled with both students' and parents' interests in mind. We cover everything from the serious issues of costs, financial aid, academic quality, and career counseling, to the richness of student life, activities, and sports.

For many students, the hardest part of the process is simply getting to know the hundreds of fine institutions available, and narrowing the field to the most appropriate, and most exciting, schools. You will quickly discover that everyone else has a strong opinion on where you ought to go to college, but no one knows better than you exactly what you are looking for. Even with the help of family, friends, and guidance counselors, it is very hard to get a clear sense of what makes these hundreds of schools different from one another.

Traditional college guidebooks work on an A to Z format, giving a little bit of basic information about a lot of schools. These books can be useful if you already know which schools interest you—but otherwise, you can't get at most of the information that they offer. If you were in a supermarket, trying to find the product you wanted with only an alphabetical listing to guide you, you would have a pretty tough time.

INTRODUCTION

Every college in this country has something special about it, and something that makes it the right place for certain students. THE ULTIMATE COLLEGE SHOPPER'S GUIDE lets know you which schools are best at the things that interest you most, whether it's a good history department, a terrific museum, a diverse student body, a leading campus daily newspaper, a top-ranked squash team, or good food.

Unlike some publications, our purpose is not to declare that any one school is qualitatively better than another. We know that every student has his or her own needs—and for each person there is a unique list of "best schools."

We searched high and low for independent authorities who could identify the truly extraordinary in their fields. We combed academic journals for department rankings, and we found an organization that tests campus food to judge the best dining halls. We even found a disabled student who had actually visited dozens of campuses to determine which were truly accessible to wheelchair-bound students.

We've also taken fundamentally important information that you may find elsewhere, such as average SAT scores and school-by-schools costs, and put it into unique new formats that make that information easier to use. Our SAT Charts, in the Admissions chapter, are listed numerically from 800 to 200, instead of school-by-school. All you need to do is look up your scores on the chart, and you will immediately see where you would be a typical student. Of course we all know that scores are only one of the many elements that schools consider, and the scores listed here reflect only the average applicant, but for the first time you get a quick profile of schools where you readily fit.

We've done the same for tuition and room and board, listing nearly three hundred schools by their

INTRODUCTION

total cost, starting at $29,200 (Middlebury College) and going all the way down to schools that are free. If you or your family is on a tight budget, you can easily and quickly identify schools that fall within the range of what you are prepared to spend. You can also get a quick sense of the schools that offer the best financial aid values, along with finding special grants for older students and students with good grades.

For more information on any school mentioned in the book, you may contact the school directly by referring to the Index of Schools. This Index lists all schools noted in the book that offer full, four-year degree programs. You may find a few schools included in various lists that do not appear in the Index; these schools do not offer full, four-year degree programs.

For each list, we have noted the source, to give context to the selections and so that you may contact it for more information. With a few exceptions, lists are in alphabetical order rather than ranked, to emphasize that these are all schools worth a good look. When no source is indicated, that means the list was generated from our own database. Approximately 300 schools provided us with up-to-date information based on our own questionnaire. The Department of Education and other authoritative sources provided general data on all these schools, as well as basic information on those schools we were unable to reach.

In each case, we tried to select the best source within the field. All have national perspectives and monitor broad groups of schools. But none is omniscient, and each has its own idiosyncratic methods of evaluation. If a school with a year-round calendar is not a member of the Association of University Summer Sessions, for example, then it won't appear on the AUSS's list of most active summer sessions. That's why any given list may well be missing schools that are equally qualified. What we do know is that nationally-recognized independent organizations feel that every school noted in this book is worthy of special mention.

Nonetheless, this is the first edition of this book, and we welcome further input from schools, students, and anyone with special knowledge and experience in the fields covered. Our mission is to help students through the morass of information to find schools that will provide what they are looking for, and we invite the submission of any data or sources that would help us fulfill that mission more effectively.

Most of all, we hope you find this book fun, and that it excites you about the wealth of opportunities that await you in college and the many wonderful colleges that can fulfill your dreams.

ADMISSIONS

NON-TRADITIONAL ESSAY QUESTIONS

The following is a selection of some of the more unusual essay questions found on applications. (Some schools give a choice of questions, and this list does not necessarily include all of the choices offered.) In addition to giving you a sense of what to expect from different applications, you can use this list for inspiration if you are having trouble thinking of an essay topic, regardless of where you are applying.

Austin College

What do you value most in a relationship? Describe the person you feel closest to and why your relationship is so strong.

Babson College

Life is filled with embarrassing and uncomfortable moments. Please describe one of yours.
(Similar questions are posed by University of Puget Sound and DePauw University.)

College of William and Mary

Creativity is vital in all areas of intellectual endeavor. It has taken many forms throughout history, from inventions like the printing press and the computer to the novels of Jane Austen to the Great Pyramids to the philosophy of Gandhi to Einstein's theory of relativity. What creation from the past is most important to you? Or, what would you like to create? Why?

ADMISSIONS

Connecticut College

Write on one of the following:

"The most beautiful thing we can experience is the mysterious. It is the source of all true art and science."

–Albert Einstein,
"What I Believe"

"It was books that taught me that the things that tormented me most were the very things that connected me with all people who were alive, or who had ever been alive."

–James Baldwin

"Lying is done with words and also with silence."

–Adrienne Rich

"The problem with the future is that it keeps turning into the present."

–Hobbes, "Calvin and Hobbes"

"No man can know where he is going unless he knows exactly where he has been and exactly how he arrived at his present place."

–Maya Angelou

"People have to believe in their capacity to act and bring about a good result. Leaders must help them keep that enlivening belief."

–John W. Gardner,
"The Tasks of Leadership"

ADMISSIONS

DePauw University
If you could form a new political party, what issues would be included in your platform and why? Please feel free to express your opinions.

Earlham College
Chinese philosopher and founder of Taoism Lao-tse wrote, "Nothing that can be said in words is worth saying." Reflect upon Lao-tse's statement as you, at the same time, think about a particular work of literature (prose or poetry) that you admire. Compose a response to Lao-tse, drawing upon the work you have in mind.

Guilford College
If you were to come upon a drowning child, you would feel compelled to do all you could to save that child, even at grave risk to yourself. Many children throughout the world suffer from a multitude of injustices. Should we feel compelled to help? To what degree? For what reasons?

Hampshire College
You are a biologist working in the field of genetic engineering. You have succeeded in altering the productivity, nutritional value, and disease resistance of certain plants and you are now poised to begin similar research on animals. Do you proceed with this work or not, and why or why not?

Harvey Mudd College
If you could travel to any time in history where you could change the course of events, to what time period would you travel, what would you change, and why?

(Similar questions are posed by Austin College,

Hampshire College, and Trinity College.)

Hollins College
Describe what you would consider to be the perfect adventure.

Mount Holyoke College
"I am constantly hearing that the future happiness of young women's personal and professional lives depends on 'juggling' and 'balancing.' " In the midst of these circus acts is a sense of self you form here, that will lead you to what you really want to do. There is no one plan that is workable. There isn't one way of doing it that is best. But there is something to be said for passion. There is something to be said about caring deeply." —Wendy Wasserstein '71, Pulitzer Prize-winning playwright; from her commencement address, Mount Holyoke College, May 27, 1990. Reflect upon this quote in light of your own beliefs.

Occidental College
You are a newspaper, radio, or television reporter. What major story would you like to report on and why? Be creative. This story could take place in the past, present, or future.

St. Michael's College
If you could have dinner and conversation with any person, living or dead, who would he or she be, and why would you select this person?

Santa Clara University
Inevitably we come face to face with an unconscious personal prejudice. Discuss a situation in which you responded to this realization.

ADMISSIONS

University of Chicago
Resolved: "All 18-year-olds in the U.S. will be assigned to one year of national service doing work deemed necessary by the government." Argue pro or con.

University of Pennsylvania
You have just completed your three-hundred-page autobiography. Please submit page 217.
(Similar questions are posed by Drew University and Mount Holyoke College.)

University of Puget Sound
If you could declare a new holiday, what would you celebrate/commemorate? Why? How would it be observed?

University of Richmond
If you were evaluating admissions applications, what insightful, revealing, probing question would you ask? Now take a moment and answer that question as it applies to you.

University of Rochester
If you could bring only two items of sentimental value from your home to college, what would you bring and why?

Wheaton College (Massachusetts)
It is the year 2002, and you just received notice of your tenth high school reunion. On the committee list you see the name of a friend whom you haven't seen since you sweated through the college application process together in your senior year. Reflecting on how your educational, family, community, and career experiences have changed over the

years, you are motivated to write a letter to your friend and let him/her know what you've been up to the last ten years. In addition to citing the developments you are proudest of, please pay some attention to the difficulties and challenges you have faced and to some of the relationships with people you've developed.

Whittier College

Imagine your twenty-five-year Whittier reunion. Among your former classmates are several millionaires, the U.S. President, a best-selling novelist, and the discoverer of a cancer cure. Yet you are the guest of honor. Why?

Willamette University

If you were given one week free from the demands of family, job, school, and other activities simply to read, name four or five books you have not read previously that you would choose to read and explain why each would be your choice.

ADMISSIONS

RX: WRITER'S BLOCK

Schools that don't require essays:
- Albany College of Pharmacy
- Alma College
- Arizona State University
- Augustana College (Illinois)
- Biola University
- Bowling Green State University
- Canisius College
- Case Western Reserve University
- City University of New York, City College
- Concordia College
- Creighton University
- DePaul University
- Eastern Illinois University
- Fairfield University
- Indiana University
- Kansas State University
- Long Island University, C.W. Post Center
- Louisiana State University
- Marquette University
- Michigan State University
- Montana State University
- Northern Illinois University
- Pennsylvania State University
- Purdue University
- Rose-Hulman Institute of Technology
- St. Louis University
- San Francisco Conservatory of Music
- Southern Illinois University
- State University of New York, Buffalo
- Stevens Institute of Technology

ADMISSIONS

University of Alabama
University of Alaska, Fairbanks
University of Arkansas
University of Kentucky
University of Oregon
University of Tennessee
University of Washington
University of Wyoming
Utah State University
Virginia Military Institute
Virginia Polytechnic Institute and State University
Worcester Polytechnic Institute

ADMISSIONS

ONE-STOP SHOPPING

Schools that are listed on the Common Application as encouraging its use:

Alfred University
Allegheny College
The American University
Antioch College
Bard College
Bates College
Beloit College
Bennington College
Boston University
Brandeis University
Bryn Mawr College
Bucknell University
Carleton College
Case Western Reserve University
Centenary College
Centre College
Claremont McKenna College
Clark University
College of Wooster
Earlham College
Eckerd College
Elmira College
Emory University
Fairfield University
Fisk University
Fordham University
Franklin and Marshall College
The George Washington University
Gettysburg College
Goucher College
Grinnell College
Guilford College
Hamilton College
Hampden-Sydney College
Hampshire College
Hartwick College
Haverford College
Hobart and William Smith Colleges
Hood College
Johns Hopkins University
Kalamazoo College
Kenyon College
Knox College
Lafayette College
Lawrence University
Lehigh University
Lewis and Clark College
Linfield College
Macalester College
Manhattan College
Manhattanville College
Mills College
Millsaps College
Morehouse College

ADMISSIONS

Mount Holyoke College
Muhlenberg College
New York University
Oberlin College
Occidental College
Ohio Wesleyan University
Pitzer College
Pomona College
Randolph-Macon College
Randolph-Macon Woman's College
Reed College
Rensselaer Polytechnic Institute
Rhodes College
Rice University
Ripon College
Rochester Institute of Technology
Rollins College
St. Lawrence University
St. Olaf College
Salem College
Sarah Lawrence College
Scripps College
Simmons College
Skidmore College
Smith College
Southern Methodist University
Southwestern University
Spelman College
Stetson University
Susquehanna University
Swarthmore College
Texas Christian University
Trinity College (Connecticut)
Trinity University
Tulane University
Union College
Ursinus College
University of Puget Sound
University of Redlands
University of Richmond
University of Rochester
University of Southern California
University of the South
University of Tulsa
Valparaiso University
Vanderbilt University
Vassar College
Wake Forest University
Washington and Lee University
Washington College
Wells College
Wesleyan University
Western Maryland College
Wheaton College (Massachusetts)
Whitman College
Willamette University
Williams College
Worcester Polytechnic Institute

Source: Common Application, National Association of Secondary School Principals

ADMISSIONS

LESS COMMON

Additional schools that accept the Common Application:
- Birmingham-Southern College
- Campbell University
- The College of Insurance
- Colorado State University
- Concordia College
- Cornell University
- Denison University
- Drake University
- Eastern Illinois University
- Furman University
- Goshen College
- Grove City College
- Gustavus Adolphus College
- Howard University
- King College
- MacMurray College
- New School for Social Research, Eugene Lang College
- Otis/Parsons School of Art and Design
- Pratt Institute
- Purdue University
- Southern Methodist University
- Stephens College
- Stevens Institute of Technology
- Temple University
- Trenton State College
- University of Arizona
- University of Arkansas
- Virginia Polytechnic Institute and State University
- Wofford College

ADMISSIONS

PERSONALITY PLUS

Although many schools offer on-campus interviews, these often are not used formally in the admissions process since not every applicant has the opportunity to be interviewed. This list indicates schools that do consider on-campus interviews when selecting students.

Adelphi University
Albright College
Alfred University
Alma College
The American University
Augustana College (Illinois)
Augustana College (South Dakota)
Austin College
Babson College
Bard College
Barnard College
Bates College
Bennington College
Biola University
Birmingham-Southern College
Bowdoin College
Bradley University
Bryn Mawr College
Bucknell University
Carleton College
Carnegie Mellon University
Claremont McKenna College
Clarkson University
Colby College
College of the Atlantic
College of the Holy Cross
The College of Insurance
Columbia University
Connecticut College
Cornell University
Denison University
DePaul University
DePauw University
Drew University
Duquesne University
Earlham College
Eckerd College
Franklin and Marshall College
Gonzaga University
Goshen College
Guilford College
Gustavus Adolphus College
Hamilton College
Hamline University
Hampshire College
Harvard University
Harvey Mudd College

ADMISSIONS

Haverford College
Hillsdale College
Hobart and William Smith Colleges
Hollins College
Hope College
Kenyon College
King College
Knox College
Lewis and Clark College
Macalester College
MacMurray College
Marymount College Tarrytown
Middlebury College
Mount Holyoke College
Muhlenberg College
New College of the University of South Florida
New Jersey Institute of Technology
New School for Social Research, Eugene Lang College
Northeast Missouri State University
Northeastern University
Northwestern University
Ohio Wesleyan University
Otis/Parsons School of Art and Design
Pratt Institute
Presbyterian College
Reed College
Rhodes College
Rose-Hulman Institute of Technology
Rosemont College
St. Anselm College
Skidmore College
Spelman College
St. John's College
State University of New York, Stony Brook
Stephens College
Stevens Institute of Technology
Stonehill College
Temple University
Trinity University
Union College
United States Air Force Academy
United States Naval Academy
University of Alabama
University of Chicago
University of Minnesota, Morris
University of Pittsburgh
University of Puget Sound
University of Rhode Island
University of Rochester
University of Southern California
University of Tulsa
University of Wyoming
Virginia Military Institute

ADMISSIONS

Washington and
  Jefferson College
Washington and Lee
  University
Webb Institute of Naval
  Architecture
Wells College
Wesleyan University

Wheaton College (Illinois)
Wheaton College (Mass-
  achusetts)
Whitman College
Whittier College
Willamette University
Yale University

ADMISSIONS

ROLL ON

Schools with rolling admissions (applications are evaluated as soon as they are received, and applicants are notified of the school's decision within two to eight weeks):

Adelphi University
Albany College of Pharmacy
Albright College
Alma College
Arizona State University
Augustana College (Illinois)
Augustana College (South Dakota)
Biola University
Bowling Green State University
Bradley University
Campbell University
City University of New York, City College
Clemson University
The College of Insurance
College of the Atlantic
Colorado State University
Concordia College
Creighton University
DePaul University
Dickinson State University
Drake University
Duquesne University
Eastern Illinois University
Eckerd College
Florida Institute of Technology
Georgia Institute of Technology
Gonzaga University
Goshen College
Grambling State University
Gustavus Adolphus College
Hamline University
Hillsdale College
Hollins College
Hope College
Howard University
Illinois State University
Illinois Wesleyan University
Indiana State University
Indiana University
Kalamazoo College
Kansas State University
King College
Knox College
Long Island University, C.W. Post Center
Louisiana State University
Lynchburg College

MacMurray College
Marquette University
Marymount College Tarrytown
Messiah College
Michigan State University
Montana State University
New College of the University of South Florida
New Jersey Institute of Technology
Northeast Missouri State University
Northeastern University
Northern Illinois University
Ohio State University
Ohio University
Otis/Parsons School of Art and Design
Pacific Lutheran University
Pennsylvania State University
Philadelphia College of Pharmacy and Science
Pratt Institute
Presbyterian College
Purdue University
Randolph-Macon College
Rose-Hulman Institute of Technology
Rosemont College
St. Anselm College
St. John's College
St. Louis University
St. Mary's College of California
St. Michael's College
St. Olaf College
San Francisco Conservatory of Music
Santa Clara University
South Dakota School of Mines and Technology
Southern Illinois University
Spelman College
State University of New York, Albany
State University of New York, Stony Brook
Stephen F. Austin State University
Stephens College
Stevens Institute of Technology
Temple University
Texas A&M University, Galveston
Texas Tech University
Thomas Aquinas College
Thomas More College
United States Air Force Academy
United States Naval Academy
University of Alabama
University of Alaska, Fairbanks
University of Arizona
University of Arkansas

ADMISSIONS

University of California, Los Angeles
University of California, Riverside
University of Cincinnati
University of Connecticut
University of Dayton
University of Georgia
University of Houston
University of Kentucky
University of Maryland
University of Massachusetts
University of Michigan
University of Missouri
University of Montana
University of Nebraska
University of New Mexico
University of North Texas
University of Oregon
University of Pittsburgh
University of Puget Sound
University of Rhode Island
University of San Diego
University of Southern California
University of Tennessee
University of Texas
University of Tulsa
University of Utah
University of Wyoming
Utah State University
Virginia Military Institute
Virginia Polytechnic Institute and State University
Washington State University
Western Michigan University
Whittier College
Worcester Polytechnic Institute

ADMISSIONS

LEGACY LEADERS

Schools where children of alumni receive preference in admissions:

- Albany College of Pharmacy
- Albright College
- Alfred University
- Allegheny College
- The American University
- Babson College
- Bates College
- Bowdoin College
- Bucknell University
- Campbell University
- Canisius College
- Carnegie Mellon University
- Case Western Reserve University
- Claremont McKenna College
- Colby College
- Colgate University
- College of the Holy Cross
- College of William and Mary
- Colorado College
- Columbia University
- Connecticut College
- Cornell University
- Davidson College
- Denison University
- DePauw University
- Dickinson College
- Emory University
- Fairfield University
- Franklin and Marshall College

ADMISSIONS

Furman University
The George Washington University
Georgia Institute of Technology
Gonzaga University
Grove City College
Guilford College
Hamilton College
Hampden-Sydney College
Harvard University
Haverford College
Hobart and William Smith Colleges
Kenyon College
Lafayette College
Lewis and Clark College
Loyola College
Macalester College
MacMurray College
Messiah College
Michigan State University
Mount Holyoke College
Muhlenberg College
New College of the University of South Florida
Ohio Wesleyan University
Philadelphia College of Pharmacy and Science
Purdue University
Rhodes College
St. Anselm College
St. Mary's College of California
St. Michael's College
Santa Clara University
Skidmore College
South Dakota School of Mines and Technology
Southern Methodist University
Stanford University

ADMISSIONS

State University of New York, Geneseo
Stonehill College
Temple University
Trinity College (Connecticut)
Union College
University of Arizona
University of Connecticut
University of Florida
University of Massachusetts
University of Michigan
University of New Hampshire
University of Notre Dame
University of Pennsylvania
University of Rhode Island
University of Richmond
University of Rochester
University of San Diego
University of Tennessee
University of Vermont
University of Virginia
University of Washington
University of Wyoming
Utah State University
Vassar College
Virginia Military Institute
Virginia Polytechnic Institute and State University
Wake Forest University
Washington and Jefferson College
Washington and Lee University
Washington University
Wesleyan University
Wheaton College (Illinois)
Whitman College
Williams College

ADMISSIONS

SPECIALIZED POLICIES

Schools that have special admissions procedures for students over age twenty-one who are returning to school to earn an undergraduate degree:

Adelphi University
Carnegie Mellon University
City University of New York, City College
Colgate University
Creighton University
Dickinson College
Franklin and Marshall College
Kansas State University
Kenyon College
Long Island University, C.W. Post Center
Louisiana State University
Muhlenberg College
Northwestern University
Pennsylvania State University
Reed College
Rhodes College
Rosemont College
Southern Illinois University
State University of New York, Albany
Stephen F. Austin State University
Thomas More College
University of California, Riverside
University of Connecticut
University of Michigan
University of Nebraska
University of New Hampshire
University of Oregon
University of Rochester

University of Tennessee
University of Tulsa
University of Utah
University of Washington
Vassar College
Washington and Lee University
Wesleyan University

Schools that have special admissions procedures for the learning disabled:
Adelphi University
Albright College
Ohio State University
Southern Illinois University
St. Louis University
Stanford University
Texas Tech University
University of California, Santa Cruz
University of Connecticut
University of Georgia
University of Tennessee
University of Utah
University of Vermont

Schools that have special admissions policies for the physically challenged:
City University of New York, City College
St. Louis University
Stanford University
University of California, Santa Cruz
University of Chicago
University of Connecticut
University of Tennessee
University of Utah

ADMISSIONS

MOST COMPETITIVE

Schools that accept the smallest percentage of applicants:

1. United States Coast Guard Academy — 11%
2. United States Naval Academy — 12%
3. United States Military Academy — 14%
4. Juilliard School — 16%
5. Princeton University — 17%
6. United States Air Force Academy — 17%
7. Harvard University — 17%
8. Cooper Union for the Advancement of Science and Art — 20%
9. Amherst College — 20%
10. Stanford University — 20%
11. University of California, Irvine — 21%
12. Yale University — 22%
13. Brown University — 23%
14. United States Merchant Marine Academy — 25%
15. Rice University — 25%
16. Dartmouth College — 27%
17. University of Virginia — 28%
18. Georgetown University — 29%
19. Williams College — 29%
20. California Institute of Technology — 30%
21. Washington and Lee University — 30%
22. Cornell University — 31%
23. California Polytechnic State University — 31%
24. Massachusetts Institute of Technology — 32%
25. Bates College — 32%

ADMISSIONS

LEAST COMPETITIVE

Schools that accept over 85% of applicants:
- Augustana College (South Dakota)
- Baylor University
- Bradley University
- Catholic University of America
- Clarkson University
- Colorado School of Mines
- Concordia College
- Creighton University
- Dickinson State University
- Drake University
- Drexel University
- Goshen College
- Hope College
- Iowa State University
- Kalamazoo College
- Louisiana State University
- Milwaukee School of Engineering
- St. Louis University
- South Dakota School of Mines and Technology
- Stephens College
- Texas A&M University
- University of Arkansas
- University of Idaho
- University of Mississippi
- University of Nebraska
- University of North Dakota
- University of Oklahoma
- University of Oregon
- University of Texas, El Paso
- University of Tulsa

ADMISSIONS

University of Wyoming
Utah State University
Valparaiso University
Washington and Jefferson College
Wells College

MOST POPULAR

Schools that receive the most applications:
  Boston University
  Cornell University
  Michigan State University
  Ohio State University
  Pennsylvania State University
  Purdue University
  Rutgers, The State University of New Jersey
  University of Arizona
  University of California, Berkeley
  University of California, Los Angeles
  University of California, San Diego
  University of California, Santa Barbara
  University of Michigan
  University of Virginia
  Virginia Polytechnic Institute and State University

ADMISSIONS

LATE ARRIVALS

Schools that admit the largest number of transfer applicants:
- Arizona State University
- Georgia State University
- Illinois State University
- New College of the University of South Florida
- Northern Illinois University
- Ohio State University
- Southern Illinois University
- University of California, Los Angeles
- University of Hawaii
- University of Houston
- University of Iowa
- University of Maryland
- University of Minnesota
- University of North Texas
- University of Texas, Arlington

ADMISSIONS

WELCOME ABOARD

Schools that admit over 80% of transfer applicants:
- Bradley University
- Case Western Reserve University
- Colorado State University
- Goshen College
- Hillsdale College
- Indiana State University
- Long Island University, C.W. Post Center
- Montana State University
- Northeastern University
- Purdue University
- St. John's College
- St. Louis University
- Stephen F. Austin State University
- Temple University
- Texas A&M University, Galveston
- University of Alabama
- University of Houston
- University of Montana
- University of Nebraska
- University of Tulsa
- University of Utah
- Utah State University
- Wells College

ADMISSIONS

BAR THE GATES

Schools that admit the smallest number of transfer applicants:
- Agnes Scott College
- Bowdoin College
- California Institute of Technology
- Carleton College
- Davidson College
- Duke University
- Haverford College
- Marlboro College
- Princeton University
- St. John's College
- Swarthmore College
- University of Judaism, Lee College
- Washington and Lee University
- Webb Institute of Naval Architecture
- Williams College

Schools that admit the lowest percentage of transfer applicants:
- California Institute of Technology
- Carleton College
- Columbia University
- Davidson College
- Fairfield University
- Harvard University
- Haverford College
- Juilliard School
- Pacific Lutheran University
- Philadelphia College of Pharmacy and Science
- Washington and Lee University
- Williams College

ADMISSIONS

TOP CHOICES

Schools where more than 70% of those accepted enroll:
- Brigham Young University
- Christian Brothers University
- Dickinson State University
- Gallaudet University
- Georgia State University
- Harvard University
- Juilliard School
- New Mexico State University
- Oregon State University
- Otis/Parsons School of Art and Design
- South Dakota School of Mines and Technology
- Texas Tech University
- Thomas Aquinas College
- United States Air Force Academy
- United States Military Academy
- United States Naval Academy
- University of Arkansas
- University of California, Irvine
- University of Minnesota
- University of Montana
- University of New Mexico
- University of North Dakota
- University of North Texas
- University of Texas, El Paso
- University of Utah
- Utah State University
- Webb Institute of Naval Architecture
- Willamette University

ADMISSIONS

SAFETIES

Schools where fewer than 30% of those accepted enroll:
- Dickinson College
- Denison University
- Drew University
- Fairfield University
- GMI Engineering and Management Institute
- Lewis and Clark College
- Muhlenberg College
- Oglethorpe University
- Rensselaer Polytechnic Institute
- Rose-Hulman Institute of Technology
- Skidmore College
- State University of New York, Albany
- Stevens Institute of Technology
- Stonehill College
- University of California, Riverside
- University of California, Santa Cruz
- University of Rochester
- Washington University

ADMISSIONS

DON'T TEST US

Schools that do not require either the SAT or the ACT for admission:
- Bard College
- Bates College
- Bowdoin College
- College of the Atlantic
- Franklin and Marshall College
- Hampshire College
- Juilliard School
- Lewis and Clark College
- Ohio State University
- St. John's College
- Union College
- University of Arkansas
- University of Puerto Rico
- Wheaton College (Massachusetts)

SAT CHART—VERBAL

SAT scores are only one of many elements that schools consider when selecting candidates for admission. This chart lists mean scores only. Therefore, each of these schools admitted numerous applicants with scores far lower (and far higher) than the figures listed here.

Certain schools have a policy of supplying only a range of SAT scores, representing the middle 50% of students accepted. A list of these schools and their middle ranges follows the main list (see page 44). For ease of reference, these schools also appear below and are marked with an asterisk. In these cases, the number listed is the midpoint of the supplied range.

Mean verbal SAT scores of students accepted:

Harvard University*	670
Yale University*	660
California Institute of Technology	650
New College of the University of South Florida	646
Williams College	646
Amherst College	642
Bryn Mawr College	640
Pomona College	640
Princeton University	640
Rice University	640
Swarthmore College	639
Vassar College	634
Columbia University*	630
Harvey Mudd College	630

ADMISSIONS

University of Chicago*	630
Wesleyan University	630
Reed College	627
Massachusetts Institute of Technology	625
Duke University	624
Dartmouth College	620
Haverford College*	620
Webb Institute of Naval Architecture	620
St. John's College*	615
Tufts University	614
Oberlin College	611
Brown University	610
Grinnell College	609
Macalester College*	605
Johns Hopkins University	603
Brandeis University	600
Claremont McKenna College (median)	600
University of Nevada	600
Wellesley College	600
College of William and Mary	593
Georgetown University	591
University of Pennsylvania	591
Bates College	590
Davidson College	590
Rhodes College*	585
Northwestern University	583
Sarah Lawrence College	580
Smith College	580
University of Notre Dame*	580
Trinity University	578
University of Virginia	573
Boston College	570
Carnegie Mellon University	570

ADMISSIONS

Columbia University, School of Engineering	570
Drew University	570
Hamilton College*	570
Hampshire College	570
Vanderbilt University	569
Yeshiva University	568
United States Air Force Academy	566
United States Military Academy	566
Emory University*	565
University of California, Berkeley*	565
Washington University*	565
Scripps College	564
Cooper Union for the Advancement of Science and Art (engineering only)	560
Earlham College*	560
The George Washington University	560
Lafayette College*	560
New School for Social Research, Eugene Lang College	560
Trinity College (Connecticut)	560
Wheaton College (Illinois)*	560
United States Coast Guard Academy	558
University of the South	558
Marlboro College	556
State University of New York College of Arts and Sciences, Geneseo	556
University of Richmond*	555
Furman University	554
Bucknell University*	553
Tulane University	552
Bennington College	550
Dickinson College*	550
Rutgers, The State University of New Jersey	550

ADMISSIONS

Syracuse University	550
Thomas Aquinas College	550
University of Minnesota, Morris	550
Boston University	546
DePauw University*	545
Georgia Institute of Technology	541
Oglethorpe University	541
University of Florida	541
Colorado School of Mines	540
Goucher College	540
Illinois Institute of Technology	540
Rose-Hulman Institute of Technology	540
Stevens Institute of Technology	540
University of Michigan*	540
Wells College*	540
State University of New York, Binghamton	535
Agnes Scott College	533
Illinois Wesleyan University	533
University of California, San Diego	532
Alfred University*	530
The American University	530
Gettysburg College	530
Hamline University	530
Lewis and Clark College*	530
Mills College	530
St. Olaf College	530
University of Rochester*	530
Mary Washington College	529
University of Miami	529
United States Merchant Marine Academy	528
College of the Atlantic	527
University of North Carolina	527
University of Tulsa	527

ADMISSIONS

Trenton State College	526
Fordham University	525
Birmingham-Southern College	524
Hobart and William Smith Colleges	523
University of California, Los Angeles	523
New Mexico Institute of Mining and Technology	522
Clark University	520
Clarkson University	520
Cornell University	520
GMI Engineering and Management Institute	520
Gustavus Adolphus College	520
Kalamazoo College*	520
Ohio Wesleyan University	520
Texas Christian University	520
University of Illinois	520
Eckerd College	519
State University of New York, Albany	518
Florida State University	517
Grove City College	517
Villanova University	516
Rhode Island School of Design	515
University of California, Santa Cruz	515
University of Texas	513
James Madison University	512
Loyola College	511
Messiah College	511
Bradley University	510
Denison University	510
Drake University	510
Florida Institute of Technology	510
Hillsdale College	510
Rollins College	510

ADMISSIONS

State University of New York, Buffalo	510
University of Scranton	510
Washington and Jefferson College	510
Auburn University	509
Fairfield University	509
Pepperdine University	508
University of Colorado	508
University of Puget Sound	508
Valparaiso University	507
Alma College	506
Catholic University of America	506
University of Judaism, Lee College	506
University of Georgia	505
University of Maryland*	505
University of Southern California*	505
Muhlenberg College	504
Stetson University	503
Pennsylvania State University	502
Pacific Lutheran University	501
University of California, Davis	501
University of New Hampshire	501
University of Wisconsin	501
Ursinus College	501
City University of New York, Queens College	500
Gonzaga University	500
Loyola University	500
Ohio University	500
Presbyterian College	500
Santa Clara University*	500
Wheaton College (Massachusetts)	500
Wofford College*	500
DePaul University	498

ADMISSIONS

Hollins College	498
San Francisco Conservatory of Music	498
Austin College	497
Randolph-Macon Woman's College	497
University of California, Santa Barbara	496
Allegheny College*	495
Hampden-Sydney College	495
St. Michael's College*	494
University of Dayton	493
University of Tennessee	493
University of Vermont	492
Drexel University	491
Concordia College	490
Providence College	490
Rosemont College	490
Adelphi University	489
St. Mary's College of California	489
Widener University	489
Indiana University of Pennsylvania	488
Marquette University	488
University of Connecticut	488
Christian Brothers University	486
North Carolina State University	486
University of Delaware	486
Duquesne University*	485
Manhattan College	485
Virginia Military Institute	485
Goshen College	484
University of Pittsburgh	484
Texas A&M University	483
St. Anselm College	482
University of San Diego	482
University of Minnesota	481

ADMISSIONS

Randolph-Macon College*	480
Hawaii Pacific University	479
Whittier College	479
Philadelphia College of Pharmacy and Science	476
Rochester Institute of Technology	476
Hofstra University	475
Milwaukee School of Engineering	475
St. Louis University*	475
University of Washington*	475
Clemson University	474
Canisius College	472
Colorado State University	470
Spelman College	470
Stonehill College	470
University of Kentucky	470
University of Denver	469
Michigan State University	468
University of Maine	468
The Citadel	467
Florida Atlantic University	467
Purdue University	467
Texas A&M University, Galveston	467
Indiana University	466
Temple University	466
University of California, Irvine	466
Bloomsburg University of Pennsylvania	465
New Jersey Institute of Technology	465
University of Arizona	465
King College	462
Ohio State University	461
University of Idaho	461
University of North Texas	460

ADMISSIONS

California Polytechnic State University	458
Hahnemann University/School of Health Science & Humanities	458
Stephen F. Austin State University	458
University of South Carolina	457
Otis/Parsons School of Art and Design	456
Hartwick College*	455
University of California, Riverside	455
University of Houston	455
Biola University	454
Bryant College	453
University of Alaska, Fairbanks	453
Bowling Green State University	451
University of Rhode Island	451
Iowa State University	450
Montana State University	450
Stephens College	450
Thomas More College	450
University of Louisville	450
University of New Mexico	450
University of Wyoming	449
Arizona State University	448
University of Wisconsin, Milwaukee	447
Northeastern University	445
Oregon State University	445
University of Alabama	445
University of the Pacific	445
University of Hawaii	444
West Virginia University	444
Albany College of Pharmacy	442
State University of New York, Stony Brook	435
St. John's University (New York)	432
Fairleigh Dickinson University	430

ADMISSIONS

Kent State University	430
Marymount College Tarrytown	430
Georgia State University	428
Pace University	428
University of Texas, Arlington	428
Howard University	427
Lynchburg College*	425
Long Island University, C.W. Post Center	424
Fisk University	422
Campbell University	420
Sacred Heart University	420
Pratt Institute	416
University of Bridgeport	416
Texas Tech University	414
Willamette University	395
California State University, Long Beach	387

ADMISSIONS

This range of scores reflects the middle 50% of all students accepted:

Harvard University	620-720
Yale University	610-710
Columbia University	590-670
University of Chicago	570-690
Haverford College	570-670
St. John's College	570-660
Macalester College	550-660
University of Notre Dame	540-620
Bucknell University	530-575
Rhodes College	530-640
Hamilton College	520-620
Emory University	520-610
University of Richmond	510-600
Washington University	510-620
Wheaton College (Illinois)	510-610
Lafayette College	500-620
Dickinson College	500-600
University of California, Berkeley	490-640
Earlham College	490-630
Wells College	490-590
DePauw University	480-610
University of Michigan	480-600
Alfred University	480-580
Lewis and Clark College	480-580
University of Rochester	470-590
Albright College	470-570
Kalamazoo College	470-570
University of Southern California	450-560
Santa Clara University	450-550
University of Maryland	445-565
St. Michael's College	445-542

ADMISSIONS

Wofford College	440-560
Allegheny College	440-550
Randolph-Macon College	440-520
Duquesne University	420-550
Hartwick College	410-500
Lynchburg College	400-449
St. Louis University	410-540
University of Washington	410-540

ADMISSIONS

SAT CHART—MATH

SAT scores are only one of many elements that schools consider when selecting candidates for admission. This chart lists mean scores only. Therefore, each of these schools admitted numerous applicants with scores far lower (and far higher) than the figures listed here.

Certain schools have a policy of supplying only a range of SAT scores, representing the middle 50% of students accepted. A list of these schools and their ranges follows the main list (see page 56). For ease of reference, these schools also appear below and are marked with an asterisk. In these cases, the number listed is the midpoint of the supplied range.

Mean math SAT scores of students accepted:

California Institute of Technology	750
Harvey Mudd College	740
Massachusetts Institute of Technology	735
Cooper Union for the Advancement of Science and Art (engineering only)	720
Columbia University, School of Engineering	710
Webb Institute of Naval Architecture	710
Yale University*	708
Harvard University*	700
Princeton University	700
Pomona College	690
Rice University	690
University of Notre Dame*	685
Johns Hopkins University	684
Duke University	682
Dartmouth College	680

ADMISSIONS

Amherst College	678
University of Pennsylvania	677
Williams College	676
Swarthmore College	673
Tufts University	673
Brown University	670
University of Chicago*	670
Columbia University*	665
Stevens Institute of Technology	665
Claremont McKenna College (median)	660
Haverford College*	660
Rose-Hulman Institute of Technology	660
Wesleyan University	660
United States Air Force Academy	658
Georgia Institute of Technology	655
Northwestern University	654
New College of the University of South Florida	653
Carnegie Mellon University	650
University of California, Berkeley*	650
University of Minnesota, Morris	650
Vassar College	649
United States Military Academy	647
College of William and Mary	645
Reed College	645
University of Richmond*	645
United States Coast Guard Academy	643
University of Virginia	641
Bates College	640
Colorado School of Mines	640
Davidson College	640
Illinois Wesleyan University	640
Wellesley College	640

Georgetown University	639
Oberlin College	638
Vanderbilt University	638
Grinnell College	636
GMI Engineering and Management Institute	635
University of Michigan*	635
Boston College	630
Bryn Mawr College	630
Bucknell University*	630
Clarkson University	630
Emory University*	630
Hamilton College*	630
Rhodes College*	630
Washington University*	630
Trinity University	628
University of California, Los Angeles	626
Yeshiva University	626
Lafayette College*	625
Macalester College*	625
Brandeis University	620
Rutgers, The State University of New Jersey	620
Trinity College (Connecticut)	620
University of Rochester*	620
State University of New York College of Arts and Sciences, Geneseo	617
University of California, San Diego	617
University of Florida	615
University of Illinois	611
DePauw University*	610
State University of New York, Binghamton	610
Wheaton College (Illinois)*	610
State University of New York, Albany	607
New Mexico Institute of Mining and Technology	603

ADMISSIONS

Tulane University	603
Drew University	600
The George Washington University	600
Smith College	600
State University of New York, Buffalo	600
Boston University	599
New Jersey Institute of Technology	597
United States Merchant Marine Academy	597
Dickinson College*	595
University of the South	595
University of Maryland*	593
Gettysburg College	592
San Francisco Conservatory of Music	592
Trenton State College	592
Villanova University	592
University of Miami	591
University of Texas	591
St. John's College*	590
Scripps College	590
Skidmore College	590
Syracuse University	590
University of Southern California*	590
University of Wisconsin	589
The American University	587
Grove City College	587
University of California, Davis	587
University of North Carolina	584
University of Colorado	583
Pennsylvania State University	581
Albright College*	580
Alfred University*	580
Bradley University	580
Denison University	580

ADMISSIONS

Florida Institute of Technology	580
Florida State University	580
Gustavus Adolphus College	580
Hamline University	580
James Madison University	580
Kalamazoo College*	580
Oglethorpe University	580
Ohio Wesleyan University	580
St. Olaf College	580
Santa Clara University*	580
Auburn University	579
University of California, Santa Barbara	579
Muhlenberg College	578
Earlham College*	575
University of Tulsa	575
City University of New York, Queens College	570
Fairfield University	570
Sarah Lawrence College	570
Willamette University	570
Hobart and William Smith Colleges	568
Pepperdine University	568
University of California, Irvine	568
Furman University	567
Mary Washington College	567
North Carolina State University	567
Alma College	566
Drexel University	565
Loyola College	565
Rochester Institute of Technology	565
University of New Hampshire	565
Ursinus College	565
Milwaukee School of Engineering	563

ADMISSIONS

Stetson University	562
College of the Atlantic	561
Valparaiso University	561
Clark University	560
Cornell University	560
Eckerd College	560
Goucher College	560
Hampshire College	560
Lewis and Clark College*	560
Rollins College	560
Thomas Aquinas College	560
University of Scranton	560
University of California, Santa Cruz	559
University of Dayton	558
University of Minnesota	558
University of Puget Sound	558
University of Vermont	558
Texas A&M University	557
Allegheny College*	555
University of Georgia	555
Wofford College*	555
Bryant College	554
Clemson University	554
Hampden-Sydney College	554
Purdue University	554
University of Connecticut	552
University of Delaware	552
Austin College	551
Fordham University	550
Hofstra University	550
Illinois Institute of Technology	550
Manhattan College	550
Philadelphia College of Pharmacy and Science	550

ADMISSIONS

Presbyterian College	550
Providence College	550
Rhode Island School of Design	550
Texas Christian University	550
Thomas More College	550
University of Nevada	550
Washington and Jefferson College	550
Albany College of Pharmacy	549
Marquette University	548
University of California, Riverside	548
DePaul University	547
Catholic University of America	546
Birmingham-Southern College	545
University of Washington*	545
Virginia Military Institute	545
Wells College*	545
Agnes Scott College	544
Messiah College	544
Concordia College	540
Drake University	540
Florida Atlantic University	540
Hillsdale College	540
New School for Social Research, Eugene Lang College	540
Pacific Lutheran University	540
University of Pittsburgh	540
St. Michael's College*	538
California Polytechnic State University	536
University of San Diego	536
Colorado State University	535
State University of New York, Stony Brook	535
Indiana University	534
Indiana University of Pennsylvania	533

ADMISSIONS

Goshen College	511
Hollins College	511
University of North Texas	511
University of South Carolina	511
Gonzaga University	510
Ohio University	510
Randolph-Macon Woman's College	510
University of Idaho	510
University of New Mexico	510
Temple University	509
Texas A&M University, Galveston	508
University of Bridgeport	508
West Virginia University	507
Pace University	506
Duquesne University*	505
Hartwick College*	505
Biola University	504
Northeastern University	504
King College	503
University of Alabama	499
University of Wisconsin, Milwaukee	498
Pratt Institute	497
St. John's University (New York)	496
Bowling Green State University	494
Rosemont College	490
Spelman College	490
Hawaii Pacific University	488
University of Judaism, Lee College	484
University of Alaska, Fairbanks	481
University of Texas, Arlington	480
Hahnemann University/School of Health Science & Humanities	473
Campbell University	470

ADMISSIONS

Canisius College	532
St. Mary's College of California	531
Bennington College	530
Iowa State University	530
Loyola University	530
Marlboro College	530
Michigan State University	530
Montana State University	530
Wheaton College (Massachusetts)	530
Christian Brothers University	529
University of Cincinnati	528
Bloomsburg University of Pennsylvania	526
Ohio State University	526
University of Denver	526
Lynchburg College*	525
The Citadel	524
University of Arizona	524
University of Tennessee	524
University of Maine	523
Adelphi University	522
Mills College	520
Randolph-Macon College*	520
St. Louis University*	520
Stonehill College	520
University of Kentucky	520
St. Anselm College	519
Whittier College	518
University of the Pacific	515
University of Wyoming	515
University of Houston	514
Oregon State University	513
Arizona State University	512
University of Rhode Island	512

ADMISSIONS

Otis/Parsons School of Art and Design	470
Texas Tech University	468
Long Island University, C.W. Post Center	463
Georgia State University	462
Kent State University	461
Howard University	460
Marymount College Tarrytown	460
California State University, Long Beach	459
Fairleigh Dickinson University	458
University of Hawaii	452
Stephens College	450
University of Louisville	450
Fisk University	447
Sacred Heart University	441
Widener University	429
Stephen F. Austin State University	418

ADMISSIONS

This range of scores reflects the middle 50% of all students accepted:

Yale University	660-750
Harvard University	650-750
University of Notre Dame	650-720
University of Chicago	620-720
Columbia University	610-720
Haverford College	610-710
University of Richmond	600-690
Bucknell University	590-670
Washington University	590-670
University of California, Berkeley	580-720
Emory University	580-680
Hamilton College	580-680
Rhodes College	580-680
University of Michigan	570-700
Lafayette College	570-680
Macalester College	570-680
University of Rochester	560-680
Wheaton College (Illinois)	560-660
DePauw University	550-670
Dickinson College	550-640
St. John's College	530-650
University of Southern California	530-650
Albright College	530-630
Santa Clara University	530-630
University of Maryland	525-660
Kalamazoo College	520-640
Alfred University	510-650
Earlham College	510-640
Lewis and Clark College	500-620
Allegheny College	500-610
Wofford College	500-610

ADMISSIONS

Lynchburg College	500-549
Wells College	490-580
St. Michael's College	482-594
University of Washington	470-620
Randolph-Macon College	470-570
Hartwick College	450-560
St. Louis University	440-600
Duquesne University	440-570

ADMISSIONS

ACT CHART

ACT scores are only one of many elements that schools consider when selecting candidates for admission. This chart lists mean scores only. Therefore, each of these schools admitted numerous applicants with scores far lower (and higher) than the figures listed here.

Certain schools have a policy of supplying only a range of ACT scores, representing the middle 50% of students accepted. A list of these schools and their middle ranges follows the main list (see page 63). For ease of reference, these schools also appear below and are marked with an asterisk. In these cases, the number listed is the midpoint of the supplied range.

ACT composite scores of students accepted:

Rose-Hulman Institute of Technology	32
Amherst College	30
Johns Hopkins University	30
Reed College	30
University of Pennsylvania	30
Wells College*	30
Wesleyan University	30
Williams College	30
New College of the University of South Florida	29
Northwestern University	29
University of Chicago*	29
Macalester College*	28.5
Brown University	28
Carnegie Mellon University	28

ADMISSIONS

Claremont McKenna College (median)	28
New School for Social Research, Eugene Lang College	28
Trinity University	28
Washington University*	28
Case Western Reserve University*	27.5
Rhodes College*	27.5
Colorado School of Mines	27
Emory University*	27
The George Washington University	27
Illinois Wesleyan University	27
State University of New York College of Arts and Sciences, Geneseo	27
Union College	27
University of Michigan*	27
University of Richmond*	27
University of Rochester*	27
Wheaton College (Illinois)*	27
Earlham College*	26.5
Kalamazoo College*	26.5
Birmingham-Southern College	26
Brigham Young University	26
Grove City College	26
Skidmore College	26
State University of New York, Buffalo	26
Trinity College (Connecticut)	26
University of Minnesota, Morris	26
Willamette University	26
DePauw University*	25.5
Lewis and Clark College*	25.5
Northeast Missouri State University	25.5
Alfred University*	25
Alma College	25

ADMISSIONS

The American University	25
Bennington College	25
Bryant College	25
Christian Brothers University	25
College of the Atlantic	25
The College of Insurance	25
Drake University	25
Hamline University	25
Hobart and William Smith Colleges	25
Illinois Institute of Technology	25
Iowa State University	25
Marquette University	25
South Dakota School of Mines and Technology	25
Southern Methodist University	25
Thomas Aquinas College	25
University of Puget Sound	25
University of Tulsa	25
University of Utah*	25
Eckerd College	24.7
University of Missouri	24.6
University of Washington*	24.5
DePaul University	24.2
Agnes Scott College	24
Allegheny College*	24
Auburn University	24
Augustana College (South Dakota)	24
Austin College	24
Bradley University	24
Canisius College	24
Colorado State University	24
Creighton University	24
Hampden-Sydney College	24

ADMISSIONS

Hawaii Pacific University	24
Hope College*	24
Indiana University	24
Purdue University	24
St. Louis University*	24
University of Dayton	24
University of Iowa	24
University of Texas	24
University of Tennessee	23.3
University of Alabama	23.2
Biola University	23
The Citadel	23
Hillsdale College	23
Hofstra University	23
Kansas State University	23
Louisiana State University	23
Ohio State University	23
Ohio University	23
Texas A&M University, Galveston	23
University of Arizona	23
University of Arkansas	23
University of Cincinnati	23
University of California, Riverside	23
University of Kansas	23
University of Nebraska	23
University of North Texas	23
University of Oklahoma	23
University of Rhode Island	23
Washington and Jefferson College	23
King College	22.8
University of Wyoming	22.6
Hollins College	22.5
Bowling Green State University	22.4

ADMISSIONS

Western Michigan University	22.3
Northern Illinois University	22.1
Arizona State University	22
Central Michigan University	22
Duquesne University	22
Illinois State University	22
Montana State University	22
Oklahoma State University	22
Oral Roberts University	22
Southern Illinois University	22
University of Houston	22
University of Mississippi	22
Virginia Military Institute	22
Wheaton College (Massachusetts)	22
Utah State University	21.9
Thomas More College	21.1
Northeastern University	21
Stephen F. Austin State University	21
Stephens College	21
University of North Dakota	21
Eastern Illinois University	20
MacMurray College	20
Tennessee State University	20
California State University, Long Beach	19
Dickinson State University	19
University of Alaska, Fairbanks	19
Idaho State University	18
New Mexico State University	18
Grambling State University	16

ADMISSIONS

This range of scores reflects the middle 50% of all students accepted:

Wells College	27-33
University of Chicago	27-31
Macalester College	27-30
Washington University	26-30
Case Western Reserve University	25-30
Rhodes College	25-30
Emory University	25-29
University of Michigan	25-29
University of Richmond	25-29
University of Rochester	25-29
Wheaton College (Illinois)	25-29
Earlham College	24-29
Kalamazoo College	24-29
Lewis and Clark College	24-27
DePauw University	23-28
Alfred University	23-27
University of Utah	23-27
University of Washington	22-27
Allegheny College	21-27
Hope College	21-27
St. Louis University	21-27

FINANCES

FINANCES

FREE!

Schools without tuition:
- Cooper Union for the Advancement of Science and Art
- United States Air Force Academy
- United States Coast Guard Academy
- United States Merchant Marine Academy
- United States Military Academy
- United States Naval Academy
- Webb Institute of Naval Architecture

CHEAP

Schools with tuition under $1,200 per year (not including out-of-state additions for public universities):
- California Polytechnic State University
- California State University, Dominguez Hills
- California State University, Long Beach
- North Carolina State University
- Stephen F. Austin State University
- Texas A&M University
- Texas A&M University, Galveston
- University of Houston
- University of North Carolina
- University of Oklahoma
- University of Texas
- University of Texas, Arlington
- University of Texas, El Paso

FINANCES

BEST BUYS

KIPLINGER'S

College of William and Mary
Colorado College
Davidson College
Earlham College
Furman University
Guilford College
Hanover College
Hendrix College
Macalester College
Mary Washington College
Miami University
New College of the University of South Florida
Rice University
St. Olaf College
Trenton State College
Trinity University
University of North Carolina
University of Virginia
Wake Forest University

Source: *Kiplinger's Personal Finance Magazine*, 1991

FINANCES

KIPLINGER'S RUNNERS UP

Beloit College
Birmingham-Southern College
College of Wooster
Cornell College
Hiram College
Knox College
Millsaps College
Northeast Missouri State University
Ripon College
Southwestern University
State University of New York, Geneseo
State University of New York, Binghamton
University of California, Berkeley
University of California, Los Angeles
University of Michigan
University of Minnesota, Morris
Washington and Lee University
Whitman College

Source: *Kiplinger's Personal Finance Magazine*, 1991

U.S. NEWS & WORLD REPORT

National Universities
1. University of North Carolina
2. Rice University
3. University of Virginia
4. University of California, Berkeley
5. University of California, Los Angeles

Liberal Arts Colleges
1. Washington and Lee University
2. Davidson College
3. Grinnell College
4. Occidental College
5. Claremont McKenna College

Source: *America's Best Colleges*, U.S. News & World Report, 1991

FINANCES

NUMERICAL COST CHART

The following lists schools in descending order of total costs, which comprises tuition and room and board, using the most recent data available (most schools provided 1991-92 costs).

$29,200	Middlebury College
23,200	Bennington College
22,920	Wesleyan University
22,800	Sarah Lawrence College
22,774	Barnard College
22,485	Tulane University
22,395	New York University
22,330	Franklin and Marshall College
22,270	Boston University
22,230	Massachusetts Institute of Technology
22,215	Bard College
22,200	Yale University
22,144	Washington University
22,120	Johns Hopkins University
22,055	Tufts University
21,985	Swarthmore College
21,981	Princeton University
21,924	University of Pennsylvania
21,845	Williams College
21,810	Colby College
21,810	University of Chicago
21,760	Hampshire College
21,750	Smith College
21,660	Bowdoin College
21,642	Columbia University
21,623	Wellesley College

FINANCES

21,550	Cornell University
21,530	Oberlin College
21,510	Vassar College
21,475	Brown University
21,475	University of Southern California
21,460	Carnegie Mellon University
21,450	Connecticut College
21,400	Bates College
21,400	University of Bridgeport
21,392	Haverford College
21,390	Dartmouth College
21,300	Pepperdine University
21,262	Stanford University
21,243	Hobart and William Smith Colleges
21,242	Georgetown University
21,210	Reed College
21,200	Hamilton College
21,120	Wheaton College (Massachusetts)
21,100	Bryn Mawr College
21,082	Colgate University
21,050	Scripps College
21,040	Trinity College (Connecticut)
20,956	The George Washington University
20,950	Pomona College
20,930	Harvard University
20,900	College of the Holy Cross
20,900	University of Rochester
20,875	Skidmore College
20,850	Mount Holyoke College
20,815	Union College
20,670	Bucknell University
20,590	Lehigh University
20,580	Drew University

FINANCES

20,422	Babson College
20,395	Vanderbilt University
20,380	Harvey Mudd College
20,375	Lafayette College
20,358	The American University
20,300	Rensselaer Polytechnic Institute
20,150	Marlboro College
19,980	Dickinson College
19,970	Brandeis University
19,970	Gettysburg College
19,928	Rhode Island School of Design
19,915	Amherst College
19,890	Claremont McKenna College
19,840	Boston College
19,745	Columbia University, School of Engineering
19,700	Stevens Institute of Technology
19,660	Duke University
19,655	University of Miami
19,500	Clark University
19,494	Carleton College
19,461	Occidental College
19,375	Muhlenberg College
19,260	University of the Pacific
19,197	Northwestern University
19,136	Whittier College
19,112	Emory University
19,100	Mills College
18,958	St. John's College
18,900	Kenyon College
18,800	Hartwick College
18,850	Alfred University
18,794	New School for Social Research, Eugene Lang College

FINANCES

18,720	Allegheny College
18,668	California Institute of Technology
18,575	Worcester Polytechnic Institute
18,530	Case Western Reserve University
18,500	Syracuse University
18,494	Ohio Wesleyan University
18,385	Goucher College
18,337	University of Vermont (out of state)
18,333	Grinnell College
18,123	Lewis and Clark College
18,112	Clarkson University
18,024	Earlham College
18,000	Fairfield University
17,840	Davidson College
17,753	Hood College
17,676	St. Mary's College of California
17,650	Fordham University
17,535	Knox College
17,450	Whitman College
17,415	Albright College
17,350	University of Notre Dame
17,320	Villanova University
17,312	Rhodes College
17,311	Catholic University of America
17,200	Macalester College
17,185	Colorado College
17,123	Northeastern University
17,100	Wells College
17,090	Illinois Institute of Technology
17,058	University of Denver
17,040	Providence College
16,928	Bryant College
16,900	University of San Diego

FINANCES

16,900	Ursinus College
16,860	University of the South
16,857	Rochester Institute of Technology
16,795	Rollins College
16,784	Pratt Institute
16,722	Kalamazoo College
16,710	Marymount College Tarrytown
16,708	DePauw University
16,700	Randolph-Macon Woman's College
16,601	Washington and Lee University
16,583	University of Michigan (out of state)
16,563	Santa Clara University
16,550	University of Puget Sound
16,427	University of California, Berkeley (out of state)
16,350	Willamette University
16,320	Cornell College
16,300	Thomas Aquinas College
16,255	St. Michael's College
16,250	Antioch College
16,200	Hollins College
16,110	Eckerd College
16,077	University of California, Santa Cruz (out of state)
15,990	Pacific Lutheran University
15,975	Stephens College
15,930	Adelphi University
15,925	Juilliard School
15,910	Denison University
15,900	Trinity University
15,890	Washington and Jefferson College
15,825	Gustavus Adolphus College

FINANCES

15,801	Augustana College (Illinois)
15,800	Manhattan College
15,720	Loyola College
15,656	Hampden-Sydney College
15,600	Rose-Hulman Institute of Technology
15,511	University of California, Riverside (out of state)
15,460	Agnes Scott College
15,439	University of California, Santa Barbara (out of state)
15,425	St. Olaf College
15,396	Stonehill College
15,380	Lynchburg College
15,318	Drexel University
15,285	Randolph-Macon College
15,272	Southern Methodist University
15,255	Drake University
15,200	Florida Institute of Technology
15,181	Hamline University
15,160	St. Anselm College
14,899	College of the Atlantic
14,770	Guilford College
14,710	Illinois Wesleyan University
14,710	Widener University
14,700	Wake Forest University
14,648	Hope College
14,640	Wofford College
14,585	Rosemont College
14,560	University of Richmond
14,448	Furman University
14,410	Alma College
14,406	Fairleigh Dickinson University
14,394	Presbyterian College

FINANCES

14,375	Yeshiva University
14,313	Duquesne University
14,295	Long Island University, C.W. Post Center
14,290	St. Louis University
14,250	Oglethorpe University
14,232	Biola University
14,196	College of William and Mary (out of state)
14,190	Hillsdale College
14,120	Hofstra University
14,120	Marquette University
14,100	Canisius College
14,100	Gonzaga University
14,074	Colorado School of Mines (out of state)
14,064	Austin College
14,062	University of Scranton
14,000	The College of Insurance
13,918	DePaul University
13,855	Stetson University
13,851	University of California, San Diego (out of state)
13,840	Bradley University
13,800	Sacred Heart University
13,620	Messiah College
13,396	Loyola University
13,440	University of New Hampshire (out of state)
13,384	University of Rhode Island (out of state)
13,352	Wheaton College (Illinois)
13,330	Pace University

FINANCES

13,290	Birmingham-Southern College
13,264	Otis/Parsons School of Art and Design
13,104	Hahnemann University/School of Health Science &Humanities
13,100	Philadelphia College of Pharmacy and Science
13,010	University of California, Irvine (out of state)
13,000	University of Virginia (out of state)
12,901	Rutgers, The State University of New Jersey (out of state)
12,800	Augustana College (South Dakota)
12,790	University of Dayton
12,788	Pennsylvania State University (out of state)
12,714	University of California, Davis (out of state)
12,652	University of Pittsburgh (out of state)
12,633	California State University, Long Beach (out of state)
12,600	Rice University
12,565	University of Maryland (out of state)
12,514	Creighton University
12,513	University of Connecticut (out of state)
12,410	Valparaiso University
12,296	University of California, Los Angeles (out of state)
12,240	GMI Engineering and Management Institute
12,230	Temple University (out of state)

FINANCES

12,150	University of Tulsa
12,100	Concordia College
12,100	MacMurray College
12,040	New Jersey Institute of Technology (out of state)
12,000	Thomas More College
11,930	University of Delaware (out of state)
11,850	Milwaukee School of Engineering
11,810	Goshen College
11,734	Michigan State University (out of state)
11,675	Virginia Military Institute (out of state)
11,628	Ohio State University (out of state)
11,583	University of Cincinnati (out of state)
11,445	University of Judaism, Lee College
11,414	Miami University (out of state)
11,250	Hawaii Pacific University
11,098	University of Wisconsin, Madison (out of state)
10,990	Purdue University (out of state)
10,936	Iowa State University (out of state)
10,752	James Madison University (out of state)
10,752	University of Massachusetts (out of state)
10,750	University of Minnesota (out of state)
10,676	University of Maine (out of state)
10,675	School for International Training
10,636	University of Arizona (out of state)

FINANCES

10,572	Arizona State University (out of state)
10,570	Spelman College
10,500	Christian Brothers University
10,458	Virginia Polytechnic Institute and State University (out of state)
10,450	King College
10,378	Texas Christian University
10,292	Indiana University (out of state)
10,182	Colorado State University (out of state)
10,138	State University of New York, Binghamton (out of state)
10,134	Georgia Institute of Technology
10,132	California State University, Dominguez Hills (out of state)
10,108	Clemson University (out of state)
9,945	Ohio University (out of state)
9,905	State University of New York, Stony Brook (out of state)
9,890	University of Illinois (out of state)
9,858	State University of New York, Buffalo (out of state)
9,759	University of Washington (out of state)
9,750	Campbell University
9,737	University of Vermont
9,730	Western Michigan University (out of state)
9,605	Washington State University (out of state)
9,586	Oral Roberts University

FINANCES

9,580	Oregon State University (out of state)
9,500	Albany College of Pharmacy
9,461	University of North Carolina (out of state)
9,425	Howard University
9,422	University of Utah (out of state)
9,410	Bowling Green State University (out of state)
9,402	University of Florida (out of state)
9,400	University of South Carolina (out of state)
9,390	University of Iowa (out of state)
9,375	University of Oregon (out of state)
9,275	New College of the University of South Florida (out of state)
9,250	Tuskegee University
9,200	San Francisco Conservatory of Music
9,158	Baylor University
9,143	Trenton State College (out of state)
9,125	University of Wisconsin, Milwaukee (out of state)
9,038	Florida State University (out of state)
9,020	Kent State University
8,945	University of Missouri (out of state)
8,937	Florida Atlantic University (out of state)
8,864	West Virginia University (out of state)
8,822	North Carolina State University (out of state)
8,759	Texas A&M University, Galveston (out of state)

FINANCES

8,729	University of California, Berkeley
8,701	Indiana State University (out of state)
8,643	University of New Mexico (out of state)
8,632	Temple University
8,625	Central Michigan University (out of state)
8,615	University of California, San Diego
8,517	State University of New York, Geneseo (out of state)
8,490	University of Colorado (out of state)
8,400	New Jersey Institute of Technology
8,378	University of California, Santa Cruz
8,310	Idaho State University (out of state)
8,304	University of Alabama (out of state)
8,290	Hanover College
8,289	California Polytechnic State University (out of state)
8,216	State University of New York, Albany (out of state)
8,194	Gallaudet University
8,154	University of Georgia (out of state)
8,150	University of Nevada (out of state)
8,080	University of Pittsburgh
8,050	State University of New York Health Science Center, Syracuse (out of state)
8,048	Illinois State University (out of state)
8,034	Texas Tech University (out of state)
8,032	University of Rhode Island

FINANCES

9,580	Oregon State University (out of state)
9,500	Albany College of Pharmacy
9,461	University of North Carolina (out of state)
9,425	Howard University
9,422	University of Utah (out of state)
9,410	Bowling Green State University (out of state)
9,402	University of Florida (out of state)
9,400	University of South Carolina (out of state)
9,390	University of Iowa (out of state)
9,375	University of Oregon (out of state)
9,275	New College of the University of South Florida (out of state)
9,250	Tuskegee University
9,200	San Francisco Conservatory of Music
9,158	Baylor University
9,143	Trenton State College (out of state)
9,125	University of Wisconsin, Milwaukee (out of state)
9,038	Florida State University (out of state)
9,020	Kent State University
8,945	University of Missouri (out of state)
8,937	Florida Atlantic University (out of state)
8,864	West Virginia University (out of state)
8,822	North Carolina State University (out of state)
8,759	Texas A&M University, Galveston (out of state)

FINANCES

8,729	University of California, Berkeley
8,701	Indiana State University (out of state)
8,643	University of New Mexico (out of state)
8,632	Temple University
8,625	Central Michigan University (out of state)
8,615	University of California, San Diego
8,517	State University of New York, Geneseo (out of state)
8,490	University of Colorado (out of state)
8,400	New Jersey Institute of Technology
8,378	University of California, Santa Cruz
8,310	Idaho State University (out of state)
8,304	University of Alabama (out of state)
8,290	Hanover College
8,289	California Polytechnic State University (out of state)
8,216	State University of New York, Albany (out of state)
8,194	Gallaudet University
8,154	University of Georgia (out of state)
8,150	University of Nevada (out of state)
8,080	University of Pittsburgh
8,050	State University of New York Health Science Center, Syracuse (out of state)
8,048	Illinois State University (out of state)
8,034	Texas Tech University (out of state)
8,032	University of Rhode Island

FINANCES

8,021	New Mexico Institute of Mining and Technology (out of state)
8,002	Pennsylvania State University
8,000	Fisk University
7,985	University of Nebraska (out of state)
7,968	Northern Illinois University (out of state)
7,955	Auburn University (out of state)
7,882	University of North Texas (out of state)
7,843	Trenton State College
7,818	University of Kentucky (out of state)
7,812	University of California, Riverside
7,808	Southern Illinois University (out of state)
7,780	New Mexico State University (out of state)
7,740	University of California, Santa Barbara
7,739	The Citadel (out of state)
7,713	University of Connecticut
7,709	University of North Dakota (out of state)
7,697	University of Maryland
7,690	University of Texas (out of state)
7,686	University of Kansas (out of state)
7,683	University of Michigan
7,662	Eastern Illinois University (out of state)
7,569	University of California, Los Angeles
7,550	Indiana University of Pennsylvania (out of state)

FINANCES

7,518	University of Arkansas (out of state)
7,488	Colorado School of Mines
7,478	University of California, Davis
7,476	College of William and Mary
7,412	University of Tennessee (out of state)
7,400	James Madison University
7,391	University of Houston (out of state)
7,359	University of Wyoming (out of state)
7,310	Montana State University (out of state)
7,300	Grove City College
7,293	University of Cincinnati
7,250	University of Montana (out of state)
7,198	Bloomsburg University of Pennsylvania (out of state)
7,150	St. John's University (New York)
7,132	Rutgers, The State University of New Jersey
7,126	Tennessee State University (out of state)
7,124	Miami University
7,022	Kansas State University (out of state)
6,954	University of Idaho (out of state)
6,890	University of New Hampshire
6,818	Stephen F. Austin State University (out of state)
6,800	University of Virginia
6,780	University of Alaska, Fairbanks (out of state)
6,760	University of Delaware
6,752	University of Hawaii (out of state)

FINANCES

6,695	Utah State University (out of state)
6,687	University of Mississippi (out of state)
6,650	University of Texas, El Paso (out of state)
6,600	Ohio University
6,594	University of California, Irvine
6,588	Ohio State University
6,538	State University of New York, Binghamton
6,514	Michigan State University
6,512	University of Maine
6,480	University of Louisville (out of state)
6,480	University of Oklahoma (out of state)
6,305	State University of New York, Stony Brook
6,295	Virginia Military Institute
6,258	State University of New York, Buffalo
6,190	Idaho State University
6,168	Iowa State University
6,168	Northeast Missouri State University (out of state)
6,160	Brigham Young University (out of state)
6,150	University of Minnesota
6,138	University of Illinois
6,106	Dickinson State University (out of state)
6,050	University of Nevada
5,997	University of Wisconsin
5,953	University of Minnesota, Morris
5,940	Grambling State University (out of state)

FINANCES

5,874	Purdue University
5,862	University of Washington
5,830	Western Michigan University
5,816	State University of New York, Albany
5,785	University of Utah
5,760	Indiana University
5,752	University of Massachusetts
5,746	Bowling Green State University
5,730	Clemson University
5,708	Washington State University
5,696	West Virginia University
5,616	Georgia State University (out of state)
5,610	Virginia Polytechnic Institute and State University
5,569	Oregon State University
5,560	University of South Carolina
5,554	Texas A&M University (out of state)
5,520	South Dakota School of Mines and Technology (out of state)
5,512	University of Colorado
5,483	Indiana State University
5,479	Central Michigan University
5,478	Colorado State University
5,470	Indiana University of Pennsylvania
5,453	California State University, Long Beach
5,400	Oklahoma State University (out of state)
5,394	University of Oregon
5,337	California Polytechnic State University
5,296	University of Alabama
5,263	University of Florida
5,254	University of Wisconsin, Milwaukee

FINANCES

5,230	University of Arizona
5,225	University of Mississippi
5,191	University of Missouri
5,166	Arizona State University
5,164	Bloomsburg University of Pennsylvania
5,160	Brigham Young University
5,100	City University of New York, Queens College (out of state)
5,090	University of Nebraska
4,917	State University of New York, Geneseo
4,899	Florida State University
4,895	University of Houston
4,872	University of Iowa
4,861	New College of the University of South Florida
4,859	Montana State University
4,850	State University of New York Health Science Center, Syracuse
4,847	University of Texas, Arlington (out of state)
4,818	Louisiana State University (out of state)
4,799	Florida Atlantic University
4,799	University of Montana
4,794	Texas Tech University
4,794	University of North Carolina
4,782	University of Arkansas
4,763	Auburn University
4,753	Louisiana State University
4,710	University of Georgia
4,677	University of New Mexico

FINANCES

4,642	University of North Texas
4,616	Texas A&M University
4,601	University of North Dakota
4,578	University of Kentucky
4,576	The Citadel
4,555	University of Wyoming
4,540	Northern Illinois University
4,532	Southern Illinois University
4,500	Webb Institute of Naval Architecture
4,460	University of Tennessee
4,450	City University of New York, City College (out of state)
4,450	University of Texas
4,449	New Mexico Institute of Mining and Technology
4,448	Illinois State University
4,444	University of Idaho
4,390	Grambling State University
4,384	Northeast Missouri State University
4,350	Eastern Illinois University
4,302	University of Hawaii
4,235	Utah State University
4,180	University of Alaska, Fairbanks
4,156	North Carolina State University
4,084	New Mexico State University
4,080	University of Oklahoma
4,008	University of Kansas
3,760	Tennessee State University
3,719	Texas A&M University, Galveston
3,699	South Dakota School of Mines and Technology
3,650	Cooper Union for the Advancement of Science and Art

FINANCES

3,578	Stephen F. Austin State University
3,556	Dickinson State University
3,530	University of Texas, El Paso
3,521	Oklahoma State University
3,308	Kansas State University
3,240	University of Louisville
3,227	University of Texas, Arlington
2,752	California State University, Dominguez Hills
1,850	City University of New York, City College
1,800	City University of New York, Queens College
1,638	Georgia State University
1,500	United States Coast Guard Academy
0	United States Air Force Academy
0	United States Merchant Marine Academy
0	United States Military Academy
0	United States Naval Academy

FINANCES

TAKE THEM FOR GRANTED

Schools where scholarship and grant packages average over $9,000:

- Alfred University
- Allegheny College
- Bard College
- Barnard College
- Bates College
- Bennington College
- Bowdoin College
- Brandeis University
- Brown University
- Bucknell University
- Carleton College
- Claremont McKenna College
- Colby College
- Colgate University
- Columbia University
- Connecticut College
- Denison University
- Drew University
- Emory University
- The George Washington University
- Hamilton College
- Hampshire College
- Haverford College
- Hobart and William Smith Colleges
- Lafayette College
- Macalester College
- Mills College
- New York University
- Ohio Wesleyan University

FINANCES

Pomona College
Reed College
Scripps College
Skidmore College
Thomas Aquinas College
Trinity College (Connecticut)
Trinity University
Tulane University
Union College
University of Chicago
University of Rochester
University of Southern California
Vanderbilt University
Vassar College
Wesleyan University
Willamette University
Williams College

FINANCES

SPREAD IT AROUND

Schools where 80% or more of undergrads receive financial aid:

- Albany College of Pharmacy
- Albright College
- Augustana College (Illinois)
- Augustana College (South Dakota)
- Austin College
- Bloomsburg University of Pennsylvania
- Bradley University
- Campbell University
- Canisius College
- Case Western Reserve University
- Clarkson University
- The College of Insurance
- Colorado School of Mines
- Concordia College
- Eckerd College
- Fisk University
- Fordham University
- Georgetown University
- Goshen College
- Grambling State University
- Hofstra University
- Illinois Institute of Technology
- Illinois Wesleyan University
- Indiana University of Pennsylvania
- Juilliard School
- King College
- MacMurray College
- Manhattan College
- Marquette University

FINANCES

Messiah College
Milwaukee School of Engineering
New College of the University of South Florida
New School for Social Research, Eugene Lang College
Oglethorpe University
Oral Roberts University
Rose-Hulman Institute of Technology
Sacred Heart University
St. Louis University
Southern Illinois University
Spelman College
State University of New York, Geneseo
State University of New York Health Science Center, Syracuse
Tennessee State University
Tulane University
Tuskegee University
United States Air Force Academy
United States Coast Guard Academy
United States Military Academy
United States Naval Academy
University of Chicago
University of Dayton
University of Illinois
University of Minnesota, Morris
University of Rochester
Webb Institute of Naval Architecture

FINANCES

RICH FOR YOUR BLOOD

Schools with total costs of over $19,500 that offer aid to fewer than 50% of students:

- Amherst College
- Babson College
- Brandeis University
- Brown University
- Bryn Mawr College
- Bucknell University
- Connecticut College
- Cornell University
- Duke University
- The George Washington University
- Hampshire College
- Haverford College
- Hobart and William Smith Colleges
- Lehigh University
- Middlebury College
- Oberlin College
- Reed College
- Scripps College
- Skidmore College
- Trinity College (Connecticut)
- Tufts University
- Wellesley College
- Wesleyan University
- Williams College
- Union College
- Vanderbilt University
- Yale University

FINANCES

SCHOLAR DOLLARS

Schools where more than 50% of financial aid is *not* awarded on the basis of need:

- Albany College of Pharmacy
- Albright College
- Augustana College (Illinois)
- Augustana College (South Dakota)
- Austin College
- Bloomsburg University of Pennsylvania
- Bradley University
- Campbell University
- Canisius College
- Case Western Reserve University
- Clarkson University
- The College of Insurance
- Colorado School of Mines
- Concordia College
- Eckerd College
- Fisk University
- Fordham University
- Georgetown University
- Goshen College
- Grambling State University
- Hofstra University
- Illinois Institute of Technology
- Illinois Wesleyan University
- Indiana University of Pennsylvania
- Juilliard School
- King College
- MacMurray College
- Manhattan College
- Marquette University

FINANCES

Messiah College
Milwaukee School of Engineering
New College of the University of South Florida
New School for Social Research, Eugene Lang College
Oglethorpe University
Oral Roberts University
Rose-Hulman Institute of Technology
Sacred Heart University
St. Louis University
Southern Illinois University
Spelman College
State University of New York, Geneseo
State University of New York Health Science Center, Syracuse
Tennessee State University
Tulane University
Tuskegee University
United States Air Force Academy
United States Coast Guard Academy
United States Military Academy
United States Naval Academy
University of Chicago
University of Dayton
University of Illinois
University of Minnesota, Morris
University of Rochester
Webb Institute of Naval Architecture

A WORD TO THE WISE

Once a school has invited you to join its freshman class, the tables turn and the school tends to want to do anything possible to persuade you to attend. If the size of your financial aid award is a part of your decision-making process, counselors often advise that you contact the school's admissions office again and ask them to review your financial aid application and improve the offer. Particularly if you are considering bids from comparable schools, the school very well may increase its financial aid package. Either way, you have nothing to lose by asking.

FINANCES

BUYER BEWARE

Schools that offer aid to many more freshman than to upperclassmen:
- Allegheny College
- Alma College
- Fairleigh Dickinson University
- The George Washington University
- Hood College
- Howard University
- Indiana State University
- Kent State University
- New Mexico Institute of Mining and Technology
- Southern Methodist University
- State University of New York, Stony Brook
- University of Houston
- University of Maryland

ELDER AID

Schools that waive tuition for senior citizens:
- Dickinson State University
- Georgia Institute of Technology
- Northeast Missouri State University
- St. Anselm College
- University of Georgia
- University of Alaska, Fairbanks

FINANCES

GRADE AID

Schools that offer automatic tuition breaks for high SAT or ACT scores and/or high class rank (in high school):
- Bard College
- Iowa State University
- MacMurray College
- Muhlenberg College

CHEAPER BY THE GENERATION

Schools that offer tuition breaks or scholarships for children of alumni:
- Albright College
- Augustana College (Illinois)
- Augustana College (South Dakota)
- Bowling Green State University
- Colorado State University
- Gonzaga University
- Grambling State University
- Indiana State University
- Iowa State University
- Louisiana State University
- St. Michael's College
- South Dakota School of Mines and Technology
- Southern Methodist University
- University of Houston
- University of Southern California
- University of Wyoming

FINANCES

FAMILY GRANTS

Schools that offer tuition breaks for siblings who attend at the same time:

- Augustana College (Illinois)
- Augustana College (South Dakota)
- Canisius College
- Catholic University of America
- Creighton University
- Fairfield University
- The George Washington University
- Gonzaga University
- King College
- Lewis and Clark College
- Loyola College
- Marquette University
- Messiah College
- Providence College
- Randolph-Macon College
- Rosemont College
- St. Anselm College
- St. Michael's College
- Stephens College
- Stonehill College
- University of Dayton
- University of Southern California

ACADEMICS

ACADEMICS

LOVE IT!

Schools that graduate at least 90% of entering freshmen:

- Albright College
- Amherst College
- Bates College
- Bowdoin College
- Brown University
- Columbia University
- Dartmouth College
- Duke University
- Harvard University
- Pomona College
- Princeton University
- Swarthmore College
- Tufts University
- University of Notre Dame
- University of Virginia
- Wesleyan University
- Williams College
- Yale University

ACADEMICS

... OR LEAVE IT

Schools where fewer than half the entering freshmen stay to graduate:

- Antioch College
- Brigham Young University
- California State University, Long Beach
- Christian Brothers University
- College of the Atlantic
- Dickinson State University
- Grambling State University
- Hawaii Pacific University
- Hofstra University
- Kent State University
- Louisiana State University
- Loyola University
- New College of the University of South Florida
- Northeast Missouri State University
- Northeastern University
- Oklahoma State University
- Oregon State University
- Southern Illinois University
- Stephen F. Austin State University
- University of Arkansas
- University of Cincinnati
- University of Houston
- University of Montana
- University of New Mexico
- University of North Dakota
- University of Oklahoma

ACADEMICS

ON MY TIME

Schools where more than 25% of undergrads attend part-time:

- Adelphi University
- Albright College
- Arizona State University
- California State University, Dominguez Hills
- California State University, Long Beach
- City University of New York, City College
- City University of New York, Queens College
- DePaul University
- Fairfield University
- Fairleigh Dickinson University
- Florida Atlantic University
- The George Washington University
- Georgia State University
- Hahnemann University/School of Health Science & Humanities
- Hawaii Pacific University
- Hood College
- Idaho State University
- Illinois Institute of Technology
- James Madison University
- Marymount College Tarrytown
- Milwaukee School of Engineering
- Montana State University
- New Jersey Institute of Technology
- North Carolina State University
- Northeastern University
- Oglethorpe University
- Pace University
- Rochester Institute of Technology

ACADEMICS

Sacred Heart University
South Dakota School of Mines and Technology
Stephens College
Temple University
Tennessee State University
Thomas More College
University of Alaska, Fairbanks
University of Bridgeport
University of Denver
University of Houston
University of Louisville
University of Nevada
University of New Mexico
University of North Dakota
University of Pittsburgh
University of Richmond
University of Texas
University of Texas, Arlington
University of Texas, El Paso
University of Utah
University of Wisconsin, Milwaukee

HARD COME, EASY GO

Schools that admit fewer than half of those who apply, but then graduate fewer than 60% of those who matriculate:

The American University
Florida Institute of Technology
New College of the University of South Florida
Northeastern University
Spelman College
University of California, Irvine

ACADEMICS
YEAR-ROUND FUN

Schools where summer enrollment equals more than 40% of fall enrollment:

- Clemson University
- Johns Hopkins University
- Southern Methodist University
- University of Hawaii
- University of Michigan
- University of Minnesota
- University of Mississippi
- University of Nebraska
- University of Nevada
- University of Oregon
- University of Vermont
- University of Washington

In addition, the following schools also have very large undergraduate summer-session enrollment (more than 7,000 students):

- Indiana University
- Pennsylvania State University
- Rutgers, The State University of New Jersey
- University of California, Berkeley
- University of Maryland
- University of Minnesota
- University of Wisconsin

Source: Association of University Summer Sessions

ACADEMICS

DEGREES BY MAIL

Top schools that offer bachelor degrees by correspondence study:

- Brigham Young University (Department of Independent Study)
- Eckerd College (Program for Experienced Learners)
- Evergreen State College
- Goddard College
- Indiana University (General Studies Degree Program, Division of Extended Studies)
- Kansas State University (Division of Continuing Education)
- Ohio University (Adult Learning Services, External Student Program)
- Skidmore College (University Without Walls)
- Stephens College (College Without Walls)
- Syracuse University (Independent Study Degree Program)
- University of Alabama (New College External Degree Program)
- University of Iowa (Center for Credit Programs)
- University of Maryland (University College, Open Learning Program)
- University of Oklahoma (College of Liberal Studies)

Source: John Bear, *College Degrees by Mail*

ACADEMICS

STUDENT-TO-FACULTY RATIOS—THE BEST

Schools that have fewer than ten students per faculty member:

- Agnes Scott College
- Antioch College
- Bard College
- Bennington College
- California Institute of Technology
- Carnegie Mellon University
- Claremont McKenna College
- College of the Atlantic
- Columbia University
- Columbia University, School of Engineering
- Cooper Union for the Advancement of Science and Art
- Fisk University
- Goucher College
- Hahnemann University/School of Health Science & Humanities
- Harvey Mudd College
- Howard University
- Johns Hopkins University
- Juilliard School
- Marlboro College
- Marymount College Tarrytown
- Massachusetts Institute of Technology
- Princeton University
- Rice University
- San Francisco Conservatory of Music
- Sarah Lawrence College

ACADEMICS

School for International Training
St. John's College (Maryland)
St. John's College (New Mexico)
State University of New York Health Science Center, Syracuse
Swarthmore College
The College of Insurance
United States Air Force Academy
United States Coast Guard Academy
United States Military Academy
University of Chicago
University of Hawaii
University of Judaism, Lee College
University of Pittsburgh
University of Southern California
Vanderbilt University
Webb Institute of Naval Architecture
Wells College
Yale University
Yeshiva University

■

Note that Yale University, which has had the very best ratio of faculty to students, is cutting 11% of its faculty positions. Many other colleges and universities are also cutting faculty, yet another sign of economically tough times in education. "And things are not going to get better for a long time," Robert H. Atwell, president of the American Council on Education, told the *New York Times*.

ACADEMICS

STUDENT-TO-FACULTY RATIOS—THE WORST

Schools that have more than 20 students per faculty member:

- Arizona State University
- Babson College
- Brigham Young University
- Bryant College
- Florida Atlantic University
- Florida State University
- Georgia State University
- Grambling State University
- Illinois State University
- Pace University
- Stephen F. Austin State University
- Tennessee State University
- Texas A&M University
- University of California, Irvine
- University of Oklahoma
- University of Texas
- University of Texas, Arlington
- University of Texas, El Paso

ACADEMICS

PREMIUM PROFS

Schools where professors' salaries average over $75,000 per year:

- California Institute of Technology
- Columbia University
- Duke University
- Harvard University
- Massachusetts Institute of Technology
- New York University
- Princeton University
- Stanford University
- University of California, Berkeley
- University of Chicago
- University of Pennsylvania
- Yale University

Source: American Association of University Professors

But keep the following in mind: "Some of the best teaching in this country goes on at places with small endowments, comparatively modest tuitions, and wonderful, overworked and underpaid faculty—places like Earlham and Kenyon, Kalamazoo and Beloit," says John M. Nicholson, associate dean of admissions and coordinator of freshman financial aid at Carleton College, quoted in *Change*.

ACADEMICS

ENGINEERING BRAIN TRUSTS

Schools with over 50 members of the National Academy of Engineering on the faculty:
- Massachusetts Institute of Technology
- Stanford University
- University of California, Berkeley

Schools with over 10 members of the National Academy of Engineering on the faculty:
- California Institute of Technology
- Carnegie Mellon University
- Cornell University
- Harvard University
- Northwestern University
- Pennsylvania State University
- Princeton University
- Purdue University
- University of Illinois
- University of Minnesota
- University of Southern California
- University of Texas
- University of Wisconsin

Source: National Academy of Engineering

ACADEMICS

WELL-ENDOWED

Schools ranked by endowment assets per full-time equivalent student:

1.	Academy of the New Church	$435,833
2.	Princeton University	$413,306
3.	Agnes Scott College	$290,106
4.	California Institute of Technology	$286,988
5.	Rice University	$279,834
6.	Harvard University	$273,769
7.	Swarthmore College	$259,631
8.	Yale University	$239,832
9.	Grinnell College	$230,834
10.	Pomona College	$227,479
11.	Macalester College	$219,115
12.	Berea College	$189,714
13.	Wellesley College	$175,095
14.	Amherst College	$168,072
15.	Wabash College	$159,734
16.	Stanford University	$157,226
17.	Massachusetts Institute of Technology	$154,463
18.	Williams College	$154,364
19.	Emory University	$154,336
20.	Rush University	$151,695
21.	Washington University	$147,839
22.	Claremont McKenna College	$141,355
23.	Smith College	$129,925
24.	Harvey Mudd College	$129,072
25.	Trinity University	$121,038

ACADEMICS

Schools with the largest endowments:
1. Harvard University $4.7 billion
2. University of Texas $3.4 billion
3. Princeton University $2.6 billion
4. Yale University $2.6 billion
5. Stanford University $2.0 billion

Source: *1991 NACUBO Endowment Study*: Prepared by Cambridge Associates, Inc.

ACADEMICS
VOLUMES AND VOLUMES

The top libraries among research universities:
1. Harvard University
2. University of California, Berkeley
3. Yale University
4. University of California, Los Angeles
5. University of Illinois
6. University of Michigan
7. University of Texas
8. Stanford University
9. Columbia University
10. Cornell University
11. University of Washington
12. University of Wisconsin
13. University of Minnesota
14. Indiana University
15. University of Chicago
16. Princeton University
17. Pennsylvania State University (all campuses)
18. Duke University
19. Rutgers, The State University of New Jersey (all campuses)
20. Ohio State University

Source: American Association of Research Libraries (Ranking is based on membership criteria index, including volumes, acquisitions, serials, staff, and expenditures.)

ACADEMICS

MEGS FOR MINDS

Schools with one or more PCs, Macintoshes, or workstations for every four students:

- Brown University
- Colby College
- Drew University
- Lafayette College
- Middlebury College
- Oberlin College
- Swarthmore College
- University of California, Berkeley
- University of California, Davis
- University of California, Los Angeles
- University of Miami
- University of Oregon
- University of Pennsylvania
- University of Wisconsin
- Wesleyan College
- Williams College

Source: *1991 Directory of Computer Facilities in Higher Education*, Austin Computation Center, University of Texas

THEY'RE SUPER

National Science Foundation Supercomputer Centers:

- Carnegie Mellon University
- Cornell University
- University of California, San Diego
- University of Illinois

Source: National Science Foundation

ACADEMICS

RESEARCH & DEVELOPMENT

Schools with the highest science and engineering R & D spending:
1. Johns Hopkins University
2. Massachusetts Institute of Technology
3. University of Michigan
4. University of Wisconsin
5. Stanford University
6. Cornell University
7. University of Minnesota
8. Texas A&M University
9. Pennsylvania State University
10. University of California, Los Angeles

Source: National Science Foundation

ACADEMICS

SCIENCE SPOTS

National Science Foundation Science and Technology Centers:
- California Institute of Technology
- Carnegie Mellon University
- Kent State University
- Michigan State University
- Northwestern University
- Rice University
- Rutgers, The State University of New Jersey
- State University of New York, Stony Brook
- University of California, Berkeley
- University of California, Davis
- University of California, Santa Barbara
- University of Chicago (2)
- University of Illinois (2)
- University of Michigan
- University of Minnesota
- University of Oklahoma
- University of Pennsylvania
- University of Rochester
- University of Southern California
- University of Texas
- University of Utah
- University of Virginia
- Virginia Polytechnic Institute and State University

NSF Science and Technology Centers study all sorts of way-out stuff, like clouds, chemistry, and climate (University of Chicago); liquid crystalline optical materials (Kent State University); and advanced cement-based materials (Northwestern University).

Source: National Science Foundation

ACADEMICS

REACH FOR THE STARS

Schools with the largest planetaria:
- Angelo State University
- Arizona State University
- Louisiana Polytechnic University
- Montana State University
- Old Dominion University
- United States Air Force Academy
- University of Arizona
- University of Arkansas
- University of Colorado
- University of North Carolina
- University of North Dakota
- Youngstown State University

Source: International Planetarium Society

ART WORLD

Schools with the most significant museums:
- Cornell University
- Harvard University
- Princeton University
- University of California, Berkeley
- University of Florida
- University of Kansas
- University of Michigan
- University of Nebraska
- University of North Carolina
- Rhode Island School of Design
- Williams College
- Yale University

Source: Association of College and University Museums

ACADEMICS

DEPARTMENT RANKINGS

Here are lists of top schools for many major majors, along with lists of schools with selected programs you may find interesting.

Keep in mind that these rankings usually reflect only one measure of what makes a good department—such as the department's reputation among knowledgeable people surveyed or the research productivity of its faculty. Too often, these rankings favor large, research-oriented departments—with lots of professors who spend all their time writing articles for academic journals. The professors at these universities may be brilliant, but unless you're really motivated—and some undergraduates *are*—you'll never meet them.

If you're looking for great teachers, make sure to consider liberal arts colleges. We've included departmental listings of liberal arts colleges in this section when available. Make sure to look at the general rankings of liberal arts schools at the end of the chapter and at the rankings of graduates' achievement in the careers chapter, too.

ACADEMICS

AGRICULTURE

AGRICULTURAL ECONOMICS

Schools with academically-influential departments:
- Cornell University
- Iowa State University
- Michigan State University
- Oklahoma State University
- Stanford University
- Texas A&M University
- University of California, Berkeley
- University of Illinois
- University of Minnesota
- University of Wisconsin

Source: Richard P. Beilock, Leo C. Polopolus, and Mario Correal, *American Journal of Agricultural Economics*

AGRICULTURE

Leading undergraduate programs:
- Cornell University
- Iowa State University
- Michigan State University
- Ohio State University
- Purdue University
- Texas A&M University
- University of California, Davis
- University of Illinois
- University of Minnesota
- University of Wisconsin

Source: *The Gourman Report*

SUSTAINABLE AGRICULTURE

Schools with undergraduate degree options in related fields:
- Ohio University
- University of California, Davis
- University of Maine
- University of Minnesota

Source: Appropriate Technology Transfer for Rural Areas

ACADEMICS

ALLIED HEALTH

In many cases, allied health programs are within a university's medical or health sciences center.

HEALTH SERVICES ADMINISTRATION

Schools that offer undergraduate programs in health services administration:

- Alfred University
- Appalachian State University
- California State University, Long Beach
- California State University, Northridge
- City University of New York, Lehman College
- Eastern Michigan University
- Florida A&M University
- Governors State University (Illinois)
- Idaho State University
- Ithaca College
- Metropolitan State College of Denver
- Oregon State University
- Pennsylvania State University
- Quinnipiac College
- Rutgers, The State University of New Jersey
- Sangamon State University
- Southwest Texas State University
- Stonehill College
- Tennessee State University
- University of Cincinnati
- University of Connecticut
- University of Kentucky
- University of Nevada
- University of New Hampshire
- University of North Carolina

ACADEMICS

University of North Carolina, Asheville
University of South Dakota
Weber State College
Western Kentucky University
Wichita State University
Winthrop College

Source: Association of University Programs in Health Administration

ACADEMICS

MEDICAL TECHNOLOGY

Leading undergraduate programs in medical technology:
- Duke University
- Hahnemann University/School of Health Science & Humanities
- Medical College of Georgia
- Michigan State University
- Northeastern University
- Ohio State University
- Southeastern Massachusetts University
- State University of New York, Buffalo
- University of Alabama, Birmingham
- University of Illinois, Chicago
- University of Iowa
- University of Kansas
- University of Kentucky
- University of Minnesota
- University of Nebraska
- University of New Hampshire
- University of North Carolina
- University of Southern Mississippi
- University of Tennessee, Memphis
- University of Texas, Houston
- University of Texas, San Antonio
- University of Vermont
- University of Washington
- University of Wisconsin
- West Virginia University

Source: Medical technology programs expert

ACADEMICS

NURSING

Top nursing schools:
- Case Western Reserve University
- Catholic University of America
- University of Arizona
- University of California, San Francisco
- University of Illinois
- University of Maryland
- University of Michigan
- University of Pennsylvania
- University of Texas
- University of Washington

Source: Patricia A. Chemings et al., *Nursing Outlook*

PHYSICAL THERAPY

Leading undergraduate programs:
- Boston University
- New York University
- Northwestern University
- Temple University
- University of California, San Francisco
- University of Minnesota
- University of North Carolina
- University of Pittsburgh
- University of Washington
- University of Wisconsin

Source: *The Gourman Report*

ACADEMICS

Many colleges and universities are in the process of changing their programs from bachelor's degree to post-baccalaureate physical therapy programs, according to the American Physical Therapy Association. The APTA encourages students pursuing a career in physical therapy to enter the profession with the higher degree. For more information, contact the APTA in Alexandria, Virginia (703) 684-2782.

PHYSICIAN'S ASSISTANT

Schools that offer accredited physician's assistant bachelor's degrees:
- Alderson-Broaddus College
- Charles R. Drew University of Medicine and Science
- Duke University
- Gannon University
- The George Washington University
- Hahnemann University/School of Health Science & Humanities
- Howard University
- King's College
- Medical College of Georgia
- Mercy College of Detroit
- St. Francis College
- St. Louis University
- State University of New York, Stony Brook
- Trevecca Nazarene College
- University of Colorado, Denver
- University of Florida
- University of Iowa
- University of Kentucky

ACADEMICS

University of Medicine & Dentistry of New Jersey
University of Nebraska
University of Oklahoma, Oklahoma City
University of Osteopathic Medicine
University of Southern California
University of Texas, Galveston
University of Texas Southwestern Medical Center, Dallas
University of Washington
University of Wisconsin
Western Michigan University
Wichita State University

Source: Committee on Allied Health Education & Accreditation, American Medical Association

PODIATRY

Schools with an undergraduate major in podiatry:
Roosevelt University
Union University
University of Wisconsin, Oshkosh

ACADEMICS

ARCHITECTURE AND PLANNING

ARCHITECTURE

Leading undergraduate programs:
- Carnegie Mellon University
- Cornell University
- Georgia Institute of Technology
- Massachusetts Institute of Technology
- Princeton University
- Rice University
- University of California, Berkeley
- University of Illinois
- University of Michigan
- University of Southern California

Source: *The Gourman Report*

ACADEMICS

CONSTRUCTION MANAGEMENT

Schools with accredited undergraduate programs in construction management:
- Arizona State University
- Auburn University
- Boise State University
- Bradley University
- Brigham Young University
- California Polytechnic State University
- California State University, Chico
- California State University, Long Beach
- California State University, Sacramento
- Clemson University
- Colorado State University
- Eastern Michigan University
- Florida International University
- Kansas State University
- Kean College of New Jersey
- Louisiana State University
- North Dakota State University
- Northeast Louisiana University
- Oregon State University
- Purdue University
- Texas A&M University
- University of Cincinnati
- University of Florida
- University of Maryland, Eastern Shore
- University of Nebraska
- University of Oklahoma
- University of Washington
- University of Wisconsin
- Virginia Polytechnic Institute and State University
- Washington State University

Source: American Council for Construction Education

ACADEMICS

URBAN AND REGIONAL PLANNING

Schools with undergraduate degree programs:
- Alabama A&M University
- Appalachian State University
- Arizona State University
- Ball State University
- Brigham Young University
- California Polytechnic State University
- California State Polytechnic University
- East Carolina University
- Eastern Washington University
- Indiana University of Pennsylvania
- Iowa State University
- Massachusetts Institute of Technology
- Miami University
- Michigan State University
- New Mexico State University
- Northern Arizona University
- Northern Michigan University
- Rutgers, The State University of New Jersey
- Southwest Missouri State University
- State University of New York, Buffalo
- University of Alabama
- University of Cincinnati
- University of Illinois
- University of Massachusetts, Boston
- University of Southern California
- University of Southern Mississippi
- University of the District of Columbia
- University of Virginia
- University of Washington
- Western Carolina University
- Western Washington University

Source: Association of Collegiate Schools of Planning

ACADEMICS

ART AND DESIGN

ART HISTORY

Universities with outstanding academic reputations (based on their Ph.D. programs):
- Bryn Mawr College
- Columbia University
- Harvard University
- Johns Hopkins University
- New York University
- Princeton University
- Stanford University
- University of California, Berkeley
- University of California, Los Angeles
- University of Michigan
- University of Pennsylvania
- Yale University

Source: *An Assessment of Research-Doctorate Programs in the United States: Humanities*, National Academy Press

ARTS SPECIALTY SCHOOLS

The tops—according to *U.S. News & World Report*:
- Art Center College of Design
- Juilliard School
- Rhode Island School of Design

Source: *America's Best Colleges*, U.S. News & World Report, 1991

ACADEMICS

ARTS ADMINISTRATION

Schools with arts administration programs:
- Alabama State University
- Alaska Pacific University
- The American University
- Arizona State University
- Arkansas State University
- Arkansas Tech University
- Auburn University
- Birmingham-Southern College
- City University of New York, Baruch College
- City University of New York, Brooklyn College
- California State University, Dominguez Hills
- California State University, Long Beach
- Columbia College
- Drexel University
- Florida State University
- Harding University
- Henderson State University
- Hendrix College
- Indiana University
- Huntingdon College
- Methodist College
- New York University
- Northern Arizona University
- Ouachita Baptist University
- Samford University
- Sangamon State University
- Simmons College
- Southern Arkansas University
- Troy State University
- University of Akron

ACADEMICS

University of Alabama
University of Alabama, Birmingham
University of Alaska, Anchorage
University of Alaska, Fairbanks
University of Arizona
University of Arkansas
University of Arkansas, Little Rock
University of California, Los Angeles
University of Central Arkansas
University of Cincinnati
University of Evansville
University of Montevallo
University of Missouri, Kansas City
University of South Alabama
University of Wisconsin
Virginia Polytechnic Institute and State University

Source: National Association of Performing Arts Management

COMPUTER GRAPHICS

Schools with an undergraduate major in computer graphics:
- Arizona State University
- Atlanta College of Art
- Bethany College (West Virginia)
- California University of Pennsylvania
- College of St. Mary
- Eastern Kentucky University
- Elmhurst College
- Hampshire College
- Marygrove College
- Millikin University
- Northern Michigan University
- Ohio State University
- Pratt Institute
- Purdue University
- School of Visual Arts
- Stockton State College
- Syracuse University
- Teikyo Marycrest University
- University of Houston

CULINARY ARTS

Johnson & Wales is the only top cooking school that offers a bachelor's degree. If you want to be a chef, consider either a degree in hotel and restaurant management (see page 147) or an associate's degree from a leading cooking school, such as the famous CIA (Culinary Institute of America in Hyde Park, New York). For more information on cooking schools, check out *The Guide to Cooking Schools*, available through the International Association of Culinary Professionals, Louisville, Kentucky (502) 581-9786.

DANCE

Schools that offer accredited bachelor's degrees in dance:

- Arizona State University
- Barnard College
- Brigham Young University
- Butler University
- California Institute of the Arts
- California State University, Fullerton
- California State University, Long Beach
- Florida State University
- Hope College
- Jacksonville University
- Loyola Marymount University
- Montclair State College
- New York University
- Ohio State University
- Ohio University
- St. Olaf College
- San Jose State University
- Southern Methodist University
- State University of New York, Brockport
- Temple University
- Towson State University
- University of Akron
- University of Arizona
- University of California, Los Angeles
- University of California, Santa Barbara
- University of Illinois
- University of Minnesota
- University of New Mexico
- University of Southern Mississippi

ACADEMICS

University of Wisconsin, Stevens Point
Western Michigan University
Wichita State University

Source: National Association of Schools of Dance

GRAPHIC DESIGN

Schools with top reputations in graphic design:
- Art Center College of Design
- California Institute of the Arts
- Illinois Institute of Technology
- School of Visual Arts
- University of Cincinnati
- University of the Arts

Source: *Educational Rankings Annual*

INDUSTRIAL AND PRODUCT DESIGN

Schools with top reputations in industrial and product design:
- Art Center College of Design
- Cranbrook Academy of Art
- Ohio State University
- Parsons School of Design
- Pratt Institute
- Rhode Island School of Design
- University of Cincinnati

Source: *Educational Rankings Annual*

MUSIC

Universities with outstanding academic reputations (based on their Ph.D. programs):

    Columbia University
    Cornell University
    New York University
    Princeton University
    University of California, Berkeley
    University of California, Los Angeles
    University of Chicago
    University of Illinois
    University of Michigan
    University of North Carolina
    University of Pennsylvania
    Yale University

Source: *An Assessment of Research-Doctorate Programs in the United States: Humanities*, National Academy Press

If the above schools have the best reputations for music research, which schools are best for music performance? You might check out the guide that *The Instrumentalist* published in its October 1990 issue (at your library). Meanwhile, follow the lead of trumpeter Michael Leonhart, who received the first Grammy Award given to the nation's most outstanding high school musician, and check out the schools where he applied:

Eastman School of Music
The Manhattan School of Music
University of Miami

THEATER

Schools with outstanding undergraduate theater programs:

- Bennington College
- Brown University
- Carnegie Mellon University
- Catholic University of America
- Cornell University
- Emerson College
- Ithaca College
- New York University
- Northwestern University
- Oberlin College
- Sarah Lawrence College
- Southern Methodist University
- State University of New York, Purchase
- University of California, Los Angeles
- University of North Carolina
- Vassar College
- Yale University

Source: New York–based theater production company

ACADEMICS

BUSINESS AND MANAGEMENT

ACCOUNTING

The top undergraduate accounting programs:
- Arizona State University
- Brigham Young University
- James Madison University
- Kansas State University
- Miami University
- Michigan State University
- Northern Illinois University
- Ohio State University
- Oklahoma State University
- Stanford University
- Texas A&M University
- University of Alabama
- University of Florida
- University of Georgia
- University of Illinois
- University of Michigan
- University of Missouri
- University of Notre Dame
- University of Pennsylvania
- University of Southern California
- University of Tennessee
- University of Texas
- University of Virginia
- University of Washington
- University of Wisconsin
- Wake Forest University

Source: *Public Accounting Report*

ACADEMICS

ACTUARIAL

Schools with top actuarial programs:
- Drake University
- Georgia State University
- University of Nebraska
- University of Wisconsin

Source: American Society of Actuaries

BUSINESS ADMINISTRATION

Top undergraduate programs:
- Carnegie Mellon University
- Indiana University
- Massachusetts Institute of Technology
- New York University
- University of California, Berkeley
- University of Illinois
- University of Michigan
- University of Pennsylvania
- University of Texas
- University of Wisconsin

Source: *The Gourman Report*

BUSINESS SPECIALTY SCHOOLS

The tops—according to *U.S. News & World Report*:
- Babson College
- Bentley College
- Bryant College

Source: *America's Best Colleges*, U.S. News & World Report, 1991

ENTREPRENEURSHIP

Schools with undergraduate degree programs:
- Babson College
- Ball State University
- Baylor University
- Boise State University
- California State University, Los Angeles
- Ferris State University
- Indiana University
- Northeastern University
- Ohio University
- San Francisco State University
- St. Mary's University
- University of Alabama
- University of Arizona
- University of Arkansas
- University of Colorado
- University of Georgia
- University of New Mexico
- University of North Texas
- University of Pennsylvania
- University of South Carolina

ACADEMICS

University of Southern California
Wichita State University
Xavier University
Youngstown State University

Source: Association of Collegiate Entrepreneurs

HOTEL AND RESTAURANT MANAGEMENT

Top undergraduate programs:
Cornell University
Iowa State University
Michigan State University
Purdue University
University of Denver
University of Houston
University of Illinois
University of Maryland
University of Massachusetts
University of Nevada

Source: *The Gourman Report*

ACADEMICS

COMMUNICATION

MASS COMMUNICATIONS

Schools with top overall academic reputations (based on their Ph.D. programs):
- Indiana University
- Michigan State University
- New York University
- Northwestern University
- Stanford University
- University of Illinois
- University of Iowa
- University of Pennsylvania
- University of Southern California
- University of Texas
- University of Wisconsin

Source: *Association for Communication Administration Bulletin*

PUBLIC RELATIONS

Schools with the top undergraduate public relations programs:
- Ball State University
- Boston University
- California State University, Fullerton
- Ohio State University
- San Diego State University
- San Jose State University
- Syracuse University
- University of Florida
- University of Maryland
- University of Southern California
- University of Wisconsin

Source: Department of Advertising/Public Relations, Marquette University

ACADEMICS

EDUCATION AND SOCIAL WORK

EDUCATION OF THE CULTURALLY DISADVANTAGED

Schools with a major in education of the culturally disadvantaged (which includes students whose education has suffered due to their cultural or socioeconomic background):

Augustana College (South Dakota)
Friends World College
Goddard College
Northeastern State University
Prescott College
Southern Connecticut State University

PHYSICAL EDUCATION

Schools with top academic reputations (based on their Ph.D. programs):
- Michigan State University
- Pennsylvania State University
- University of California, Berkeley
- University of California, Los Angeles
- University of Illinois
- University of Iowa
- University of Maryland
- University of Massachusetts
- University of Michigan
- University of Wisconsin

Source: Cynthia A. Hasbrook and John W. Loy, *Quest*

SOCIAL WORK

Top departments based on research productivity, adjusted by faculty size:
- Florida State University
- State University of New York, Albany
- University of California, Berkeley
- University of Chicago
- University of Georgia
- University of Illinois
- University of Kansas
- University of Michigan
- University of Minnesota
- University of Southern California
- University of Texas, Arlington
- University of Washington
- University of Wisconsin
- Washington University

Source: Kevin J. Corcoran and Stuart A. Kirk, *Journal of Social Work Education*

TEACHER EDUCATION

Colleges of education with top reputations:
- Michigan State University
- Ohio State University
- Stanford University
- University of California, Los Angeles
- University of Georgia
- University of Illinois
- University of Minnesota
- University of Texas
- University of Wisconsin

Source: Charles West, University of Illinois, in *Illini-Week*

ACADEMICS

ENGINEERING AND COMPUTER SCIENCE

COMPUTER SCIENCE

Universities with outstanding academic reputations (based on their Ph.D. programs):
- Carnegie Mellon University
- Cornell University
- Massachusetts Institute of Technology
- Stanford University
- University of California, Berkeley
- University of Illinois

Source: *Changing Times*

CHEMICAL ENGINEERING

Universities with outstanding academic reputations (based on their Ph.D. programs):
- California Institute of Technology
- Carnegie Mellon University
- Massachusetts Institute of Technology
- Northwestern University
- Princeton University
- Purdue University
- University of California, Berkeley
- University of Delaware
- University of Houston
- University of Illinois
- University of Minnesota
- University of Pennsylvania

Source: *An Assessment of Research-Doctorate Programs in the United States: Engineering,* National Academy Press

CIVIL ENGINEERING

Universities with outstanding academic reputations (based on their Ph.D. programs):
- California Institute of Technology
- Colorado State University
- Cornell University
- Massachusetts Institute of Technology
- Northwestern University
- Princeton University
- Stanford University
- University of California, Berkeley
- University of Illinois
- University of Michigan
- University of Texas
- University of Washington

Source: *An Assessment of Research-Doctorate Programs in the United States: Engineering,* National Academy Press

ELECTRICAL ENGINEERING

Universities with outstanding academic reputations (based on their Ph.D. programs):

- California Institute of Technology
- Carnegie Mellon University
- Cornell University
- Massachusetts Institute of Technology
- Pennsylvania State University
- Purdue University
- Stanford University
- University of Arizona
- University of California, Berkeley
- University of California, Los Angeles
- University of California, Santa Barbara
- University of Florida
- University of Illinois
- University of Michigan
- University of Minnesota
- University of Rochester
- University of Southern California
- University of Wisconsin

Source: Institute for Scientific Information

ENGINEERING SPECIALTY SCHOOLS

The tops—according to *U.S. News & World Report*:
- Cooper Union for the Advancement of Science and Art
- Harvey Mudd College
- Rose-Hulman Institute of Technology

Source: *America's Best Colleges*, U.S. News & World Report, 1991

ENVIRONMENTAL ENGINEERING

Schools that offer undergraduate degrees in environmental engineering, environmental resources engineering, or civil and environmental engineering:
- California Polytechnic State University
- Florida Institute of Technology
- Humboldt State University
- Michigan Technological University
- Montana College of Mineral Science and Technology
- Northwestern University
- Pennsylvania State University
- Rensselaer Polytechnic Institute
- University of Central Florida
- University of Florida
- University of Wisconsin
- Vanderbilt University

Source: American Academy of Environmental Engineers

MECHANICAL ENGINEERING

Universities with outstanding academic reputations (based on their Ph.D. programs):
- Brown University
- California Institute of Technology
- Cornell University
- Massachusetts Institute of Technology
- Princeton University
- Purdue University
- Stanford University
- University of California, Los Angeles
- University of Illinois
- University of Michigan
- University of Minnesota
- University of Wisconsin

Source: *An Assessment of Research-Doctorate Programs in the United States: Engineering,* National Academy Press

POLYMER ENGINEERING (I.E., PLASTICS)

Schools that offer an undergraduate curriculum:
- Case Western Reserve University
- Stevens Institute of Technology
- University of Akron
- University of Lowell
- University of Massachusetts

Source: Stevens Institute of Technology Polymer Processing Institute

ACADEMICS

HUMANITIES

CLASSICS

Universities with outstanding academic reputations (based on their Ph.D. programs):

- Brown University
- Bryn Mawr College
- Columbia University
- Cornell University
- Harvard University
- Princeton University
- Stanford University
- University of California, Berkeley
- University of Michigan
- University of North Carolina
- University of Pennsylvania
- University of Texas
- Yale University

Source: *An Assessment of Research-Doctorate Programs in the United States: Humanities,* National Academy Press

ACADEMICS

ENGLISH

Universities with outstanding academic reputations (based on their Ph.D. programs):

- Brown University
- Cornell University
- Harvard University
- Indiana University
- Johns Hopkins University
- Northwestern University
- Princeton University
- Rutgers, The State University of New Jersey
- Stanford University
- University of California, Los Angeles
- University of Chicago
- University of Michigan
- University of North Carolina
- University of Pennsylvania
- University of Virginia
- University of Wisconsin

Source: *An Assessment of Research-Doctorate Programs in the United States: Humanities,* National Academy Press

FOLKLORE AND MYTHOLOGY

Schools with an undergraduate major in folklore and mythology:
- Eastern Washington University
- Friends World College
- Hampshire College
- Harvard University
- Marlboro College
- New College of the University of South Florida
- Pitzer College
- Prescott College
- Sarah Lawrence College
- Shimer College
- University of Pennsylvania

FRENCH

Universities with outstanding academic reputations (based on their Ph.D. programs):
- Columbia University
- Cornell University
- Indiana University
- New York University
- Princeton University
- University of California, Berkeley
- University of Michigan
- University of Pennsylvania
- Yale University

Source: *An Assessment of Research-Doctorate Programs in the United States: Humanities,* National Academy Press

ACADEMICS

GERMAN

Universities with outstanding academic reputations (based on their Ph.D. programs):
- Cornell University
- Indiana University
- Princeton University
- Stanford University
- University of California, Berkeley
- University of Texas
- University of Wisconsin
- Yale University

Source: *An Assessment of Research-Doctorate Programs in the United States: Humanities,* National Academy Press

LINGUISTICS

Universities with outstanding academic reputations (based on their Ph.D. programs):
- Massachusetts Institute of Technology
- Ohio State University
- Stanford University
- University of California, Berkeley
- University of California, Los Angeles
- University of California, San Diego
- University of Chicago
- University of Illinois
- University of Massachusetts
- University of Pennsylvania
- University of Texas

Source: *An Assessment of Research-Doctorate Programs in the United States: Humanities,* National Academy Press

PHILOSOPHY

Universities with outstanding academic reputations (based on their Ph.D. programs):
- Brown University
- Cornell University
- Harvard University
- Massachusetts Institute of Technology
- Princeton University
- Stanford University
- University of California, Berkeley
- University of California, Los Angeles
- University of Chicago
- University of Massachusetts
- University of Michigan
- University of Pittsburgh

Source: *An Assessment of Research-Doctorate Programs in the United States: Humanities,* National Academy Press

SPANISH

Universities with outstanding academic reputations (based on their Ph.D. programs):

- Brown University
- Cornell University
- Harvard University
- Indiana University
- Stanford University
- University of California, Berkeley
- University of California, Los Angeles
- University of Kansas
- University of Michigan
- University of Pennsylvania
- University of Texas
- University of Wisconsin
- Yale University

Source: *An Assessment of Research-Doctorate Programs in the United States: Humanities,* National Academy Press

NATURAL SCIENCES

ASTROPHYSICS

Schools that offer degrees in astrophysics:
- Bennington College
- Boston University
- Brown University
- City University of New York, Brooklyn College
- Colgate University
- Columbia University
- Massachusetts Institute of Technology
- Marlboro College
- Michigan State University
- Northwestern University
- Montana State University
- New Mexico Institute of Mining and Technology
- Princeton University
- San Francisco State University
- United States Military Academy
- University of Akron
- University of Chicago
- University of Minnesota
- University of New Mexico
- University of Oklahoma
- University of Virginia
- University of Wisconsin
- Wesleyan University
- Williams College

Source: *Careers in Space*

BIOLOGICAL SCIENCES

The top twenty-five universities, based on research influence:

- Brandeis University
- California Institute of Technology
- Columbia University
- Cornell University
- Duke University
- Harvard University
- Johns Hopkins University
- Massachusetts Institute of Technology
- New York University
- Princeton University
- Stanford University
- University of California, Berkeley
- University of California, Los Angeles
- University of California, San Diego
- University of California, San Francisco
- University of California, Santa Cruz
- University of Chicago
- University of Colorado
- University of Massachusetts
- University of Oregon
- University of Washington
- Vanderbilt University
- Washington University
- Yale University

Source: Institute for Science Information

ACADEMICS

BIOCHEMISTRY

Universities with outstanding academic reputations (based on their Ph.D. programs):
- Brandeis University
- Cornell University
- Duke University
- Harvard University
- Massachusetts Institute of Technology
- Stanford University
- University of California, Berkeley
- University of California, Davis
- University of California, Los Angeles
- University of California, San Diego
- University of California, San Francisco
- University of Chicago
- University of Illinois
- University of Michigan
- University of Pennsylvania
- University of Washington
- University of Wisconsin
- Yale University

Source: *An Assessment of Research-Doctorate Programs in the United States: Biological Sciences*, National Academy Press

BOTANY

Universities with outstanding academic reputations (based on their Ph.D. programs):
- Cornell University
- Duke University
- Michigan State University
- University of California, Berkeley
- University of California, Davis
- University of California, Riverside
- University of Illinois
- University of Michigan
- University of Texas
- University of Wisconsin
- Yale University

Source: *An Assessment of Research-Doctorate Programs in the United States: Biological Sciences*, National Academy Press

CELLULAR AND MOLECULAR BIOLOGY

Universities with outstanding academic reputations (based on their Ph.D. programs):
- California Institute of Technology
- Columbia University
- Harvard University
- Massachusetts Institute of Technology
- Stanford University
- University of California, Berkeley
- University of Colorado
- University of Washington
- University of Wisconsin
- Yale University

Source: *An Assessment of Research-Doctorate Programs in the United States: Biological Sciences*, National Academy Press

CHEMISTRY—COLLEGES

The top undergraduate institutions based on research productivity:
- Amherst College
- College of Wooster
- Franklin and Marshall College
- Harvey Mudd College
- Hope College
- Lafayette College
- Lebanon Valley College
- Pomona College
- Pratt Institute
- Williams College

Source: Claude H. Yoder and James N. Spencer, *Journal of Chemical Education*

CHEMISTRY—UNIVERSITIES

Universities that graduate the most American Chemical Society–certified bachelor graduates:
- Harvard University
- Illinois State University
- Massachusetts Institute of Technology
- Ohio State University
- University of California, San Diego
- University of Delaware
- University of Illinois
- University of Minnesota
- University of Texas
- University of Washington

Source: *Chemical and Engineering News*

LIBERAL ARTS SCIENCE LEADERS

Fifty liberal arts colleges that produce a large number of influential scientists:

    Albion College
    Alma College
    Amherst College
    Antioch College
    Barnard College
    Bates College
    Beloit College
    Bowdoin College
    Bryn Mawr College
    Bucknell University
    Carleton College
    Colgate University
    College of the Holy Cross
    College of Wooster
    Colorado College
    Davidson College
    Denison University
    DePauw University
    Earlham College
    Franklin and Marshall College
    Grinnell College
    Hamilton College
    Hampton University
    Harvey Mudd College
    Haverford College
    Hope College
    Kalamazoo College
    Kenyon College
    Lafayette College

ACADEMICS

Macalester College
Manhattan College
Middlebury College
Mount Holyoke College
Oberlin College
Occidental College
Ohio Wesleyan University
Pomona College
Reed College
St. Olaf College
Smith College
Swarthmore College
Trinity College (Connecticut)
Union College
Vassar College
Wabash College
Wellesley College
Wesleyan University
Wheaton College (Illinois)
Whitman College
Williams College

Source: *Maintaining America's Scientific Productivity: The Necessity of Liberal Arts Colleges*, Oberlin College

MATH

Universities with outstanding academic reputations (based on their Ph.D. programs):

- Brown University
- Columbia University
- Cornell University
- Harvard University
- Massachusetts Institute of Technology
- New York University
- Princeton University
- Stanford University
- University of California, Berkeley
- University of Chicago
- University of Michigan
- University of Wisconsin
- Yale University

Source: *Changing Times*

ACADEMICS

MICROBIOLOGY

Universities with outstanding academic reputations (based on their Ph.D. programs):

- Columbia University
- Duke University
- Johns Hopkins University
- Massachusetts Institute of Technology
- New York University
- Rutgers, The State University of New Jersey
- Stanford University
- University of Alabama
- University of California, Davis
- University of California, Los Angeles
- University of California, San Diego
- University of California, San Francisco
- University of Chicago
- University of Illinois
- University of Michigan
- University of Minnesota
- University of Pennsylvania
- University of Washington
- University of Wisconsin
- Yale University

Source: *An Assessment of Research-Doctorate Programs in the United States: Biological Sciences*, National Academy Press

PHYSIOLOGY

Universities with outstanding academic reputations (based on their Ph.D. programs):
- Duke University
- Harvard University
- University of California, Davis
- University of California, Los Angeles
- University of California, San Francisco
- University of Michigan
- University of Pennsylvania
- University of Virginia
- University of Washington
- Washington University
- Yale University

Source: *An Assessment of Research-Doctorate Programs in the United States: Biological Sciences*, National Academy Press

PHYSICS/ASTRONOMY—COLLEGES

The top undergraduate institutions based on research productivity:

- Bryn Mawr College
- Colgate University
- Haverford College
- Indiana University of Pennsylvania
- Ithaca College
- Oakland University
- Texas Christian University
- Union College
- University of Michigan, Dearborn
- Wellesley College

Source: John Mateja, *Council on Undergraduate Research*

ACADEMICS

PHYSICAL SCIENCE

The top twenty-five universities, based on research influence:

- Boston University
- California Institute of Technology
- Columbia University
- Cornell University
- Harvard University
- Indiana University
- Johns Hopkins University
- Massachusetts Institute of Technology
- Northeastern University
- Princeton University
- Stanford University
- State University of New York, Stony Brook
- University of Arizona
- University of California, Berkeley
- University of California, San Diego
- University of California, Santa Barbara
- University of California, Santa Cruz
- University of Chicago
- University of Colorado
- University of Houston
- University of Oregon
- University of Pennsylvania
- University of Pittsburgh
- University of Utah
- Yale University

Source: Institute for Scientific Information

ACADEMICS

PLANETARY SCIENCE

Schools that offer undergraduate degrees in planetary science:
- California Institute of Technology
- Florida Institute of Technology
- Johns Hopkins University
- Massachusetts Institute of Technology
- Montana State University

Source: *Careers in Space*

STATISTICS

Universities with the largest number of influential faculty:
- Cornell University
- Iowa State University
- North Carolina State University
- Stanford University
- Texas A&M University
- University of California, Berkeley
- University of Chicago
- University of Florida
- University of Michigan
- Virginia Polytechnic Institute and State University

Source: Jean D. Gibbons, *The American Statistician*

ZOOLOGY

Universities with outstanding academic reputations (based on their Ph.D. programs):

- Duke University
- Harvard University
- Stanford University
- University of California, Berkeley
- University of California, Los Angeles
- University of Chicago
- University of Texas
- University of Washington
- University of Wisconsin
- Yale University

Source: *An Assessment of Research-Doctorate Programs in the United States: Biological Sciences*, National Academy Press

SOCIAL SCIENCES

AFRICAN STUDIES

Schools that receive government funding in order to serve as National Resource Centers for Africa:

- Boston University
- Cornell University
- Indiana University
- Michigan State University
- Stanford University
- University of California, Los Angeles
- University of Florida
- University of Illinois
- University of Wisconsin
- Yale University

Source: African Studies Association, Emory University

ANTHROPOLOGY

Universities with outstanding academic reputations (based on their Ph.D. programs):

- Harvard University
- Northwestern University
- Stanford University
- University of Arizona
- University of California, Berkeley
- University of California, Los Angeles
- University of Chicago
- University of Michigan
- University of Pennsylvania
- Yale University

Source: *An Assessment of Research-Doctorate Programs in the United States: Social & Behavioral Sciences*, National Academy Press

ECONOMICS

Universities with the largest number of influential faculty:

- Carnegie Mellon University
- Columbia University
- Cornell University
- Duke University
- Harvard University
- Massachusetts Institute of Technology
- Michigan State University
- New York University
- Northwestern University
- Ohio State University
- Princeton University
- Stanford University
- University of California, Berkeley
- University of California, Los Angeles
- University of California, San Diego
- University of Chicago
- University of Michigan
- University of Minnesota
- University of Pennsylvania
- University of Rochester
- University of Wisconsin
- Yale University

Source: Jean D. Gibbons and Mary Fish, *Journal of Economic Education*

EAST ASIAN STUDIES

Schools that receive government funding in order to serve as National Resource Centers for East Asia:

- Columbia University
- Harvard University
- Indiana University
- Princeton University
- Stanford University
- University of California, Berkeley
- University of California, Los Angeles
- University of Chicago
- University of Hawaii, Manoa
- University of Michigan
- University of Pittsburgh
- University of Southern California
- University of Washington

Source: Center for International Education, U.S. Department of Education

GEOGRAPHY

The top universities based on research influence:
- Clark University
- Ohio State University
- Pennsylvania State University
- Syracuse University
- University of California, Berkeley
- University of California, Los Angeles
- University of Chicago
- University of Illinois
- University of Minnesota
- University of Washington
- University of Wisconsin

Source: B. L. Turner II and William B. Meyer, *Professional Geographer*

HISTORY

Universities with outstanding academic reputations (based on their Ph.D. programs):

- Brandeis University
- Brown University
- Columbia University
- Cornell University
- Duke University
- Harvard University
- Indiana University
- Johns Hopkins University
- Northwestern University
- Princeton University
- Stanford University
- University of California, Berkeley
- University of California, Los Angeles
- University of Chicago
- University of Michigan
- University of North Carolina
- University of Pennsylvania
- University of Rochester
- University of Virginia
- University of Wisconsin
- Yale University

Source: *An Assessment of Research-Doctorate Programs in the United States: Social & Behavioral Sciences*, National Academy Press

INTERNATIONAL STUDIES

Schools that receive government funding in order to serve as National Resource Centers for international studies:

Columbia University
Duke University
Johns Hopkins University
Marquette University
Michigan State University
Princeton University
Tufts University
University of Denver
University of Iowa
University of Minnesota
University of Pennsylvania
University of Washington
University of Wisconsin
Yale University

Source: Center for International Education, U.S. Department of Education

ACADEMICS

LATIN AMERICAN STUDIES

Schools that receive government funding in order to serve as National Resource Centers for Latin America:

- Brown University
- Columbia University
- Cornell University
- Florida International University
- New Mexico State University
- New York University
- San Diego State University
- Stanford University
- Tulane University
- University of California, Berkeley
- University of California, Los Angeles
- University of California, San Diego
- University of Chicago
- University of Connecticut
- University of Florida
- University of Illinois
- University of Massachusetts
- University of New Mexico
- University of Pittsburgh
- University of Texas
- University of Wisconsin
- University of Wisconsin, Milwaukee

Source: Latin American Studies Association, University of Pittsburgh

ACADEMICS

LIBRARY AND INFORMATION SCIENCE

Top universities based on research productivity:
- Indiana University
- Louisiana State University
- Rutgers, The State University of New Jersey
- University of Arizona
- University of California, Los Angeles
- University of Illinois
- University of Iowa
- University of Michigan
- University of North Carolina
- University of Wisconsin

Source: Danny P. Wallace, *Library Journal*

MID-EAST STUDIES

Schools that receive government funding in order to serve as National Resource Middle East Centers:

- Columbia University
- Harvard University
- New York University
- Ohio State University
- Portland State University
- Princeton University
- University of Arizona
- University of California, Berkeley
- University of California, Los Angeles
- University of Chicago
- University of Michigan
- University of Pennsylvania
- University of Texas
- University of Utah
- University of Washington

Source: Middle Eastern Studies Association of North America, University of Arizona

ACADEMICS

NATIVE AMERICAN STUDIES

Schools with large Native American studies and culture programs:

- Bemidji State University
- Cornell University
- Dartmouth College
- California State Polytechnic Institute
- California State University, Long Beach
- California State University, Northridge
- Iowa State University
- Oklahoma State University
- University of Alaska, Fairbanks
- University of Arizona
- University of California, Davis
- University of California, Los Angeles
- University of Illinois, Chicago
- University of North Dakota
- University of Wisconsin, La Crosse
- University of Wisconsin, Milwaukee

Source: Charlotte Heth and Susan Guyette, *Issues for the Future of American Indian Studies*

POLITICAL SCIENCE

Universities with outstanding academic reputations (based on their Ph.D. programs):
- Cornell University
- Harvard University
- Massachusetts Institute of Technology
- Northwestern University
- Princeton University
- Stanford University
- University of California, Berkeley
- University of Chicago
- University of Michigan
- University of Minnesota
- University of North Carolina
- University of Rochester
- University of Wisconsin
- Yale University

Source: *An Assessment of Research-Doctorate Programs in the United States: Social & Behavioral Sciences*, National Academy Press

ACADEMICS

PSYCHOLOGY

The top ten departments according to research productivity per faculty member:
- Brown University
- Cornell University
- Harvard University
- Johns Hopkins University
- Princeton University
- Stanford University
- University of California, Davis
- University of California, Riverside
- University of Illinois
- Yale University

The following universities are among the top ten in total research productivity:
- Rutgers, The State University of New Jersey
- University of California, Berkeley
- University of California, Los Angeles
- University of Minnesota
- University of Texas
- University of Wisconsin

Source: George S. Howard, David A. Cole, and Scott E. Maxwell, *American Psychologist*

SLAVIC STUDIES

Schools that receive government funding in order to serve as National Resource Centers for Russian, Eurasian, and East European Studies:

- Columbia University
- Emory University
- Harvard University
- Indiana University
- Middlebury College
- Ohio State University
- University of California, Berkeley
- University of Illinois
- University of Kansas
- University of Michigan
- University of North Carolina
- University of Pennsylvania
- University of Pittsburgh
- University of Texas
- University of Virginia
- Yale University

Source: *AAASS Newsletter*, American Association for the Advancement of Slavic Studies, Stanford University

SOCIOLOGY

Universities with outstanding academic reputations (based on their Ph.D. programs):
- Columbia University
- Harvard University
- Stanford University
- State University of New York, Stony Brook
- University of Arizona
- University of California, Berkeley
- University of California, Los Angeles
- University of Chicago
- University of Michigan
- University of North Carolina
- University of Pennsylvania
- University of Texas
- University of Washington
- University of Wisconsin

Source: *An Assessment of Research-Doctorate Programs in the United States: Social & Behavioral Sciences*, National Academy Press

ACADEMICS

SOUTHEAST ASIAN STUDIES

Schools that receive government funding in order to serve as National Resource Centers for Southeast Asia:
- Arizona State University
- Cornell University
- Northern Illinois University
- Ohio University
- University of California, Berkeley
- University of Hawaii, Manoa
- University of Michigan
- University of Washington
- University of Oregon
- University of Wisconsin

Source: Center for International Education, U.S. Dept. of Education

SOUTHERN ASIAN STUDIES

Schools that receive government funding in order to serve as National Resource Centers for South Asia:
- Columbia University
- Cornell University
- Syracuse University
- University of California, Berkeley
- University of Chicago
- University of Michigan
- University of Pennsylvania
- University of Texas
- University of Virginia
- University of Washington
- University of Wisconsin

Source: Center for International Education, U.S. Dept. of Education

ACADEMICS

WESTERN EUROPEAN STUDIES

Columbia University
Cornell University
Indiana University
Kalamazoo College
New School for Social Research
New York University
University of California, Berkeley
University of Minnesota
University of Pittsburgh
Vanderbilt University
Yale University

Source: Center for International Education, U.S. Department of Education

ACADEMICS

SELECTED RANKINGS

There must be a lot of room at the top. The colleges and universities in these "top" lists add up to over 200 schools. That means two things: (1) there are lots of fine schools, and (2) experts disagree about what's best of the best.

For you, the large number of great schools means that you can follow your own interests and needs and still end up at a school with a good reputation. We recommend that you identify schools that meet your other criteria (from location to extracurricular activities), then scan these lists to see how they rank. That way, you can tell your parents that your number one choice is on so-and-so's list of top schools—*then* tell them it has its own golf course. (Remember also to check out the "best buys" lists on pages 68–71.)

U.S. NEWS TOP 25 LIBERAL ARTS COLLEGES

1. Williams College
2. Swarthmore College
3. Amherst College
4. Bowdoin College
5. Pomona College
6. Wellesley College
7. Wesleyan University
8. Haverford College
9. Middlebury College
10. Smith College
11. Bryn Mawr College
12. Carleton College
13. Vassar College
14. Claremont McKenna College
15. Oberlin College
16. Grinnell College
17. Colgate University
18. Mount Holyoke College
19. Barnard College
20. Colby College
21. Davidson College
22. Washington and Lee University
23. College of the Holy Cross
24. Occidental College
25. Hamilton College

Source: *America's Best Colleges*, U.S. News & World Report, 1991

ACADEMICS

U.S. NEWS TOP REGIONAL LIBERAL ARTS COLLEGES

North
1. Simon's Rock College of Bard
2. Cedar Crest College
3. St. Mary's College of Maryland
4. Trinity College (District of Columbia)
5. Westminster College
6. St. Anselm College
7. Rosemont College
8. St. Joseph College
9. St. Vincent College
10. Marymount College Tarrytown

South
1. Wofford College
2. Spelman College
3. Berry College
4. Transylvania University
5. Presbyterian College
6. Wesleyan College
7. Converse College
8. Morehouse College
9. Arkansas College
10. Spring Hill College

ACADEMICS

Midwest
1. Marietta College
2. Ohio Wesleyan University
3. Wittenberg University
4. Hillsdale College
5. Hiram College
6. North Park College
7. Monmouth College
8. College of the Ozarks
9. Mount Union College
10. Taylor University

West
1. Southwestern University
2. Pacific University
3. Texas A&M University, Galveston
4. Evergreen State College
5. Alaska Pacific University
6. Mount St. Mary's College
7. Fresno Pacific College
8. Northwest Nazarene College
9. Phillips University
10. Texas Lutheran College

Source: *America's Best Colleges*, U.S. News & World Report, 1991

ACADEMICS

U.S. NEWS TOP 25
NATIONAL UNIVERSITIES

1. Harvard University
2. Yale University
3. Stanford University
4. Princeton University
5. California Institute of Technology
6. Massachusetts Institute of Technology
7. Duke University
8. Dartmouth College
9. Columbia University
10. University of Chicago
11. Johns Hopkins University
12. Cornell University
13. University of Pennsylvania
14. Northwestern University
15. Rice University
16. University of California, Berkeley
17. Brown University
18. Washington University
19. Vanderbilt University
20. Georgetown University
21. University of Virginia
22. University of Michigan
23. University of California, Los Angeles
24. Carnegie Mellon University
25. University of North Carolina

Source: *America's Best Colleges*, U.S. News & World Report, 1991

ACADEMICS

U.S. NEWS TOP REGIONAL UNIVERSITIES

North
1. Worcester Polytechnic Institute
2. Alfred University
3. Villanova University
4. Fairfield University
5. Rutgers, The State University of New Jersey
6. Providence College
7. Ithaca College
8. Trenton State College
9. St. Michael's College
10. Hood College
11. Susquehanna University
12. Loyola College
13. St. Joseph's College (Pennsylvania)
14. Simmons College
    Manhattan College

South
1. Wake Forest University
2. University of Richmond
3. Stetson University
4. Berea College
5. University of Alabama, Huntsville
6. Rollins College
7. Samford University
8. Florida International University
9. The Citadel
10. Mercer University
11. University of Central Florida
12. James Madison University
13. Loyola University

14. University of North Carolina, Asheville
15. Appalachian State University
    Winthrop College

Midwest

1. Illinois Wesleyan University
2. Valparaiso University
3. St. Mary's College (Indiana)
4. Michigan Technological University
5. DePaul University
6. St. Norbert College
7. Creighton University
8. Butler University
9. John Carroll University
10. University of Dayton
    Northeast Missouri State University
11. Oakland University
13. University of Minnesota, Duluth
14. Ohio Northern University
15. University of Michigan, Dearborn
16. Calvin College

West

1. Trinity University
2. Santa Clara University
3. University of San Diego
4. Loyola Marymount University
5. University of Puget Sound
6. St. Mary's College of California
7. Whittier College
8. Pacific Lutheran University
9. University of Redlands
10. Seattle University

ACADEMICS

    University of Alaska, Fairbanks
12. University of Colorado, Denver
13. California Polytechnic State University
14. Linfield College
15. University of the Pacific

Source: *America's Best Colleges*, U.S. News & World Report, 1991

ACADEMICS

THE *NATIONAL REVIEW* TOP 50 LIBERAL ARTS SCHOOLS

Asbury College
Baylor University
Birmingham-Southern College
Boston University
Brigham Young University
Calvin College
Centre College
Claremont McKenna College
College of William and Mary
Columbia University
Davidson College
Franciscan University of Steubenville
Furman University
Gonzaga University
Grove City College
Gustavus Adolphus College
Hampden-Sydney College
Hanover College
Hillsdale College
Hope College
Houghton College
Lawrence University
Lynchburg College
Millsaps College
Mount St. Mary's College of Maryland
Oglethorpe University
Pepperdine University
Providence College
Rhodes College
St. Anselm College

ACADEMICS

St. John's College
St. John's University (Minnesota)
St. Mary's College of Maryland
St. Olaf College
St. Vincent College
Southwestern University
Thomas Aquinas College
Thomas More College
Transylvania University
Trinity University
Union College
University of Chicago
University of Dallas
University of Notre Dame
University of the South
Wabash College
Washington and Lee University
Wheaton College (Illinois)
Whitman College
Wofford College

Source: *The National Review College Guide: America's Top 50 Liberal Arts Schools*

ACADEMICS

CARNEGIE FOUNDATION: LIBERAL ARTS COLLEGES I

These are primarily undergraduate schools that are considered highly selective and award more than half of their baccalaureate degrees in the arts and sciences:

Agnes Scott College
Albion College
Albright College
Allegheny College
Alma College
Amherst College
Antioch College
Augustana College (Illinois)
Austin College
Barat College
Bard College
Barnard College
Bates College
Beloit College
Benedictine College
Bennington College
Bethany College (West Virginia)
Birmingham-Southern College
Blackburn College
Borromeo College of Ohio
Bowdoin College
Bryn Mawr College
Bucknell University
Carleton College
Carroll College
Centenary College of Louisiana
Centre College
Chatham College
Chestnut Hill College
Claremont McKenna College
Coe College
Colby College
Colgate University
College of Mount Saint Vincent
College of the Holy Cross
College of Wooster
Colorado College
Connecticut College
Cornell College
Davidson College
DePauw University
Denison University
Dickinson College
Drew University
Earlham College
Eckerd College
Emmanuel College
Franklin and Marshall College

ACADEMICS

Furman University
Gettysburg College
Goddard College
Gordon College
Goshen College
Goucher College
Grinnell College
Guilford College
Gustavus Adolphus College
Hamilton College
Hamline University
Hampden-Sydney College
Hampshire College
Hanover College
Hartwick College
Haverford College
Hendrix College
Hobart and William
  Smith Colleges
Hollins College
Hope College
Houghton College
Juniata College
Kalamazoo College
Kenyon College
King College
Knox College
Lafayette College
Lake Forest College
Lawrence University
Lebanon Valley College
Lewis and Clark College
Luther College
Macalester College
MacMurray College
Manhattanville College

Marlboro College
Marymount Manhattan
  College
Middlebury College
Mills College
Millsaps College
Mount Holyoke College
Muhlenberg College
Nebraska Wesleyan
  University
Neumann College
Oberlin College
Occidental College
Oglethorpe University
Pitzer College
Pomona College
Principia College
Radcliffe College
Randolph-Macon
  College
Randolph-Macon
  Woman's College
Reed College
Regis College
Rhodes College
Ripon College
Rockford College
St. John's College
  (Maryland)
St. John's College
  (New Mexico)
St. John's University
St. Lawrence University
St. Olaf College
Salem College
Sarah Lawrence College

ACADEMICS

Scripps College
Skidmore College
Smith College
State University of New York College of Arts and Sciences, Purchase
Swarthmore College
Sweet Briar College
Thomas More College
Trinity College (Connecticut)
Union College
University of Dallas
University of the South
Ursinus College
Vassar College
Virginia Military Institute
Wabash College
Wartburg College
Washington and Jefferson College
Washington and Lee University
Washington College
Wellesley College
Wells College
Wesleyan University
Western Maryland College
Westmont College
Wheaton College (Illinois)
Wheaton College (Massachusetts)
Whitman College
Willamette University
Williams College

Source: Carnegie Foundation for the Advancement of Teaching

ACADEMICS

CARNEGIE FOUNDATION: RESEARCH UNIVERSITIES I

These schools give a high priority to research, offer a full range of baccalaureate programs, and are committed to graduate education through the doctoral degree. These schools receive considerable federal research money and graduate a large number of Ph.D.'s:

- Boston University
- California Institute of Technology
- Carnegie Mellon University
- Case Western Reserve University
- Colorado State University
- Columbia University
- Cornell University
- Duke University
- Georgia Institute of Technology
- Harvard University
- Howard University
- Indiana University
- Johns Hopkins University
- Louisiana State University
- Massachusetts Institute of Technology
- Michigan State University
- New Mexico State University
- New York University
- North Carolina State University
- Northwestern University
- Ohio State University
- Oregon State University
- Pennsylvania State University
- Princeton University
- Purdue University
- Rutgers, The State University of New Jersey
- Stanford University
- State University of New York, Stony Brook
- Texas A&M University
- University of Arizona
- University of California, Berkeley
- University of California, Davis
- University of California, Irvine
- University of California, Los Angeles
- University of California, San Diego
- University of California, San Francisco
- University of Chicago

ACADEMICS

University of Cincinnati
University of Colorado
University of Connecticut
University of Florida
University of Georgia
University of Hawaii
University of Illinois, Chicago
University of Illinois
University of Iowa
University of Kentucky
University of Maryland
University of Miami
University of Michigan
University of Minnesota
University of Missouri
University of New Mexico
University of North Carolina
University of Pennsylvania
University of Pittsburgh
University of Rochester
University of Southern California
University of Tennessee
University of Texas
University of Utah
University of Virginia
University of Washington
University of Wisconsin
Virginia Polytechnic Institute and State University
Vanderbilt University
Washington University
Yale University
Yeshiva University

Source: Carnegie Foundation for the Advancement of Teaching

ACADEMICS

THE PUBLIC IVYS

Public institutions that are considered to have the admissions selectivity, undergraduate educational excellence, and academic prestige of Ivy League and other leading private schools:

    College of William and Mary
    Miami University
    University of California, Berkeley
    University of California, Davis
    University of California, Irvine
    University of California, Los Angeles
    University of California, Riverside
    University of California, San Diego
    University of California, Santa Barbara
    University of California, Santa Cruz
    University of Michigan
    University of North Carolina
    University of Texas
    University of Vermont
    University of Virginia

Other leading public institutions:

    Georgia Institute of Technology
    New College of the University of South Florida
    Pennsylvania State University
    State University of New York, Binghamton
    University of Colorado
    University of Illinois
    University of Pittsburgh
    University of Washington
    University of Wisconsin

Source: Richard Moll, *The Public Ivys*

STUDENT LIFE

STUDENT LIFE

FOR WOMEN ONLY

Women's colleges:
- Agnes Scott College
- Barnard College
- Bryn Mawr College
- Hollins College
- Marymount College Tarrytown
- Mills College
- Mount Holyoke College
- Randolph-Macon Woman's College
- Rosemont College
- Scripps College
- Smith College
- Spelman College
- Wellesley College
- Wells College

GIRLS, GIRLS, GIRLS

Coed colleges whose student body is at least 70% female:
- Goucher College
- Hahnemann University/School of Health Science & Humanities
- Hood College
- Sarah Lawrence College
- Stephens College

STUDENT LIFE

WHERE THE BOYS ARE

Coed colleges whose student body is at least 70% male:

- California Institute of Technology
- Clarkson University
- Colorado School of Mines
- Cooper Union for the Advancement of Science and Art
- Drexel University
- Georgia Institute of Technology
- GMI Engineering and Management Institute
- Harvey Mudd College
- Illinois Institute of Technology
- Milwaukee School of Engineering
- New Jersey Institute of Technology
- New Mexico Institute of Mining and Technology
- Rensselaer Polytechnic Institute
- Stevens Institute of Technology
- United States Air Force Academy
- United States Coast Guard Academy
- United States Merchant Marine Academy
- United States Military Academy
- United States Naval Academy
- Webb Institute of Naval Architecture
- Worcester Polytechnic Institute

STUDENT LIFE

FOR MEN ONLY

Men's colleges:
- Hampden-Sydney College
- Morehouse College
- Rose-Hulman Institute of Technology
- The Citadel
- Virginia Military Institute
- Wabash College

AFRICAN-AMERICAN

Schools whose student body is at least 15% African-American (excluding historically black colleges):
- California State University, Dominguez Hills
- Christian Brothers University
- City University of New York, City College
- Georgia State University
- Hahnemann University/School of Health Science & Humanities
- Illinois Institute of Technology
- Oral Roberts University
- Pace University
- St. John's University (New York)
- Temple University
- University of Maryland

Highly selective historically black colleges:
- Morehouse College
- Spelman College
- Hampton University
- Florida A&M University

Source: *Black Issues in Higher Education*

STUDENT LIFE

ASIAN

Schools whose student body is at least 20% Asian:

- California Institute of Technology
- Columbia University, School of Engineering
- Cooper Union for the Advancement of Science and Art
- Harvey Mudd College
- Hawaii Pacific University
- Illinois Institute of Technology
- Juilliard School
- Massachusetts Institute of Technology
- New York University
- Otis/Parsons School of Art and Design
- San Francisco Conservatory of Music
- Stanford University
- State University of New York, Stony Brook
- Stevens Institute of Technology
- University of California, Berkeley
- University of California, Irvine
- University of California, Los Angeles
- University of California, Riverside
- University of California, San Diego
- University of Chicago
- University of Hawaii
- University of Southern California
- University of Washington

STUDENT LIFE

HISPANIC

Schools whose student body is at least 15% Hispanic:
- California State University, Dominguez Hills
- New Mexico State University
- Occidental College
- St. Mary's College of California
- University of California, Berkeley
- University of California, Los Angeles
- University of Miami
- University of New Mexico
- University of Texas, El Paso
- Whittier College

STUDENT LIFE

NATIVE AMERICAN

Four-year colleges with the largest number of Native American students:

- Bemidji State University
- Brigham Young University
- California State University, Northridge
- Central State University
- Eastern Montana College
- Eastern Washington University
- Montana State University
- Northeastern State University
- Northern Arizona University
- Oklahoma State University
- Pembroke State University
- San Diego State University
- Southeastern Oklahoma State University
- University of Alaska, Fairbanks
- University of Arizona
- University of Montana
- University of New Mexico
- University of North Dakota

Source: *Issues for the Future of American Indian Studies*, University of California, Los Angeles

STUDENT LIFE

WHITE BRED

Schools where 95% or more of the student body is caucasian:

- Augustana College (South Dakota)
- Bloomsburg University of Pennsylvania
- Brigham Young University
- Bryant College
- Central Michigan University
- Dickinson College
- Dickinson State University
- Grove City College
- Gustavus Adolphus College
- Hampden-Sydney College
- Hollins College
- Miami University
- Montana State University
- St. Michael's College
- Stonehill College
- Thomas More College
- University of Maine
- University of New Hampshire
- University of Scranton
- University of the South

STUDENT LIFE

MOST PREPPY

Schools where more than 40% of students come from private, non-parochial schools:
- Amherst College
- Babson College
- Bennington College
- Biola University
- Christian Brothers University
- Connecticut College
- Goucher College
- Hampden-Sydney College
- Hobart and William Smith Colleges
- Pace University
- Rollins College
- Sarah Lawrence College
- Skidmore College
- Stevens Institute of Technology
- Trinity College (Connecticut)
- Tulane University
- University of the South
- Vassar College
- Wheaton College (Massachusetts)
- Widener University
- Williams College

STUDENT LIFE

LEAST PREPPY

Schools where more than 90% of students come from public schools:

- Arizona State University
- Augustana College (South Dakota)
- Austin College
- California State University, Long Beach
- Concordia College
- Eastern Illinois University
- Gustavus Adolphus College
- Indiana University of Pennsylvania
- Iowa State University
- MacMurray College
- North Carolina State University
- Pacific Lutheran University
- Texas A&M University
- Texas Tech University
- University of Idaho
- University of Minnesota, Morris
- University of Oregon
- University of Texas, Arlington
- University of Wyoming
- Utah State University
- Western Michigan University

STUDENT LIFE

MODERN MATURITY

Schools where the average age of undergrads is 24 or older:
- California State University, Dominguez Hills
- California State University, Long Beach
- City University of New York, City College
- The College of Insurance
- Georgia State University
- Hawaii Pacific University
- New Mexico State University
- Pacific Lutheran University
- San Francisco Conservatory of Music
- School for International Training
- Temple University
- Trenton State College
- University of Alaska, Fairbanks
- University of Houston
- University of Louisville
- University of New Mexico
- University of Texas, Arlington
- University of Texas, El Paso
- University of Utah

STUDENT LIFE

GLOBAL VILLAGES

Schools with the largest numbers of foreign students:
1. University of Southern California
2. University of Texas
3. Boston University
4. University of Wisconsin
5. University of Pennsylvania
6. Columbia University
7. Ohio State University
8. University of Illinois
9. University of California, Los Angeles
10. University of Minnesota
11. Southern Illinois University
12. Texas A&M University

Schools with the highest proportion of foreign students:
1. New Jersey Institute of Technology
2. Massachusetts Institute of Technology
3. Hawaii Pacific University
4. Columbia University
5. University of Pennsylvania
6. Stanford University
7. Howard University
8. University of Southern California
9. The George Washington University
10. Harvard University

Source: Institute of International Education

STUDENT LIFE

STUDENTS OF MERIT

Schools with the largest number of freshmen who are National Merit Scholars:
1. Harvard University
2. Rice University
3. University of Texas
4. Stanford University
5. Yale University
6. Princeton University
7. Texas A&M University
8. University of Florida
9. Massachusetts Institute of Technology
10. Carleton College
11. Duke University
12. University of Chicago
13. University of Oklahoma
14. Brigham Young University
15. Georgia Institute of Technology
16. University of California, Berkeley
17. Northwestern University
18. University of Houston
19. Cornell University
20. Brown University

Source: *Chronicle of Higher Education Almanac*

STUDENT LIFE

CAMPUS GREEN

Schools with very active Green Party chapters:

- Carleton College
- Humboldt State University
- Northeastern Missouri State
- Ohio University
- University of California, San Diego
- University of Colorado
- University of Michigan
- University of Minnesota
- University of Washington
- University of West Florida
- University of Wisconsin
- University of Wisconsin, Eau Claire
- West Virginia University

Source: Green Party USA

THEY SAY "NO"

States with the toughest marijuana laws:

- Alabama
- Arkansas
- Georgia
- Missouri
- Nevada
- Rhode Island
- Texas

Source: *High Times Magazine*

STUDENT LIFE

THE GRASS IS GREENER

States where marijuana is decriminalized:
- California
- Colorado
- Maine
- Minnesota
- Mississippi
- Nebraska
- New York
- North Carolina
- Ohio
- Oregon

Source: *High Times Magazine*

Cities where marijuana is decriminalized:
- Ann Arbor, Michigan
- Berkeley, California
- Madison, Wisconsin

Source: National Organization for the Reform of the Marijuana Laws (NORML)

Schools with the largest marijuana rallies:
- University of Florida
- University of Michigan
- University of Wisconsin

Source: National Organization for the Reform of the Marijuana Laws

STUDENT LIFE

PC PATROL

The most politically correct schools:
- Brown University
- Duke University
- Harvard University
- Haverford College
- Middlebury College
- Mount Holyoke College
- Smith College
- Stanford University
- University of California, Berkeley
- University of Michigan
- Wellesley College
- Wesleyan University
- Williams College
- Yale University

Source: National Association of Scholars

NON PC

The least politically correct schools:
- California Institute of Technology
- Claremont McKenna College
- Hillsdale College
- St. John's College
- St. Thomas Aquinas College
- University of Chicago
- Washington and Lee College

Source: National Association of Scholars

CORRECT CRITERIA

The battle over "political correctness" and what it means is being played out to some degree on most campuses. PC schools tend to favor a more multi-cultural-based curriculum. Concurrently, some say these schools are likely to be more sensitive to racial concerns, gay/lesbian/bisexual rights, women's rights, and other issues of social justice.

Schools on the least PC list favor more traditional, core-curriculum oriented degree requirements. While these schools share a somewhat conservative approach to education, the social and political environment varies widely.

Students concerned about issues relating to political correctness should explore individual schools in depth, rather than reaching conclusions from these lists alone.

BIRCH FORESTS

Schools with New American Clubs (affiliated with The John Birch Society):

- Biola College
- Brigham Young University
- Drexel University
- Hampden-Sydney College
- Mississippi State University
- Temple University
- Truett McConnell College
- University of California, Davis
- University of California, Irvine
- University of Massachusetts
- University of North Carolina, Asheville
- University of Texas

Source: The John Birch Society

STUDENT LIFE

PRO-CHOICE

Schools with the most active pro-choice movements:
- Arizona State University
- Boston College
- California State University, Northridge
- Catholic University of America
- Cleveland State University
- Columbia University
- Duke University
- Emory University
- Georgetown University
- The George Washington University
- Howard University
- Hunter College
- Louisiana State University
- Marquette University
- Miami University
- Oberlin College
- Ohio State University
- Southwestern University
- Texas Woman's University
- Trinity College (Connecticut)
- University of Alabama
- University of Alabama, Birmingham
- University of California, Los Angeles
- University of California, Santa Barbara
- University of Connecticut
- University of Colorado
- University of Florida
- University of Iowa
- University of New Hampshire

University of Miami
University of Pennsylvania
University of Texas
University of Wisconsin
University of Wisconsin, Milwaukee
Vanderbilt University
Yale University

Source: National Abortion Rights Action League

PRO-LIFERS

Schools with the most active pro-life groups:
Catholic University of America
Cornell University
Dordt College
Franciscan University of Steubenville
Indiana University
Texas A&M University
Thomas More College
University of Illinois
University of Wisconsin
Villanova University

Source: American Collegians for Life

STUDENT LIFE

AMNESTY ACTIVISTS

Schools with the most active Amnesty International groups:
- Boston University
- Columbia University
- Georgetown University
- James Madison University
- Northwestern University
- Southern Methodist University
- University of California, Berkeley
- University of Florida
- University of Minnesota
- University of Washington

Source: Amnesty International USA

TOP G.O.P.'S

Schools with the most active Republican clubs:
- Ball State University
- Colorado State University
- Illinois State University
- Marquette University
- Mississippi State University
- Ohio State University
- Texas A&M University
- University of California, Berkeley
- University of Southern California
- University of Texas

Source: College Republican National Committee

STUDENT LIFE

DEMOCRAT FRATS

Schools with the most active Democratic clubs:
- Columbia University
- Georgetown University
- Harvard University
- Louisiana State University
- Oberlin College
- Southern Illinois University
- Spelman College
- State University of New York, Geneseo
- University of California, Berkeley
- University of Colorado
- University of Florida
- University of Michigan
- University of Minnesota
- University of Rochester

Source: College Democrats of America

STUDENT LIFE

ROTC-LESS

Schools that have banned ROTC:
- Colby College
- Harvard University
- Pitzer College
- Rutgers, The State University of New Jersey (no scholarships)
- University of Wisconsin, River Falls
- Yale University

Source: Lesbian and Gay Rights Project, American Civil Liberties Union

Schools with a high degree of anti-ROTC activism:
- Alfred University
- California State University, Chico
- California State University, Northridge
- California State University, Sacramento
- California State University, San Bernardino
- California State University, San Jose
- City University of New York, John Jay College of Criminal Justice
- Dartmouth College
- DePauw University
- Indiana University (all campuses)
- Johns Hopkins University
- Lynchburg College
- Massachusetts Institute of Technology
- Northern Illinois University
- Northwestern University
- San Diego State University

STUDENT LIFE

State University of New York, Oswego
Syracuse University
University of California, Berkeley
University of California, Los Angeles
University of California, Santa Cruz
University of Cincinnati
University of Colorado
University of Connecticut
University of Illinois
University of Kansas
University of Minnesota
University of Pennsylvania
University of Pittsburgh
University of Rhode Island
University of Southern California
University of Texas, Arlington
University of Virginia
University of Washington
University of Wisconsin
Washington University

Source: Lesbian and Gay Rights Project, American Civil Liberties Union

STUDENT LIFE

Schools that have given ROTC a deadline to leave campus:
- Amherst College
- California State University, Chico
- California State University, Sacramento
- City University of New York, John Jay College of Criminal Justice
- Dartmouth College
- Lynchburg College
- Massachusetts Institue of Technology
- State University of New York, Cortland
- State University of New York, Oswego

Source: Lesbian and Gay Rights Project, American Civil Liberties Union

ROTC IN THE MULTICULTURAL ERA

ROTC controversy on campuses today focuses on its policy of excluding gays and lesbians from the armed services.

The level of protest activity varies from campus to campus. In some cases it is initiated by the campus gay/lesbian/bisexual alliance, while in other cases, it's the student government or even a faculty member who galvanizes support in the school community.

This was the case at University of Indiana when Dr. Michael V. W. Gordon, Vice Chancellor and Dean of students, spoke in support of a resolution to sever ROTC ties. He related the need for ROTC to be inclusive to his own experience as a black man who served in ROTC immediately after the military ended its policy of discrimination against blacks.

STUDENT LIFE

PRO ROTC

Schools with the most active Army ROTC programs:
- Campbell University
- The Citadel
- Clarkson College
- Indiana University of Pennsylvania
- Lehigh University
- Massachusetts Institute of Technology
- Northeastern University
- Norwich University
- St. John's University (Minnesota)
- Seattle University
- South Carolina State College
- Syracuse University
- Texas A&M University
- University of California, Los Angeles
- University of Kentucky
- University of Miami
- University of North Dakota
- University of Puerto Rico
- University of Washington
- Virginia Military Institute

Source: U.S. Army ROTC Command, Fort Monroe, Virginia

STUDENT LIFE

STATES OF BLISS

Top states in which students from different schools work together on progressive environmental action:

- California
- Florida
- Illinois
- Massachusetts
- Michigan
- New Jersey
- New York
- North Carolina
- Ohio
- Pennsylvania

Source: Students for Environmental Action Coalition (SEAC)

ENVIRONMENTAL IS ELEMENTAL

With over 33,000 students on 1,500 campuses, SEAC is the largest and most active student environmental action group in the nation. The following schools have the most active SEAC groups:

- Columbia University
- Baylor University
- Boston University
- Brandeis University
- Brown University
- Cleveland State University

STUDENT LIFE

College of the Atlantic
Duke University
Emory University
Furman University
Harvard University
Hendrix College
James Madison University
Johns Hopkins University
Kansas State University
Macalester College
Marshall University
Michigan State University
Mississippi State University
New York University
Northeast Missouri State University
Northeastern University
Northland College
Ohio University
Princeton University
Southern Illinois University, Edwardsville
State University of New York, Potsdam
Stockton State College
Susquehanna University
Trinity University
Tufts University
Tulane University
University of California, Berkeley
University of California, Los Angeles
University of California, San Diego
University of Colorado
University of Delaware
University of Georgia
University of Idaho

STUDENT LIFE

University of Illinois
University of Maine
University of Michigan
University of Nebraska
University of New Mexico
University of North Carolina
University of North Carolina, Greensboro
University of San Francisco
University of South Carolina
University of Virginia
University of Wyoming
Vanderbilt University
Wellesley College
Wheaton College (Massachusetts)
Yale University

Source: Students for Environmental Action Coalition

STUDENT LIFE

WAYNE'S WORLD

The top college TV stations:
- Bemidji State University, KBSU-TV
- Berry College, WBCS-TV
- Buena Vista College, Innovation Video
- Indiana University–Purdue University, Fort Wayne, College Cable Access
- Ithaca College, ICTV
- Northern Arizona University, U-TV
- San Francisco State University, TV-35
- Southern Missouri State University, MSTV
- Temple University, Channel 55
- Washington State University, Cable 8
- Western Michigan University, EduCable

Source: National Association of College Broadcasters

STUDENT LIFE

WCOL

The top college radio stations:
- Brown University, WBRU-FM
- California State University, San Jose, KSJS-FM
- Dartmouth College, WFRD-FM/WDCR-AM
- Georgia State University, WRAS-FM
- Loyola University, Los Angeles KXLU-FM
- Loyola University, Chicago, WLUW-FM
- Northwestern University, WNUR-FM
- Rice University, KTRU-FM
- Seton Hall University, WSOU-FM
- University of Dayton, WVUD-FM
- University of Kansas, KJHK-FM
- University of San Francisco, KUSF-FM
- University of Virginia, WUVA-FM
- University of Washington, KCMU-FM

Source: National Association of College Broadcasters

MUSIC MECCAS

Best college towns and cities for underground music:
- Athens, Georgia
- Austin, Texas
- Lincoln, Nebraska
- Minneapolis, Minnesota
- Norman, Oklahoma
- Raleigh, North Carolina
- Seattle, Washington

Source: *nachur ov realitees*

STUDENT LIFE

BETTER DEAD THAN READ

Havens for Dead Heads:
- Albany State College
- Bryn Mawr College
- Bucknell University
- State University of New York, Buffalo
- Ithaca College
- Lehigh University
- Ohio University
- Stanford University
- State University of New York, Binghamton
- Swarthmore College
- Syracuse University
- University of California, Berkeley
- University of California, Los Angeles
- University of California, Santa Cruz
- University of Colorado
- University of Minnesota
- University of Oregon
- University of Richmond
- University of Washington
- University of Pennsylvania
- West Chester State University
- Worcester Polytechnic Institute

Source: *Unbroken Chain*, the longest-running Grateful Dead magazine in America

STUDENT LIFE

READ ALL ABOUT IT

The best campus dailies:
- Arizona State University, *State Press*
- Indiana University, *Indiana Daily Student*
- Kansas State University, *Kansas State Collegian*
- University of California, Berkeley, *The Daily Californian*
- University of California, Los Angeles, *Daily Bruin*
- University of Georgia, *The Red & Black*
- University of Illinois, *The Daily Illini*
- University of Iowa, *Daily Iowan*
- University of Kansas, *The University Daily Kansan*
- University of Minnesota, *The Minnesota Daily*
- University of Nebraska, *Daily Nebraskan*
- University of North Carolina, *The Daily Tar Heel*
- University of Pennsylvania, *The Daily Pennsylvanian*
- University of Texas, Arlington, *The Shorthorn*
- University of Texas, *Daily Texan*

Source: *Gannett Center Journal*, Columbia University

STUDENT LIFE

UNDERGROUND PRESS

Schools with the top alternative/progressive student-run newspapers:

    Evergreen State College, *Evergreen Free Press*
    Massachusetts Institute of Technology, *The Thistle*
    Southern Illinois University, *Satyagraha*
    University of California, Davis, *Third World Forum*
    University of Florida, *The Gainesville Iguana*
    University of Kansas, *Take This!*
    University of Oregon, *Student Insurgent*
    University of Texas, *Polemicist*
    Wesleyan University, *Hermes*

Source: New Liberation News Service

According to Jason Pramis, the director of the New Liberation News Service, a radical news wire founded in the sixties, most progressive papers share a dedication to democratic social change. On college campuses, these publications tend to cover issues relating to the environment, race relations, sexuality, and underground culture.

STUDENT LIFE

CONSERVATIVELY PRESSED

The ten largest (and most widely read) conservative college newspapers and magazines:

Columbia University (*The Federalist Paper*)
Dartmouth College (*The Dartmouth Review*)
Duke University (*Duke Review*)
Harvard University (*The Harvard Salient*)
University of California, Berkeley (*Berkeley Review*)
University of Illinois (*The Orange and Blue Observer*)
University of Michigan (*Michigan Review*)
University of Texas (*University Review of Texas*)
University of Wisconsin, Milwaukee (*The U.W.M. Times*)
Stanford University (*Stanford Review*)

Source: The Collegiate Network

STUDENT LIFE

IN TUNE

Schools with the top men's a cappella groups:
- Amherst College—Zumbyes
- Brown University—Jaborwockes
- Columbia University—Kingsmen
- Harvard University—Krokodiloes
- Princeton University—Tiger Tones
- Stanford University—Fleet Street Singers
- Tufts University—Beelzebubs
- University of California, Berkeley—Men's Octet
- University of Pennsylvania—Penn Six–5000
- Yale University—Whiffenpoofs

Schools with the top women's a cappella groups:
- Columbia University—Metrotones
- Colgate University—Swinging Gates
- Duke University—Out of the Blue
- Harvard University—Radcliffe Pitches
- Mount Holyoke—V-8's
- Smith College—Notables
- Tufts University—Jackson Jills
- University of California, Berkeley—Golden Overtones
- University of North Carolina—Loreleis
- Vassar College—Measure for Measure
- Wellesley College—Tupelos

Source: Contemporary A Cappella Society

STUDENT LIFE

BRIDGE BANDITS

Schools with highly competitive bridge teams:
- Brown University
- California Institute of Technology
- College of William and Mary
- Columbia University
- Cornell University
- Harvard University
- Johns Hopkins University
- Lehigh University
- Massachusetts Institute of Technology
- Princeton University
- Purdue University
- Rensselaer Polytechnic Institute
- Rice University
- Stanford University
- University of California, Los Angeles
- University of Miami
- University of Michigan
- University of Minnesota
- University of North Carolina
- University of Pennsylvania
- University of Texas
- University of Virginia
- University of Washington
- Virginia Polytechnic Institute and State University
- Yale University

Source: American Contract Bridge League

STUDENT LIFE

National Bridge Conference winners:
- California Institute of Technology
- Johns Hopkins University
- Rice University
- University of Michigan
- Yale University

Source: American Contract Bridge League

BRIDGE IS BACK

Bridge is a highly cerebral card game that tends to attract people with a mathematical bent. Although its popularity peaked on campus in the late 1950's, it seems to be gaining new interest and élan. Top celebrity bridge players include Clint Eastwood, Lee Iacocca, and Martina Navratilova. In an effort to attract a new generation of bridge players, the American Contract Bridge League and the Association of Collegiate Unions are working together to sponsor lessons and organize bridge teams at colleges throughout the United States.

GRAD MASTERS

Schools with the top chess teams:
- Columbia University
- Harvard University
- University of Chicago
- Yale University

Source: U.S. Chess Federation

STUDENT LIFE

COMEDY U.

Schools that have participated in the National College Comedy Festival:

- Brandeis University
- Brown University
- College of William and Mary
- Cornell University
- Harvard University
- Kenyon College
- Skidmore College
- Stanford University
- Swarthmore College
- Tufts University
- University of Arizona
- University of Maryland
- University of Michigan
- University of Notre Dame
- University of Pennsylvania
- University of Southern California
- University of Virginia
- Vassar College
- Williams College
- Yale University

Source: National College Comedy Festival

STUDENT LIFE

THAT'S DEBATABLE

The top schools for parliamentary debate:
- Columbia University
- Harvard University
- Johns Hopkins University
- Princeton University
- Wesleyan University
- University of Maryland
- Yale University

Source: American Parliamentary Debate Association

The top schools in individual events competition:
- Arizona State University
- Bradley University
- Colorado College
- Cornell University
- Eastern Michigan University
- George Mason University
- Illinois State University
- Kansas State University
- Ohio University
- Seton Hall University
- Southwest Baptist University
- University of Texas
- University of Texas, Arlington
- University of Wisconsin
- University of Wisconsin, Eau Claire

Source: *Intercollegiate Speech Tournament Results*

STUDENT LIFE

The top schools for cross-examination debate:
- Central State University
- Cornell University
- Emory University
- Emporia State University
- Florida State University
- Kansas State University
- Macalester College
- Marist College
- Northwestern State University of Louisiana
- Southern Utah State University
- Southern Illinois University
- United States Air Force Academy
- University of California, Los Angeles
- University of Missouri, Kansas City
- University of Vermont
- Wheaton College (Illinois)

Source: Executive Secretary's Report, Cross-Examination Debate Association

STUDENT LIFE

MARCH ON

The top college marching bands:
- Florida A&M University
- Ohio State University
- University of Tennessee
- University of Illinois
- University of Southern California
- University of Michigan
- University of Texas
- University of Oklahoma

Source: Bill Foster, past president of College Band Directors National Association and director of the Florida A&M University Marching Band since 1946

BAND TOGETHER

Schools with the largest college marching bands (number of members in parentheses):
- Florida State University (400)
- Purdue University (386)
- Texas Tech University (380)
- University of Georgia (371)
- University of Texas (338)

Source: *USA Today* research

STUDENT LIFE

CAMPUS CRUSADERS

Schools with the largest Campus Crusade for Christ ministries:

- Auburn University
- Bowling Green State University
- Colorado State University
- Cornell University
- Indiana University
- Indiana University of Pennsylvania
- James Madison University
- Kansas State University
- Miami University
- Pennsylvania State University
- Purdue University
- St. Cloud State University
- Syracuse University
- University of Alabama
- University of Arizona
- University of Kansas
- University of Minnesota
- University of North Carolina
- University of Southern California
- University of Texas
- University of Washington
- Virginia Polytechnic Institute and State University

Source: Campus Crusade for Christ

STUDENT LIFE

CHRISTIAN LEADERS

The most competitive Christian colleges:
- Anderson University
- Asbury College
- Azusa Pacific University
- Belhaven College
- Bethel College (Minnesota)
- Bethel College (Kansas)
- Biola University
- Calvin College
- Campbell University
- Covenant College
- Dallas Baptist University
- Eastern College
- Eastern Mennonite College
- Fresno Pacific College
- Geneva College
- George Fox College
- Gordon College
- Goshen College
- Grand Canyon University
- Greenville College
- Houghton College
- John Brown University
- King College
- The King's College
- LeTourneau University
- Malone College
- Messiah College
- Mississippi College
- North Park College
- Northwestern College (Iowa)

Northwestern College (Minnesota)
Northwest Nazarene College
Palm Beach Atlantic College
Point Loma Nazarene College
Roberts Wesleyan College
Seattle Pacific University
Sioux Falls College
Southern California College
Tabor College
Taylor University
Trinity College (Illinois)
Westmont College
Wheaton College (Illinois)
Whitworth College
William Jennings Bryan College

Source: Christian College Coalition

CHRISTIAN CAMPUSES

The largest Christian colleges:
1. Campbell University
2. Mississippi College
3. Seattle Pacific University
4. Azusa Pacific University
5. Biola University
6. Wheaton College (Illinois)
7. Messiah College
8. Dallas Baptist University
9. Point Loma Nazarene University
10. Cedarville College

Source: Christian College Coalition

STUDENT LIFE

INTERVARSITY LEADERS

Schools with the most active Intervarsity chapters:

- Appalachian State University
- California Polytechnic State University
- College of William and Mary
- North Carolina State University
- Northwestern University
- Occidental College
- University of California, Berkeley
- University of California, San Diego
- University of Delaware
- University of Illinois
- University of Illinois, Chicago
- University of Minnesota
- University of North Carolina
- University of Wisconsin
- Wayne State University

With chapters at over 800 schools, Intervarsity is one of the largest and, some say, most low-key of the evangelical Christian groups on campus.

"They are never rah-rah or yippy skippy over Jesus," says a Columbia University junior. "They never try to cram the Bible down your throat. Intervarsity is simply cooler than many of the other conservative Christian groups."

Source: Intervarsity Christian Fellowship

STUDENT LIFE

TRUE CATHOLICS

Schools that practice complete fidelity to the teachings of the Holy Roman Catholic Church:

- Christendom College
- Magdalen College
- Franciscan University of Steubenville
- Thomas Aquinas College
- The Thomas More College
- University of Dallas

The people who attend the schools listed above look at institutions such as Georgetown University and University of Notre Dame as schools that have "left the fold" and, in effect, betrayed their Catholic mission.

"Unlike most other 'Catholic' colleges in this country, we recognize that when the Church speaks in the person of the Holy Father, the Pope, that the Church speaks with the authority of God. Therefore we have an obligation to adhere to all Vatican teachings," explains Regis Martin, S.T.D., Professor of Theology at Franciscan University of Steubenville.

STUDENT LIFE

JEWISH COMMUNITIES

Schools with the largest number of Jewish students:

- The American University
- Boston University
- Brandeis University
- California State University, Northridge
- Columbia University
- Cornell University
- City University of New York, Brooklyn College
- City University of New York, Queens College
- Duke University
- Emory University
- The George Washington University
- Harvard University
- Michigan State University
- New York University
- Ohio State University
- Pennsylvania State University
- Rutgers, The State University of New Jersey
- San Diego State University
- San Francisco State University
- State University of New York, Albany
- State University of New York, Binghamton
- State University of New York, Buffalo
- State University of New York, Stony Brook
- Temple University
- Tulane University
- Tufts University
- University of California, Berkeley
- University of California, Davis
- University of California, Los Angeles

University of California, San Diego
University of Cincinnati
University of Florida
University of Illinois
University of Maryland
University of Massachusetts
University of Miami
University of Michigan
University of Minnesota
University of Pennsylvania
University of Pittsburgh
University of South Florida
University of Texas
University of Wisconsin
Washington University
Yeshiva College/Stern College for Women

Source: *The Hillel Guide to Jewish Life on Campus*

Schools where over 25% of the student body is Jewish:

The American University
Barnard College
Boston University
Brandeis University
Brown University
Carnegie Mellon University
Curry College
California State University, Northridge
Columbia University
The George Washington University
Harvard University
Haverford College

New York University
Oberlin College
Sarah Lawrence College
Simmons College
State University of New York, Albany
State University of New York, Binghamton
Tulane University
Tufts University
University of California, Berkeley
University of California, Los Angeles
University of Maryland
University of Pennsylvania
Vassar College
Washington University
Yale University
Yeshiva College/Stern College for Women

Source: *The Hillel Guide to Jewish Life on Campus*

STUDENT LIFE

HILLEL HOTBEDS

Schools with the most active Hillel organizations:

- Boston University
- Brandeis University
- Brown University
- California State University, Northridge
- Carnegie Mellon University
- Columbia University
- Cornell University
- The George Washington University
- Harvard University
- Hofstra University
- Northwestern University
- Rutgers, The State University of New Jersey
- Stanford University
- State University of New York, Binghamton
- State University of New York, Buffalo
- State University of New York, Stony Brook
- University of California, Berkeley
- University of California, Los Angeles
- University of California, San Diego
- University of California, Santa Barbara
- University of Cincinnati
- University of Chicago
- University of Florida
- University of Maryland
- University of Massachusetts
- University of Miami
- University of Michigan
- University of Pennsylvania
- University of Pittsburgh

University of Rochester
University of Southern California
University of Texas
University of Washington
University of Wisconsin
Washington University

Source: *The Hillel Guide to Jewish Life on Campus*

MEETING QUAKERS

Schools under the care of Friends:
  Barclay College
  Bryn Mawr College
  Earlham College
  Friends University
  George Fox College
  Guilford College
  Haverford College
  Malone College
  Swarthmore College
  Whittier College
  William Penn College
  Wilmington College

Source: Friends Council on Education

STUDENT LIFE

MUSLIM STUDENTS

Schools with the most active Muslim Student Associations:
- American University
- Arizona State University
- Colorado State University
- George Mason University
- The George Washington University
- Louisiana State University
- Massachusetts Institute of Technology
- New Mexico State University
- State University of New York, Buffalo
- University of California, Los Angeles
- University of Cincinnati
- University of Colorado
- University of Illinois
- University of Maryland
- University of Wisconsin

Source: The Islamic Society of North America

STUDENT LIFE

ONE BIG FAMILY

Schools where more than 90% of undergrads live on campus:

- Alma College
- Amherst College
- Bates College
- The Citadel
- Claremont McKenna College
- Colby College
- Columbia University, School of Engineering
- Connecticut College
- Dartmouth College
- DePauw University
- Dickinson College
- Drew University
- Duke University
- Fisk University
- Gustavus Adolphus College
- Hamilton College
- Hampshire College
- Harvard University
- Harvey Mudd College
- Haverford College
- Hollins College
- Illinois Wesleyan University
- Kalamazoo College
- Lafayette College
- Massachusetts Institute of Technology
- Messiah College
- Middlebury College
- Mount Holyoke College
- Muhlenberg College

STUDENT LIFE

Ohio Wesleyan University
Pomona College
Princeton University
Randolph-Macon College
Scripps College
Smith College
St. Olaf College
Swarthmore College
Trinity College (Connecticut)
United States Air Force Academy
United States Coast Guard Academy
United States Merchant Marine Academy
United States Military Academy
United States Naval Academy
University of Richmond
University of the South
Ursinus College
Vassar College
Virginia Military Institute
Webb Institute of Naval Architecture
Wellesley College
Wells College
Williams College

STUDENT LIFE

A LIFE OF ONE'S OWN

Schools where fewer than 15% of students live on campus:

- Albany College of Pharmacy
- California State University, Dominguez Hills
- California State University, Long Beach
- City University of New York, City College
- City University of New York, Queens College
- Cooper Union for the Advancement of Science and Art
- Florida Atlantic University
- Georgia State University
- Hawaii Pacific University
- New Jersey Institute of Technology
- Pace University
- Sacred Heart University
- St. John's University (New York)
- San Francisco Conservatory of Music
- University of Cincinnati
- University of Houston
- University of Louisville
- University of Minnesota
- University of Nevada
- University of New Mexico
- University of Texas
- University of Texas, Arlington
- University of Texas, El Paso
- University of Utah
- University of Wisconsin, Milwaukee

STUDENT LIFE

SPRAWLING

Schools with campuses of 5,000 or more acres (total acreage is listed):

Berry College	28,000
United States Air Force Academy	18,325
United States Military Academy	16,000
University of the South	10,000
Duke University	8,500
Stanford University	8,200
New Mexico State University	6,250
Michigan State University	5,239
Texas A&M University	5,142
Pennsylvania State University	5,013
Tuskegee University	5,000

STUDENT LIFE

PERSONAL SPACE

Schools with over half an acre per student:
- Amherst College
- Bard College
- Bennington College
- Carleton College
- Duke University
- Earlham College
- Hamilton College
- Hampden-Sydney College
- Hampshire College
- Kenyon College
- Knox College
- Marlboro College
- Montana State University
- St. John's College (New Mexico)
- Stanford University
- Tuskegee University
- United States Air Force Academy
- United States Military Academy
- University of the South
- Wells College
- Williams College

STUDENT LIFE

THE BIG POND

Schools with more than 25,000 undergrads:
- Arizona State University
- Brigham Young University
- California State University, Long Beach
- Indiana University
- Michigan State University
- Northeastern University
- Ohio State University
- Pennsylvania State University
- Texas A&M University
- University of Arizona
- University of Florida
- University of Illinois
- University of Maryland
- University of Minnesota
- University of Wisconsin

STUDENT LIFE

SMALL AND COZY

Schools with fewer than eight hundred undergrads:
- Agnes Scott College
- Albany College of Pharmacy
- Antioch College
- Bennington College
- College of the Atlantic
- The College of Insurance
- Harvey Mudd College
- Juilliard School
- King College
- Marlboro College
- Mills College
- New College of the University of South Florida
- New School for Social Research, Eugene Lang College
- Otis/Parsons School of Art and Design
- Randolph-Macon Woman's College
- Rosemont College
- San Francisco Conservatory of Music
- School for International Training
- Scripps College
- St. John's College (Maryland)
- St. John's College (New Mexico)
- State University of New York Health Science Center, Syracuse
- University of Judaism, Lee College
- Webb Institute of Naval Architecture
- Wells College

STUDENT LIFE

ALL IN THE SAME BOAT

Schools with campuses of fewer than ten acres:
- Albany College of Pharmacy
- Barnard College
- The College of Insurance
- Cooper Union for the Advancement of Science and Art
- Hahnemann University/School of Health Science & Humanities
- Hawaii Pacific University
- Juilliard School
- Milwaukee School of Engineering
- New School for Social Research, Eugene Lang College
- Otis/Parsons School of Art and Design
- Pace University
- San Francisco Conservatory of Music
- School for International Training
- State University of New York Health Science Center, Syracuse

STUDENT LIFE

HEAVY HISTORY

The oldest schools, listed by year of founding:

Harvard University	1636
College of William and Mary	1693
St. John's College (Maryland)	1696
Yale University	1701
University of Pennsylvania	1740
University of Delaware	1743
Princeton University	1746
Washington and Lee University	1749
Columbia University	1754
Brown University	1764
Rutgers, The State University of New Jersey	1766
Dartmouth College	1769
Dickinson College	1773
Hampden-Sydney College	1776
Washington and Jefferson College	1781

STUDENT LIFE

SIXTIES CHILDREN

Schools founded in the sixties:
- California State University, Dominguez Hills
- College of the Atlantic
- The College of Insurance
- Florida Atlantic University
- Hampshire College
- Hawaii Pacific University
- New College of the University of South Florida
- Oral Roberts University
- Sacred Heart University
- St. John's College (New Mexico)
- School for International Training
- Texas A&M University, Galveston
- Thomas Aquinas College
- University of California, Irvine
- University of California, Santa Cruz

STUDENT LIFE

CAMPUS CUISINE

Schools with award-winning residence-hall food:
   Ashland University
   Kansas State University
   Lawrence University
   Southern Methodist University
   University of California, Irvine
   University of California, Los Angeles
   University of Kansas
   University of San Diego

Source: The National Association of College and University Food Services

Schools with award-winning specialty restaurants or shops:
   Louisiana State University
   Pennsylvania State University
   State University of New York, Morrisville
   Texas Tech University

Source: The National Association of College and University Food Services

STUDENT LIFE

PIZZA FACE

Schools with Pizza Huts on campus:
- Anderson University
- Arizona State University
- Babson College
- Boise State University
- Buena Vista College
- Butler University
- California State University, Fullerton
- California State University, Stanislaus
- Case Western Reserve University
- Central Missouri State University
- College of William and Mary
- Colorado College
- Cornell University
- David Lipscomb University
- Denison University
- Earlham College
- Emerson College
- George Mason University
- The George Washington University
- Georgetown University
- Grand Valley State College
- Hamline University
- Hunter College
- Indiana University/Purdue University at Indianapolis
- St. Louis University
- Southern Illinois University
- State University of New York, Farmingdale
- Texas A&I University
- Texas Christian University

STUDENT LIFE

Troy State University
Tulane University
University of California, Davis
University of California, Riverside
University of Denver
University of Evansville
University of Hartford
University of Louisville
University of Lowell
University of North Carolina
University of North Carolina, Greensboro
University of South Carolina
University of Tennessee, Martin
University of Texas, Arlington
Washington University
Weber State University
Western Washington University
Winthrop College

Source: New Concepts Department, Pizza Hut

STUDENT LIFE

A WHEELCHAIR GUIDE

The best schools for students who use wheelchairs.

Comprehensive service:
- Edinboro University of Pennsylvania
- Louisiana Tech University
- St. Andrews Presbyterian College
- University of Houston
- University of Illinois
- University of Kentucky
- University of South Carolina
- Wright State University

Intermediate service:
- Arizona State University
- Ball State University
- Boston University
- Dowling College
- East Carolina University
- Kent State University
- Memphis State University
- Michigan State University
- Southern Illinois University
- University of California, Davis
- University of Connecticut
- University of Missouri
- University of North Carolina
- University of North Carolina, Greensboro

Basic service:
- Colorado State University

STUDENT LIFE

Emory University
Emporia State University
Hofstra University
Hope College
Marquette University
Montana State University
Ohio State University
Ramapo College of New Jersey
State University of New York, Stony Brook
Stephen F. Austin State University
Temple University
Texas A&I University
Texas A&M University
University of Arizona
University of Delaware
University of Kansas
University of North Dakota

Source: *Colleges That Enable*

Jason Tweed, co-author of *Colleges That Enable*, is confined to a wheelchair, and he evaluated the services schools offer the wheelchair-bound student.

"Full service" schools offer the most comprehensive services and are best for students who have never lived away from home before. This may include attendant care, academic assistance, transportation, or special support services such as wheelchair repair. "Intermediate service" schools provide a good transition for students who have not been independent before but want to become moderately so at school. "Basic service" schools are those which may not have as extensive support services but were found to be enthusiastic and committed to helping wheelchair-bound students in any way possible. For more information, contact Jason Tweed at (215) 376-1015.

STUDENT LIFE

A HELPING HAND

Schools with scholarships for disabled students:

- Arizona State University (Andrew Brown Scholarships, Disabled Students Resources Regents Scholarships, Merriam Scholarships)
- College of St. Elizabeth (Genevieve A. Walsh Scholarship)
- Francis Marion College (Ralph K. Anderson III Scholarship)
- Goldey-Beacom College (Esther S. Marshall Scholarship)
- Hofstra University (Rosalie Giannone Scholarship, John Brennan Memorial Scholarship, Robert B. Betts Distinguished Academic Scholarship)
- Iowa State University (Elizabeth R. Hansen Scholarship)
- Kent State University (Richard T. Cunningham Spinal Cord Injury Scholarship, Telephone Pioneers Scholarship, Akron YMCA Scholarship)
- Old Dominion University (Hugh Vivius Vaughan Scholarship)
- South Dakota School of Mines and Technology (Ivan E. Landstrom Memorial Scholarship)
- Southern Illinois University (Shubert Scholarship)
- Texas A&M University (Will Rogers Memorial Scholarship, Howard Allen Johnston Endowed Scholarship)

University of Arizona (Wheelchair Athletic Scholarship, CeDrr Academic Scholarship, CeDrr Minority Scholarship, Margaret Modine Encouragement Grant)

University of California, Davis

University of Colorado (Robert Wilkerson Scholarship)

University of Houston (Terry Brayton Scholarship)

University of Illinois (Athletic Scholarships, Academic Scholarships)

University of Texas, Arlington (Andrew David Beck Memorial Wheelchair Scholarship, Wheelchair Athletic Scholarship, Allan Saxe Scholarship)

Wright State University (Michael Emrick Scholarship, Campus Scholarship, Dan Byrnes Wheelchair Basketball Scholarship, White Prize, Heines Merker Scholarship)

Source: *Sports 'n Spokes*

LEARNING DISABILITIES

There are over 250 schools with programs and services designed to help the learning disabled student. As might be expected, the depth of the offerings and the kinds of facilities and services that are available vary from campus to campus. Brown University, for example, is one of the only schools to offer a program to help the "gifted" learning disabled student.

For more information on what's out there, contact the Learning Disabilities Association of America, 4156 Library Road, Pittsburgh, PA 15234, (412) 341-1515.

STUDENT LIFE

DEAF JAM

Schools with the largest number of deaf students:
- California State University, Northridge
- City University of New York (four branches)
- Gallaudet University
- Rochester Institute of Technology

Schools with college and career programs for deaf students:
- Abilene Christian University
- Arizona State University
- Bakersfield College
- Boise State University
- Boston University
- Bloomsburg University of Pennsylvania
- California State Polytechnic University
- California State University, Long Beach
- California State University, Northridge
- Central College
- City University of New York (four branches)
- Colorado State University
- East Carolina University
- East Central University
- Eastern Kentucky University
- Eastern New Mexico University
- Florida State University
- Gallaudet University
- Gardner Webb College
- Georgia State University
- Illinois State University
- Jacksonville State University
- Lamar University
- Lee College

STUDENT LIFE

Lenoir-Rhyne College
Madonna University
Mankato State University
Michigan State University
Northeastern University
Northern Illinois University
Oklahoma State University
Pennsylvania State University
Rochester Institute of Technology
San Diego State University
San Francisco State University
Southern Illinois State University
Stephen F. Austin State University
Tennessee Temple University
Tufts University
University of Arizona
University of California, Davis
University of Colorado
University of Florida
University of Iowa
University of Kentucky
University of North Florida
University of Minnesota
University of Nebraska
University of Texas
University of Tennessee
University of Vermont
University of Wisconsin, Milwaukee
Utah State University
Weber State University
Western Oregon State College

Source: *College and Career Programs for Deaf Students*, Gallaudet University, and The National Institute for the Deaf

STUDENT LIFE

GAY LIFE ON CAMPUS

Schools with courses in gay/lesbian/bisexual studies:

- Alfred University
- Amherst College
- Arizona State University
- Bucknell University
- California State University, San Bernardino
- California State University, San Jose
- City College of San Francisco
- Colorado College
- The George Washington University
- Grinnell College
- Hampshire College
- Iowa State University
- Mankato State University
- Miami University
- Michigan State University
- New York University
- Northwestern University
- Ohio State University
- Ohio University
- Pace University
- Pennsylvania State University
- Pitzer College
- Southern Oregon State College
- State University of New York, Albany
- State University of New York, Cortland
- State University of New York, New Paltz
- State University of New York, Stony Brook
- University of Alabama
- University of California, Berkeley

STUDENT LIFE

University of California, Davis
University of California, Irvine
University of Illinois
University of Iowa
University of Michigan
University of Minnesota
University of Northern Iowa
University of Oklahoma
University of Oregon
University of Wisconsin

Source: National Gay and Lesbian Task Force

What constitutes a lesbian/gay/bisexual course will vary from school to school. Depending on what the course deals with, it could be housed in one of any number of departments from anthropology to women's studies. Colorado College, for example, offers "Gay Literature and Film" through the English Department. California State University, San Bernardino, offers "Psychology of Gays and Lesbians" through the Psychology Department and at Alfred University, students can sign up at the Human Studies Department for "Gay American History."

Schools with lesbian/gay/bisexual student services offices:

Mankato State University
Ohio State University
University of Massachusetts
University of Michigan
University of Pennsylvania
Western Michigan University

Source: National Gay and Lesbian Task Force

STUDENT LIFE

Schools at which gay/lesbian students are eligible to benefit from the Markowski-Leach Scholarship Fund:

San Francisco State University
Stanford University
University of California, Berkeley

The Markowski-Leach Scholarship Fund was established in 1991 by two San Francisco men, Thomas Markowski and James Leach, who were long-time companions. Both died of AIDS. They established this fund for lesbian and gay students at San Francisco State University and other Bay Area institutions.

The first awards were distributed in the fall of 1992. For more information on the fund's eligibility requirements, contact San Francisco State University Development Office at (415) 338-2517.

Source: San Francisco State University

Schools with chapters of the lesbian sorority Lambda Delta Lambda:

Ball State University*
California State University, Long Beach
California State University, San Diego
San Francisco State University
University of California, Los Angeles
University of Delaware
University of Nebraska*

*chapters in formation

Source: Lambda Delta Lambda

STUDENT LIFE

Schools that provide "married student" housing for gay and lesbian couples:
- Brandeis University
- Harvard University
- Massachusetts Institute of Technology
- Miami University
- Occidental College
- Stanford University
- University of California, Berkeley
- University of California, Irvine
- University of California, Los Angeles
- University of Cincinnati
- University of North Dakota
- University of Oregon*

*for families with children only

Source: American Civil Liberties Union/National Gay and Lesbian Task Force's Family Project

STUDENT LIFE

NON-DISCRIMINATING

Schools with non-discrimination policies that include sexual orientation:

- Agnes Scott College
- Amherst College
- Antioch College
- Arizona State University
- Babson College
- Barnard College
- Beloit College
- Boston University
- Bowdoin College
- Brown University
- Bryn Mawr College
- California Institute of Technology
- California State University (20 campuses)
- Carleton College
- Carnegie Mellon University
- City University of New York (17 campuses)
- Claremont McKenna College
- Colby College
- College of William and Mary
- Colorado College
- Colorado State University
- Columbia University
- Cornell University
- Cornell College
- Dartmouth College
- Denison University
- Duke University
- Emory University
- The George Washington University
- Goddard College
- Grinnell College
- Hamline University
- Hampshire College
- Harvard University
- Haverford College
- Hood College
- Indiana University
- Iowa State University
- Kalamazoo College
- Kenyon College
- Knox College
- Lawrence University
- Macalester College
- Mankato State University
- Massachusetts Institute of Technology
- Michigan State University
- Mount Holyoke College
- New York University
- Northeastern University
- Northwestern University
- Oakland University
- Oberlin College
- Ohio State University

Ohio Wesleyan University
Oklahoma University
Oregon State University
Pennsylvania State University
Pitzer College
Pomona College
Portland State University
Princeton University
Radford University
Rensselaer Polytechnic Institute
Rollins College
Rutgers, The State University of New Jersey
St. Cloud State University
St. John's University
St. Lawrence University
San Francisco State University
Smith College
Southern Illinois University
Stanford University
State University of New York (includes all 64 SUNY campuses)
Swarthmore College
Syracuse University
Temple University
Texas A&M University
Trinity College (Connecticut)
Tufts University
Tulane University
University of Akron
University of Arizona
University of Arkansas
University of Chicago
University of California (all)
University of Cincinnati
University of Connecticut
University of Delaware
University of Hawaii
University of Houston
University of Illinois
University of Iowa
University of Kansas
University of Maine
University of Massachusetts
University of Michigan
University of Minneapolis
University of Minnesota
University of Missouri
University of Montana
University of Nebraska
University of New Hampshire
University of North Carolina
University of North Dakota
University of Oregon
University of Pennsylvania
University of Pittsburgh
University of Rhode Island
University of St. Thomas (Minnesota)
University of Texas

STUDENT LIFE

University of Utah
University of Vermont
University of Virginia
University of Washington
University of Wisconsin
Vassar College
Virginia Polytechnic Institute and State University
Wabash College
Washington State University
Wellesley College
Wesleyan University
West Chester State College (and all 14 other Pennsylvania state colleges)
West Virginia University
Western Illinois University
Western Michigan University
Williams College
Yale University

Source: National Gay and Lesbian Task Force

ATHLETICS

ATHLETICS

ON THE BALL

Schools where at least half the undergrads participate in intercollegiate sports:

- California Institute of Technology
- City University of New York, City College
- Connecticut College
- Florida Atlantic University
- Fordham University
- Gallaudet University
- Hampshire College
- Lehigh University
- Mount Holyoke College
- Stevens Institute of Technology
- United States Coast Guard Academy
- United States Merchant Marine Academy
- University of Puget Sound
- University of Virginia
- Washington and Jefferson College
- Williams College

ATHLETICS

ATHLETES INTO SCHOLARS

The National Consortium for Academics and Sports, a growing group of over 80 colleges and universities, was founded in 1985 in order to "Keep the Student in the Student Athlete."

They have their work cut out for them. According to a recent Louis Harris poll, over 32% of high school male football and basketball players think that they will play professionally. The reality is that one in 10,000 high school athletes becomes a professional.

In joining the Consortium, a school agrees to bring back "tuition-free" their own former student-athletes who competed in revenue-generating sports but were unable to complete their studies. In exchange, these "returning" athletes agree to counsel high school athletes about the world of college sports, encouraging them to pursue their education and plan carefully for their futures.

Here is a list of schools that belong to the Consortium:

Auburn University
Boise State University
Boston College
Boston University
Bradley University
California State University, Dominguez Hills
California State University, Long Beach
California State University, Sacramento
Canisius College
Cleveland State University
DePaul University
Duquesne University
Florida A&M University
Florida International University

ATHLETICS

Fordham University
George Mason University
The George Washington University
Georgetown University
Georgia Institute of Technology
Gonzaga University
Grambling State University
Hofstra University
Iona College
Indiana University—Purdue University, Indianapolis
Ithaca College
Kansas State University
La Salle University
Lehigh University
Loyola Marymount University
Manhattan College
Marist College
New York University
Occidental College
Northeast Louisiana University
Northeastern University
Pennsylvania State University
St. John's University (New York)
St. Mary's College of California
Santa Clara University
Seattle University
Seton Hall University
Southern Methodist University
Temple University
Texas A&M University
University of California, Berkeley
University of California, Davis

ATHLETICS

University of California, Irvine
University of California, San Diego
University of California, Santa Barbara
University of Central Florida
University of Cincinnati
University of Colorado, Colorado Springs
University of Connecticut
University of Denver
University of Georgia
University of South Florida
University of Hartford
University of Kentucky
University of Maryland
University of Mississippi
University of Missouri, St. Louis
University of Nebraska
University of Nevada
University of Nevada, Reno
University of North Carolina
University of the Pacific
University of Portland
University of Rhode Island
University of South Carolina
University of San Francisco
University of St. Thomas (Minnesota)
University of Texas, Arlington
University of Texas
University of Tulsa
University of Utah
Virginia Commonwealth University
West Virginia University

Source: Center for the Study of Sport in Society and National Consortium for Academics and Sports

ATHLETICS

PROBATION

These schools are under sanction by the NCAA. The relevant sports are noted, and the dates in parentheses indicate when the sanctions expire. Although sanctions vary from school to school, probation often primarily restricts the school's tournament eligibility:

Auburn University —Basketball, Tennis (11/22/93)
Hampton University—Football (2/1/93)
Howard University—Football (12/25/93)
Memphis State University—Football (8/7/92)
Miami University— Basketball (1/17/93)
Oklahoma State University—Football (1/9/93)
Simpson College—Wrestling (9/30/95)
Southeastern Louisiana University—Basketball (10/2/94)
Texas A&M University— Basketball (11/11/93)
Tulane University—Tennis (8/23/93)
University of the District of Columbia — Football, Basketball (9/25/94)
University of Florida—Football, Basketball (9/24/92)
University of Illinois—Basketball (11/12/93)
University of Lowell—Ice Hockey (2/1/93)
University of Maryland—Basketball (8/3/93)
University of Michigan—Baseball (3/26/93)
University of Minnesota—Football, Basketball, Wrestling (3/29/93)
University of Missouri—Basketball (11/7/92)
University of Nevada—Basketball (8/31/92)

ATHLETICS

University of Texas, El Paso—Basketball (10/30/94)
University of the Pacific—Basketball (4/3/93)
University of Tennessee—Football (10/5/93)
Upsala College—Basketball (9/7/95)

Source: NCAA

ARCHERY

Schools with archery clubs:
    Arizona State University
    Barnard College
    California State University, Long Beach
    Case Western Reserve University
    City University of New York, Baruch College
    Furman University
    James Madison University
    Miami University
    Michigan State University
    Millersville University
    North Carolina State University
    Purdue University
    Texas A&M University
    Trenton State College
    University of California, Davis
    University of California, Los Angeles
    University of Illinois
    University of Southern Maine
    University of Texas
    University of Virginia
    University of Akron
    University of Michigan
    Virginia Polytechnic Institute and State University

Source: National Archery Association

ATHLETICS

BADMINTON'S BEST

In the world of competitive sports, Arizona State University is a badminton dynasty. With a competitive program in place for twenty-three years, Arizona State has won thirty-four men's and women's team titles, fourteen men's and women's singles crowns, and eleven men's doubles and six women's doubles championships. Over the years, the badminton program has produced more All-Americans than any school in the country: seventy women and fifty-two men.

ATHLETICS

BASEBALL

Division I Champions
1. Louisiana State University
2. Wichita State University
3. Creighton University
   University of Florida
5. California State University, Fresno
   California State University, Long Beach
7. Clemson University
   Florida State University

Division II Champions
1. Jacksonville State University
2. Southern Missouri State University
3. University of California, Riverside
4. Longwood College
5. Florida Southern College
   Southern Illinois University
7. American International College
   Shippensburg University

Division III Champions
1. University of Southern Maine
2. Trenton State College
3. University of Wisconsin, Oshkosh
4. Methodist College
5. California State University, San Bernardino
   Marietta College
7. Ithaca College
   Simpson College

Source: NCAA (1991 results)

BASKETBALL

The top-ranked basketball teams:

Division I (Men's)
1. Duke University
2. Indiana University
3. University of Michigan
4. Ohio State University
5. University of Cincinnati
6. University of Kentucky
7. University of Kansas
8. University of California, Los Angeles
9. Oklahoma State University
10. University of Arkansas
11. University of Southern California
12. University of North Carolina
13. Seton Hall University
14. Florida State University
15. University of Massachusetts
16. University of Arizona
17. Memphis State University
18. University of Missouri
19. University of Alabama
20. Michigan State University
21. Georgia Institute of Technology
22. University of Texas, El Paso
23. Georgetown University
24. Syracuse University
25. Louisiana State University

Source: *USA Today*/CNN Poll (1992 results)

Division I (Women's)

1. Stanford University
2. University of Virginia
3. Western Kentucky University
4. Southwest Missouri State University
5. University of Tennessee
6. University of Mississippi
7. Vanderbilt University
8. University of Maryland
9. University of Miami
10. University of Iowa
11. West Virginia University
12. University of Southern California
13. Stephen F. Austin State University
14. Pennsylvania State University
15. Texas Tech University
16. Purdue University
17. University of Alabama
18. University of California, Los Angeles
19. Clemson University
20. The George Washington University
21. University of California, Santa Barbara
22. University of Vermont
23. University of Texas
24. Creighton University
25. University of Kansas

Source: *USA Today*/CNN poll; (1992 results)

BIATHLON

Schools with biathlon programs:
- Alaska Pacific University
- Dartmouth College
- Northern Michigan University

Source: United States Biathlon Association

BLIND ATHLETES

Schools with top programs for blind athletes:
- Ball State University
- Western Michigan University

Source: United States Association for Blind Athletes

BOWLING FOR SCHOLARS

Schools that offer bowling scholarships or financial aid for bowlers:
- Arizona State University
- Central Missouri State University
- Michigan State University
- Saginaw Valley State University (men's only)
- University of Florida
- University of Houston
- University of Nebraska
- West Texas State University
- Wichita State University

ATHLETICS

BOWLING

Top-ranked bowling teams:

Men's
1. William Paterson College
2. Wichita State University
3. San Jose State University
4. Vincennes University
5. Saginaw Valley State University
6. West Texas State University
7. University of Cincinnati
8. Ohio State University
9. Arizona State University
10. University of Nebraska
11. West Virginia University
12. University of Florida

Women's
1. West Texas State University
2. University of Nebraska
3. Wichita State University
4. Illinois State University
5. University of Florida
6. California State University, Sacramento
7. Erie Community College
8. Michigan State University
9. William Paterson College
10. Southwest Missouri State University
11. California State University, Fresno
12. Ohio State University

Source: Young American Bowling Alliance (1992 results)

ATHLETICS

COLLEGE BOWL

Bowling is more popular on campuses than you might have imagined. During the average school year, one in three college students will bowl. Over 200 schools offer competitive bowling teams. Just as the Ivy League schools were athletic powerhouses in many sports in earlier times, Yale University was the first school to recognize bowling as an intercollegiate sport in 1916.

ATHLETICS

BOXING

Schools that are members of the National Collegiate Boxing Association:

- Boston College
- Central Connecticut State University
- The Citadel
- Gettysburg College
- Iowa State University
- Lehigh University
- Lock Haven University of Pennsylvania
- Miami University
- Ohio University
- Pennsylvania State University
- St. John's College (Maryland)
- Santa Clara University
- Shippensburg University
- Texas A&M University
- United States Air Force Academy
- United States Military Academy
- United States Naval Academy
- University of California, Berkeley
- University of Nevada
- Virginia Military Institute
- Westfield State College
- West Chester University
- Western New England College
- Xavier University

Source: United States Amateur Boxing Federation

ATHLETICS

CHEERLEADING

Schools that offer cheerleading scholarships:
- The American University
- Angelo State University
- Auburn University
- Austin Peay State University
- Baptist College
- Cameron University
- Central Missouri State University
- Clemson University
- Cleveland State University
- Cumberland College
- Dallas Baptist University
- Ferris State University
- Florida Atlantic University
- Fort Hays State University
- Georgia State University
- Howard Payne University
- James Madison University
- Kent State University
- Limestone College
- Livingston College
- Louisiana State University
- Louisiana Tech University
- Memphis State University
- Mississippi College
- Missouri Southern State College
- Montana State University
- Moorhead State University
- Nicholls State University
- Northeast Louisiana University
- Ohio State University

ATHLETICS

Pepperdine University
Pittsburg State University
St. Peter's College
Sam Houston State University
Southwestern Oklahoma State University
Southern Arkansas University
Sul Ross State University
Tennessee Technological University
Texas A&I University
University of Alabama
University of Alabama, Huntsville
University of Central Arkansas
University of Cincinnati
University of Detroit
University of Florida
University of Georgia
University of Hawaii
University of Miami
University of Mississippi
University of North Alabama (captain gets tuition)
University of Northern Colorado
University of South Carolina
Southern Arkansas University
University of Texas
University of Texas, Arlington
University of Texas, San Antonio
University of Toledo
Wichita State University

Source: *Cheer News Today*, The National Magazine for Today's Cheerleaders

ATHLETICS

CHEERLEADING CHAMPIONS

Schools with championship cheerleading teams:
- Carson-Newman College
- Clemson University
- Cumberland College
- Delta State University
- Florida State University
- George Mason University
- Georgia Institute of Technology
- North Carolina State University
- James Madison University
- Kansas State University
- Louisiana State University
- Memphis State University
- Mississippi College
- Moorhead State University
- Ohio State University
- Pittsburg State University
- Sam Houston State University
- Temple University
- University of Alabama
- University of Alabama, Birmingham
- University of Cincinnati
- University of Florida
- University of Georgia
- University of Kentucky
- University of Mississippi
- University of North Carolina, Wilmington
- University of Texas
- Wright State University

Source: Universal Cheerleaders' Association

ATHLETICS

FENCING

Schools with the top fencing teams (men's and women's combined):

1. Pennsylvania State University
2. Columbia University/Barnard College
3. University of Notre Dame
4. Yale University
5. University of Pennsylvania
6. Temple University
7. Fairleigh Dickinson University
8. University of North Carolina
9. Wayne State University
10. University of Wisconsin
11. Stanford University
12. United States Air Force Academy
13. University of Illinois
14. University of Detroit, Mercy
15. California State University, Long Beach
16. Johns Hopkins University
17. New York University
18. United States Naval Academy
19. Ohio State University
20. Duke University

Source: NCAA (1991 results)

ATHLETICS

CREW

Schools with the top rowing teams:

Men's
- Brown University
- Cornell University
- Georgetown University
- Harvard University
- Northeastern University
- Princeton University
- Stanford University
- Temple University
- United States Naval Academy
- University of California, Berkeley
- University of Pennsylvania
- University of Washington
- University of Wisconsin
- Yale University

Women's
- Boston University
- Cornell University
- The George Washington University
- Harvard University
- Princeton University
- United States Naval Academy
- University of California, Berkeley
- University of Pennsylvania
- University of Virginia
- University of Washington

Lightweight (Men's)
Harvard University
Massachusetts Institute of Technology
Princeton University
University of California, Santa Barbara
University of Pennsylvania
University of Rochester
Yale University

Lightweight (Women's)
Harvard University
University of California, Davis
University of Rhode Island
University of Central Florida
Washington University
Western Washington University

Source: United States Rowing Association

CYCLING

Schools with the most competitive cycling programs:
Indiana University
Stanford University
University of Colorado
University of California, Berkeley

Source: National Collegiate Cycling Association

FIELD HOCKEY

The top schools for women's field hockey:

Division I
- Northeastern University
- Northwestern University
- Old Dominion University
- Pennsylvania State University
- Temple University
- University of Iowa
- University of Maryland
- University of Massachusetts
- University of North Carolina
- West Chester University

Division III
- Bloomsburg University of Pennsylvania
- Hartwick College
- Hobart and William Smith Colleges
- Ithaca College
- Lock Haven University
- Messiah College
- Salisbury State University
- State University of New York, Cortland
- Trenton State College

Source: NCAA (Note: there is no Division II)

FIGURE SKATING

The University of Delaware is the only school in the country that runs a figure skating training program. Figure skating is not an intercollegiate sport; most competitive skaters train under the direction of a coach at select rinks and skating centers.

ATHLETICS

FOOTBALL

The top twenty-five teams, according to the Coaches Poll:

1. University of Washington
2. University of Miami
3. Pennsylvania State University
4. Florida State University
5. University of Alabama
6. University of Michigan
7. University of California, Berkeley
8. University of Florida
9. East Carolina University
10. University of Iowa
11. Syracuse University
12. University of Notre Dame
13. Texas A&M University
14. University of Oklahoma
15. University of Tennessee
16. University of Nebraska
17. Clemson University
18. University of California, Los Angeles
19. University of Georgia
20. University of Colorado
21. University of Tulsa
22. Stanford University
23. Brigham Young University
24. United States Air Force Academy
25. North Carolina State University

Source: *USA Today*/CNN (1991-1992 results)

GOLF

The top schools for golf:

Division I (Men's)
1. Oklahoma State University
2. University of North Carolina
3. Arizona State University
4. Wake Forest University
5. Brigham Young University
6. Georgia Institute of Technology
7. University of Southern California
8. University of Nevada
9. University of Arkansas
10. University of Texas
11. University of Texas, El Paso
12. University of Central Florida
13. Clemson University
14. North Carolina State University
15. University of New Mexico
16. University of South Carolina
17. Stanford University
18. University of Arizona
19. Northwestern University
20. University of Florida

Division II (Men's)
1. Florida Southern College
2. Columbus College
3. Abilene Christian University
4. Troy State University
5. Florida Atlantic University
6. Valdosta State College

ATHLETICS

7. Bryant College
8. Jacksonville State University
9. California State University, Stanislaus
10. Indiana University of Pennsylvania

Division III (Men's)

1. Methodist College
2. Gustavus Adolphus College
3. Ohio Wesleyan University
4. University of California, San Diego
5. California State University, San Bernardino
6. Allegheny College
7. Wittenberg University
8. Skidmore College
9. Salem State College
10. Washington and Lee University

Women's:

1. University of California, Los Angeles
2. San Jose State University
3. University of Arizona
4. University of South Florida
5. University of Georgia
6. Stanford University
7. University of Texas
8. Lamar University
9. University of Tulsa
10. University of Kentucky
11. New Mexico State University
12. Southern Methodist University
13. Duke University
14. Florida State University
15. University of Florida

Source: NCAA (1991 results)

ATHLETICS

GYMNASTICS

Schools with top gymnastics teams:

Men's
1. University of Oklahoma
2. Pennsylvania State University
3. University of California, Los Angeles
4. University of Minnesota
5. Stanford University
6. Ohio State University
7. University of Nebraska
8. University of Iowa

Women's
1. University of Alabama
2. University of Utah
3. University of Georgia
4. Oregon State University
5. Pennsylvania State University
6. University of Florida
7. Louisiana State University
8. Brigham Young University
9. Arizona State University
10. Auburn University
11. University of Arizona
12. Utah State University

Source: NCAA (1991 results)

ICE HOCKEY

Schools with top ice hockey teams:
- Boston University
- Clarkson University
- Colorado College
- Harvard University
- Lake Superior State University
- Michigan State University
- Northern Michigan University
- Miami University
- Providence College
- St. Lawrence University
- University of Alaska
- University of Maine
- University of Michigan
- University of Minnesota
- University of New Hampshire
- University of Wisconsin

Source: NCAA (1992 data)

ATHLETICS

HOCKEY-ETTES

Schools with ice hockey programs for women:
- Bowdoin College (Division III)
- Brown University (Division I)
- Colby College (Division III)
- Colgate University (Club)
- College of the Holy Cross (Club)
- Colorado College (Club)
- Connecticut College (Club)
- Cornell University (Division I)
- Dartmouth College (Division I)
- Hamilton College (Club)
- Harvard University (Division I)
- Lake Forest College (Club)
- Massachusetts Institute of Technology (Club)
- Middlebury College (Division III)
- Northeastern University (Division I)
- Princeton University (Division I)
- Providence College (Division I)
- Rensselaer Polytechnic Institute (Club)
- Rochester Institute of Technology (Division III)
- St. Cloud State University (Club)
- St. Lawrence University (Division III)
- Skidmore College (Club)
- University of Colorado (Club)
- University of Connecticut (Club)

Source: USA Hockey

ATHLETICS

JUDO

Schools with the most competitive judo teams:
- California State University, Fresno
- Ohio State University
- San Jose State University
- Seattle University
- State University of New York, Brockport
- Texas A&M University
- United States Naval Academy
- University of California, Berkeley
- University of Indiana
- University of Texas, El Paso

Source: United States Collegiate Judo Association

ATHLETICS

LACROSSE

Schools that consistently field top teams:

Men's
- Cornell University
- Hobart and William Smith Colleges
- Johns Hopkins University
- Syracuse University
- University of Maryland
- United States Naval Academy
- University of Massachusetts
- University of North Carolina
- University of Virginia

Women's
- Harvard University
- Pennsylvania State University
- Temple University
- University of Delaware
- University of Maryland
- University of Massachusetts
- University of Virginia

Source: United States Intercollegiate Lacrosse Association

LUGE

Schools that accommodate the luge athlete:
- Dartmouth College
- Drexel University
- Ohio State University
- Skidmore College
- Stanford University
- St. Lawrence University
- University of Utah
- University of Colorado

Source: United States Luge Association

LUGE IT OR LEAVE IT

There are currently fifteen internationally certified luge runs throughout the world, one of which is located in the United States at the Olympic Sports Complex, Lake Placid, New York. If you want to get involved in luge and still go to school, it's a good idea to attend a college in the Lake Placid area. In addition, though, the schools listed above have arranged academic credit swaps with these New York schools or worked out individual arrangements with their luge athletes. For more information, contact United States Luge Association, Lake Placid, New York (518) 523-2171.

ATHLETICS

RACQUETBALL

Schools that offer racquetball scholarships:
- Arizona State University
- Ferris State University
- Memphis State University
- Southwest Missouri State University
- University of California, Sacramento

The top schools for men's racquetball:
1. Southwest Missouri State University
2. Memphis State University
3. University of California, Sacramento
4. Ferris State University
5. University of Arizona
6. Arizona State University
7. Pennsylvania State University
8. Brigham Young University

The top schools for women's racquetball:
1. Southwest Missouri State University
2. Memphis State University
3. University of California, Sacramento
4. Ferris State University
5. University of Arizona
6. Arizona State University
7. Pennsylvania State University
8. Brigham Young University

Source: American Amateur Racquetball Association (1991 results)

RIFLE

Schools with the top-ranked rifle teams (men's and women's combined):
1. West Virginia University
2. University of Alaska, Fairbanks
3. Murray State University
4. United States Naval Academy
5. Xavier College
6. Tennessee Technological University
7. United States Military Academy
8. Ohio State University

Source: NCAA (1992 results)

ATHLETICS

RUGBY

Schools with the top rugby clubs and teams:

Men's
- Bowling Green State University
- Brown University
- California Polytechnic State University
- California State University, Long Beach
- Harvard University
- Kansas State University
- Louisiana State University
- Ohio State University
- Pennsylvania State University
- San Diego State University
- Stanford University
- United States Air Force Academy
- United States Military Academy
- United States Naval Academy
- University of California, Berkeley
- University of Cincinnati
- University of Colorado
- University of Kansas
- University of Wisconsin

Women's
- Boston College
- Carleton College
- Colorado State University
- Dartmouth College
- Grinnell College
- James Madison University
- Kansas State University
- Luther College

Mankato State University
Reed College
Shippensburg University of Pennsylvania
Stanford University
Texas A&M University
United States Air Force Academy
University of California, Santa Cruz
University of Connecticut
University of Michigan
University of Wyoming
Washington State University
Western Washington University
Source: *Rugby*

SKIING

Schools with the top skiing teams (men's and women's combined):

1. University of Colorado
2. University of Vermont
3. University of Utah
4. University of Wyoming
5. Dartmouth College
6. University of New Mexico
7. University of Alaska
8. Williams College
9. Middlebury College
10. University of New Hampshire
11. St. Lawrence University
12. St. Olaf College
13. Bates College
14. University of Wisconsin
15. Keene State College
16. Colby College

Source: NCAA (1991 results)

ATHLETICS

BUMMING AROUND

Good schools for ski bums:
- Colorado College
- Montana State University
- University of Colorado
- University of Utah
- University of Vermont
- University of Washington
- Western State College of Colorado
- Western Washington University

Source: Editors of *Skiing*

ATHLETICS

SOARING

Schools with Collegiate Soaring Association member clubs:

- Brown University
- Cornell University
- Embry Riddle Aeronautical University
- Georgia Institute of Technology
- Iowa State University
- Kent State University
- Massachusetts Institute of Technology
- Michigan State University
- Mississippi State University
- Ohio State University
- Oklahoma State University
- Pennsylvania State University
- Princeton University
- Rensselaer Polytechnic Institute
- United States Naval Academy
- University of California, San Diego
- University of Illinois
- University of Michigan
- University of Nevada, Reno
- Wright State University

Soaring is sometimes called sailplane flying or gliding. Sailplanes operate without a motor, using the power of the air itself to stay up, and no previous flying experience is necessary to fly one.

For more information on college soaring, contact the Collegiate Soaring Association, Inc. (CSA), 3428 34th Street, Washington, D.C. 20008

Source: Collegiate Soaring Association

ATHLETICS

SOCCER

Schools that participated in Division I championships (Men's)
- Adelphi University
- Boston University
- California State University, Fresno
- Clemson University
- Columbia University
- Florida International University
- Furman University
- North Carolina State University
- Old Dominion University
- Rutgers, The State University of New Jersey
- Santa Clara University
- Seton Hall University
- Southern Methodist University
- Stanford University
- University of Evansville
- University of Hartford
- University of North Carolina
- University of North Carolina, Charlotte
- University of Portland
- University of San Francisco
- University of Tulsa
- University of Wisconsin
- Wake Forest University
- Yale University

ATHLETICS

Schools that participated in Division I championships (Women's)
- Colorado College
- North Carolina State University
- Santa Clara University
- University of California, Santa Barbara
- University of Central Florida
- University of Connecticut
- University of Hartford
- University of Massachusetts
- University of North Carolina
- University of Virginia
- University of Wisconsin

Source: NCAA (1991 results)

SOFTBALL

Schools with top women's softball teams:

Division I
1. University of Arizona
2. University of California, Los Angeles
3. California State University, Fresno
4. California State University, Long Beach
5. Florida State University
6. University of Missouri
7. University of Nevada
8. University of Utah

Division II
1. Augustana College (South Dakota)
2. Bloomsburg University of Pennsylvania
3. Portland State University
4. Southeast Missouri State University

Division III
1. Central College
2. Eastern Connecticut State University
3. Hope College
4. Trenton State College
5. Capital University
6. Luther College

Source: NCAA (1991 results)

SQUASH

Top collegiate squash teams (Men's):
    Cornell University
    Dartmouth College
    Franklin & Marshall College
    Harvard University
    Princeton University
    Trinity College
    United States Naval Academy
    University of Pennsylvania
    Williams College
    Yale University

Top collegiate squash teams (Women's):
    Brown University
    Dartmouth College
    Franklin and Marshall College
    Harvard College
    Princeton University
    Trinity College
    Tufts University
    University of Pennsylvania
    Williams College
    Yale University

Source: National Intercollegiate Squash Racquets Association (1992 data)

SURFING

Schools with the top surfing teams:
- Flagler College
- Florida Atlantic University
- Florida Institute of Technology
- Pepperdine University
- Point Loma Nazarene University
- San Diego State University
- University of California, San Diego
- University of California, Santa Barbara
- University of Central Florida
- University of Florida
- University of North Florida
- University of South Florida
- University of San Diego

Source: National Scholastic Surfing Association (1992 data)

SWIMMING AND DIVING

Division I (Men's)
1. University of Texas
2. Stanford University
3. University of Florida
4. University of Southern California
5. University of Tennessee
6. University of Michigan
7. University of Arizona
8. Southern Methodist University
9. Arizona State University
10. University of California, Los Angeles

Division II (Men's)
1. California State University, Bakersfield
2. Oakland University
3. Clarion University of Pennsylvania
4. Shippensburg University
5. University of California, Davis
6. California State University, Chico
7. State University of New York, Buffalo
8. California Polytechnic State University
9. University of North Dakota
10. Ashland University

Division III (Men's)
1. Kenyon College
2. Claremont McKenna College
3. University of California, San Diego
4. Wheaton College (Illinois)
5. Denison University

6. Hope College
7. Johns Hopkins University
8. Wabash College
9. Emory University
10. Millikin University
11. Williams College
12. Allegheny College

Division I (Women's)
1. University of Texas
2. Stanford University
3. University of Florida
4. University of California, Berkeley
5. University of California, Los Angeles
6. Southern Methodist University
7. University of Arizona
8. University of Georgia
9. University of Southern California
10. University of Miami
11. Brigham Young University
12. Ohio State University
13. Arizona State University
14. Louisiana State University

Division II (Women's)
1. Oakland University
2. Florida Atlantic University
3. Northern Michigan University
4. University of North Dakota
5. Clarion University of Pennsylvania
6. California Polytechnic State University
7. State University of New York, Buffalo
8. United States Naval Academy

9. Bloomsburg University of Pennsylvania
10. Edinboro University of Pennsylvania

Division III (Women's)
1. Kenyon College
2. University of California, San Diego
3. Williams College
4. Allegheny College
5. Emory University
6. Ithaca College
7. Denison University
8. Gettysburg College
9. Hope College
10. Pomona-Pitzer Colleges
11. St. Olaf College
12. Wheaton College (Illinois)

Source: NCAA (1991 results)

ATHLETICS

SYNCHRONIZED SWIMMING

Schools with synchronized swimming programs:

California State University, Sacramento
Carleton College
Florida State University
Keuka College
Michigan State University
University of Michigan
Millersville University
Northwestern University
Ohio State University
Pennsylvania State University
San Diego State University
Smith College
Stanford University
University of Arizona
University of California, Berkeley
University of California, Davis
University of Colorado
University of Connecticut
University of Illinois
University of Iowa
University of Notre Dame
University of Pennsylvania
University of Richmond
Vassar College
Wheaton College (Massachusetts)

Source: Synchro USA (1992 data)

ATHLETICS

TABLE TENNIS

Schools with top table tennis teams:

Men's
- Albion College
- Anderson College
- Augusta College
- Massachusetts Institute of Technology
- Rensselaer Polytechnic Institute
- University of Arizona
- University of Houston
- University of Illinois
- University of Maryland
- University of Minnesota
- University of Oregon
- Washburn University

Women's
- Augusta College
- Ball State University
- California State University, Long Beach
- College of Staten Island
- Florida International University
- Massachusetts College of Pharmacy
- New Mexico State University
- North Carolina State University
- Rensselaer Polytechnic Institute
- University of California, Irvine
- University of Illinois, Chicago

Source: United States Table Tennis Association (1992 results)

TENNIS

Schools with top tennis teams:

Men's
1. University of Southern California
2. Stanford University
3. University of Georgia
4. University of Kentucky
5. Texas Christian University
6. University of California, Los Angeles
   Mississippi State University
8. University of North Carolina
9. Louisiana State University
10. University of Notre Dame

Women's
1. University of Florida
2. Stanford University
3. University of Texas
4. Duke University
5. University of Georgia
6. University of California, Berkeley
7. University of California, Los Angeles
8. University of Arizona
9. Arizona State University
10. Indiana University

Source: Intercollegiate Tennis Coaches Association (1992 results)

ATHLETICS

TRACK AND FIELD

CROSS COUNTRY

Schools with the top cross country teams:

Division I (Men's)
1. University of Arkansas
2. Iowa State University
3. University of Wisconsin
4. Weber State College
   University of Arizona
6. University of Michigan
7. University of Texas
8. East Tennessee State University
9. Michigan State University
10. Pennsylvania State University

Division I (Women's)
1. Villanova University
2. University of Arkansas
3. Northern Arizona University
4. Cornell University
5. University of Oregon
6. Georgetown University
   University of Wisconsin
8. North Carolina State University
9. Providence College
10. Baylor University

ATHLETICS

Division II (Men's)
1. University of Lowell
2. Kearney State College
3. Humboldt State University
4. Shippensburg University
   University of California, Davis
6. Slippery Rock University
7. Augustana College (South Dakota)
8. South Dakota State University
9. Edinboro University of Pennsylvania
10. University of California, Riverside

Division II (Women's)
1. California Polytechnic State University
2. University of California, Davis
3. South Dakota State University
4. North Dakota State University
5. University of North Dakota
6. Springfield College
7. Ashland University
8. Edinboro University of Pennsylvania
9. St. Cloud State University
10. University of California, Riverside

Source: NCAA (1992 results)

ATHLETICS

INDOOR TRACK AND FIELD

Top ranked schools:

Division I (Men's)
1. University of Arkansas
2. Clemson University
3. University of Florida
4. University of Texas, El Paso
5. Louisiana State University
   Georgetown University
7. University of North Carolina
8. Baylor University
9. Iowa State University
10. Indiana University
    Ohio State University
    Southern Methodist University

Division I (Women's)
1. University of Florida
2. Stanford University
3. Villanova University
4. Louisiana State University
   Providence College
   University of Wisconsin
7. Georgia Tech University
   University of Houston
   University of Nebraska
10. University of Texas

ATHLETICS

Division II (Men's)
1. St. Augustine's College
2. Abilene Christian University
   Norfolk State University
4. Mankato State University
5. Augustana College (South Dakota)
   University of California, Riverside
7. University of South Dakota
8. California Polytechnic State University
   Kutztown University

Division II (Women's)
1. Alabama A&M University
2. Abilene Christian University
   California State University, Los Angeles
4. Norfolk State University
5. North Dakota State University
6. St. Cloud University
7. University of Wisconsin, Parkside
8. California State University, Bakersfield
   North Carolina Central University
   Pittsburg State University

Source: NCAA (1992 results)

OUTDOOR TRACK AND FIELD

Division I (Men's)
1. University of Tennessee
2. Washington State University
3. University of Oregon
4. Brigham Young University
5. University of Texas
6. Louisiana State University
7. University of Arkansas
8. Georgetown University
9. Texas Christian University
10. University of Georgia

Division I (Women's)
1. Louisiana State University
2. University of Texas
3. University of Nebraska
4. University of California, Los Angeles
5. University of Tennessee
6. University of Florida
7. Villanova University
8. Brigham Young University
9. Florida State University
10. University of Arkansas

Division II (Men's)

1. St. Augustine's College
2. Angelo State University
3. Hampton College
4. California Polytechnic State University
5. New York Institute of Technology
6. California State University, Los Angeles
7. North Dakota State University
8. Southeast Missouri State University
9. Norfolk State University
10. Abilene Christian University

Division II (Women's)

1. California Polytechnic State University
2. Alabama A&M University
3. Norfolk State University
4. California State University, Los Angeles
5. Southeast Missouri State University
6. Abilene Christian University
7. North Dakota State University
8. Hampton University
9. St. Augustine's College
10. Seattle Pacific University

Source: NCAA (1991 results)

ULTIMATE (FRISBEE)

Schools with the top ultimate (Frisbee) teams:
1. Stanford University
2. University of North Carolina, Wilmington
3. University of Arizona
4. Cornell University
5. Carleton College
6. University of Texas
7. University of California, Santa Cruz
8. University of California, Santa Barbara
9. University of Wisconsin
10. Georgia Institute of Technology
11. California Polytechnic State University
12. University of California, Berkeley
13. Harvard University
14. University of Virginia
15. Los Positas College
16. University of Kansas
17. Columbia University
18. Humboldt State University
19. University of Georgia
20. East Carolina University

Source: Ultimate Players Association (1992 results)

ATHLETICS

VOLLEYBALL

Schools with top volleyball teams:

Men's
- Ball State University
- California State University, Northridge
- California State University, Long Beach
- Indiana University—Purdue University, Fort Wayne
- Pennsylvania State University
- Pepperdine University
- Stanford University
- University of California, Los Angeles
- University of California, Santa Barbara
- University of Hawaii
- University of Southern California

Women's
- Arizona State University
- Brigham Young University
- California State University, Long Beach
- Louisiana State University
- Stanford University
- University of California, Los Angeles
- University of Hawaii
- University of Nebraska
- University of the Pacific
- University of Texas

Source: United States Volleyball Association

WATER POLO

Men's
1. University of California, Berkeley
2. University of California, Los Angeles
3. Pepperdine University
4. University of California, Irvine
5. California State University, Long Beach
6. Stanford University
7. University of Southern California
8. University of the Pacific
9. University of California, San Diego
10. University of California, Santa Barbara
11. California State University, Fresno
12. United States Air Force Academy
13. Slippery Rock University
14. United States Naval Academy
15. Brown University
16. University of California, Davis
17. Princeton University
18. Bucknell University
19. Chaminade University of Honolulu
20. University of Massachusetts
21. Washington and Lee University
22. Claremont-Harvey Mudd-Scripps Colleges
23. University of California, Riverside
24. University of Arkansas, Little Rock
25. Iona College

Source: American Water Polo Coaches Association (1991 results)

ATHLETICS

Schools with Women's Water Polo:
Amherst College
Brown University
Bucknell University
California Polytechnic State University
California State University, Long Beach
Claremont-Harvey Mudd-Scripps Colleges
Harvard University
Massachusetts Institute of Technology
Northwestern University
Ohio State University
Pomona-Pitzer Colleges
Princeton University
Queens College
Slippery Rock University
Stanford University
United States Naval Academy
University of California, Berkeley
University of California, Davis
University of California, Irvine
University of California, Riverside
University of California, San Diego
University of California, Santa Barbara
University of Findlay
University of Michigan
University of Redlands
University of Wisconsin

Source: United States Water Polo

ATHLETICS

WEIGHTLIFTING

Schools with the top weightlifting programs (men's and women's combined). Particularly strong women's programs are noted with an asterisk:
- Arizona State University
- Augsburg College
- Indiana University
- Louisiana State University*
- Missouri Western State College
- Pennsylvania State University
- Stanford University
- United States Air Force Academy*
- University of Maryland*
- University of Missouri

Source: The United States Weightlifting Federation

WHEELCHAIR

Schools with wheelchair athletic programs:
- Ball State University
- Edinboro University of Pennsylvania
- University of Arizona
- University of Houston
- Wright State University

Source: *Sports 'n Spokes*

WINDSURFING

Schools with windsurfing programs or clubs:
- Cornell University
- Drexel University
- Duke University
- Kansas State University
- University of Florida
- Old Dominion University
- Rollins College
- University of California, Los Angeles
- United States Coast Guard Academy
- University of Delaware
- University of Iowa
- University of Rhode Island
- University of Virginia
- Western Washington University
- Yale University

Schools with windsurfing teams:
- Eckerd College
- Stanford University
- United States Naval Academy

Source: Mistral

ATHLETICS

WRESTLING

Top-ranked wrestling teams:

Division I
1. University of Iowa
2. Oklahoma State University
3. Pennsylvania State University
4. Iowa State University
5. Ohio State University
6. Arizona State University
7. University of Wisconsin
8. Clarion University of Pennsylvania
9. North Carolina State University
10. University of Northern Iowa
11. University of Nebraska
12. Purdue University
13. University of Oklahoma
14. Syracuse University
15. Cornell University

Source: USA Wrestling (1992 results)

WOMEN'S WINNERS

Division I schools with the most NCAA team titles:
- University of Texas (14)
- Stanford University (11)
- University of California, Los Angeles (11)
- University of North Carolina (9)
- Louisiana State University (8)
- Old Dominion University (6)
- University of Utah (6)

Division I schools with the most individual titles:
- University of Florida (74)
- University of Texas (72)
- Stanford University (66)
- University of California, Los Angeles (24)
- Louisiana State University (23)
- University of Tennessee (23)

Division II schools with the most team titles:
- California Polytechnic State University (15)
- California State University, Northridge (12)
- Abilene Christian University (8)
- California State Polytechnic University (4)
- California State University, Bakersfield (4)
- Southern Illinois University (4)

ATHLETICS

Division II schools with the most individual titles:
California State University, Northridge (62)
Abilene Christian University (44)
California Polytechnic State University (42)
Alabama A&M University (23)
United States Air Force Academy (21)

Division III schools with the most team titles:
Trenton State College (13)
University of California, San Diego (10)
Kenyon College (8)
Christopher Newport College (6)
University of St. Thomas (Minnesota) (5)

Division III schools with the most individual titles:
Kenyon College (81)
Williams College (34)
Christopher Newport College (29)
State University of New York, Cortland (20)
Boston University (19)
University of California, San Diego (19)

Source: NCAA (1990-91 results)

MEN'S WINNERS

Division I schools with the most team men's titles:

    University of Southern California (66)
    University of California, Los Angeles (55)
    Oklahoma State University (40)
    Stanford University (33)
    University of Michigan (26)
    Yale University (25)
    University of Texas, El Paso (21)
    University of Denver (19)
    Indiana University (19)
    Ohio State University (18)
    Michigan State University (17)
    University of California, Berkeley (17)
    University of Houston (17)
    University of Wisconsin (17)
    University of Illinois (16)
    Pennsylvania State University (16)

Division I schools with the most individual men's titles:

    University of Southern California (261)
    University of Michigan (191)
    Ohio State University (176)
    Stanford University (139)
    University of California, Los Angeles (136)
    Oklahoma State University (132)
    Indiana University (114)
    University of Illinois (108)
    Yale University (104)
    Michigan State University (96)

University of Oklahoma (89)
University of Texas (89)
Iowa State University (87)
University of Iowa (83)
Pennsylvania State University (83)

Division II schools with the most team men's titles:
California Polytechnic State University (20)
California State University, Northridge (18)
University of California, Irvine (15)
California State University, Bakersfield (14)
Florida Southern College (14)

Division II schools with the most individual men's titles:
California State University, Northridge (101)
California State University, Bakersfield (82)
California Polytechnic State University (73)
Oakland University (62)
University of California, Irvine (61)

Division III schools with the most team men's titles:
California State University, Stanislaus (14)
Hobart and William Smith Colleges (12)
Kenyon College (12)
North Central University (9)
Glassboro State University (9)

ATHLETICS

Division III schools with the most individual men's titles:
- Kenyon College (87)
- Johns Hopkins University (38)
- St. Lawrence University (30)
- University of California, San Diego (28)
- Lincoln College (Pennsylvania) (25)

Source: NCAA (1990-91 results)

CAREERS

CAREERS

GRATEFUL GIVERS

Schools with the highest percentages of alumni (listed in parentheses) who give money:

- Dartmouth College (52%)
- Duke University (52%)
- University of Notre Dame (47.3%)
- Lehigh University (45.8%)
- Princeton University (42.8%)
- Clark University (42.6%)
- Rice University (42.4%)
- Yale University (41.7%)
- University of Alabama (39.4%)
- University of Arizona (36.8%)
- University of Montana (36.2%)
- Massachusetts Institute of Technology (35.6%)

Source: *Chronicle of Higher Education Almanac*

CAREERS
BIZ WHIZZES

Schools that send at least 12% of their graduates to business school:
- Albright College
- Clemson University
- Columbia University
- Duquesne University
- Eckerd College
- Florida Institute of Technology
- Hawaii Pacific University
- Hillsdale College
- New York University
- St. John's College (New Mexico)
- Stetson University
- University of Montana
- University of Oregon
- University of Puget Sound
- University of Tulsa
- Washington University
- Whitman College
- Widener University

CAREERS

LEGAL EAGLES

Schools that send at least 12% of their graduates to law school:

- Alma College
- Brandeis University
- Bryn Mawr College
- Bucknell University
- Claremont McKenna College
- Columbia University
- Duke University
- Emory University
- Georgetown University
- Harvard University
- New School for Social Research, Eugene Lang College
- Northwestern University
- Occidental College
- St. John's College (New Mexico)
- Trinity University
- University of California, Irvine
- University of California, Santa Barbara
- University of Louisville
- University of Oregon
- University of Pennsylvania
- Vanderbilt University
- Washington and Jefferson College
- Washington University
- Widener University
- Willamette University

CAREERS

DOCTOR DENS

Schools that send at least 10% of their graduates to medical school:

- Albright College
- Amherst College
- Brown University
- Bryn Mawr College
- City University of New York, City College
- Creighton University
- Emory University
- Fisk University
- Harvard University
- Haverford College
- Johns Hopkins University
- Kenyon College
- King College
- Muhlenberg College
- Northwestern University
- Occidental College
- Stanford University
- Swarthmore College
- University of California, Irvine
- Ursinus College
- Washington and Jefferson College
- Washington University
- Willamette University
- Yeshiva University

CAREERS

CEO SOURCES

Schools that have graduated the largest number of CEOs (by total number):

1. Yale University
2. Princeton University
3. Harvard University
4. Northwestern University
5. Cornell University
6. Columbia University
   Stanford University
7. University of Michigan
8. Dartmouth College
9. University of Illinois
   University of Missouri
   University of Texas

Source: *Fortune*, 1990

Schools that have graduated the most CEOs (as a percentage of all graduates):

1. Yale University
2. Princeton University
3. Washington and Lee University
4. Harvard University
5. Dartmouth College
6. Northwestern University
7. Davidson College
8. Wesleyan University
9. Amherst College
10. Columbia University

Source: *Fortune*, 1990

CAREERS

WHERE THE BOSSES WERE

Schools that have graduated the most business executives:

1. City University of New York (entire system)
2. Yale University
3. Harvard University
4. University of Wisconsin
5. University of California (entire system)
6. Princeton University
7. University of Pennsylvania
8. University of Michigan
9. University of Illinois
10. New York University
11. Cornell University
12. University of Minnesota

Source: Standard & Poor's Executive College Survey

CAREERS

DOCTORATES IN THE HOUSE

Schools with the largest number of graduates who have Ph.D.'s:

1. City University of New York, City College
2. Harvard University
3. Massachusetts Institute of Technology
4. Cornell University
5. University of Chicago
6. Yale University
7. Princeton University
8. Oberlin College
9. University of Rochester
10. Brown University

Source: *Chronicle of Higher Education*

Schools with the highest percentage of graduates who went on to earn Ph.D.'s:

1. Harvey Mudd College
2. California Institute of Technology
3. Reed College
4. Massachusetts Institute of Technology
5. Swarthmore College
6. Haverford College
7. Oberlin College
8. New College of the University of South Florida
9. University of Chicago
10. University of California, San Diego

Source: *Chronicle of Higher Education*

CAREERS

TEACHING TEACHERS

Schools that produce the most teachers:
- Berry College
- Boston College
- Boston University
- Bucknell University
- California Lutheran University
- Central State University
- Chicago State University
- Coe College
- Drake University
- Emory University
- Fitchburg State College
- Fort Valley State College
- Georgia State University
- Illinois State University
- Mercer University
- Mills College
- National College of Education
- Oklahoma State University
- Pennsylvania State University
- Roosevelt University
- San Francisco State University
- Temple University
- University of California, Berkeley
- University of Denver
- University of Georgia
- University of Illinois
- University of Northern Colorado
- West Chester University

Source: *Places Where Teachers Are Taught*

CAREERS

HI TECH

Schools with the largest number of graduates listed in *Who's Who in Science and Technology*:

1. California Institute of Technology
2. University of Chicago
3. Massachusetts Institute of Technology
4. Harvard University
5. Harvey Mudd College
6. Wesleyan University
7. Yale University
8. Princeton University
9. Swarthmore College
10. Columbia University
11. University of California, San Diego
12. Cornell University
13. Amherst College
14. Stanford University
15. Reed College
16. Haverford College
17. Wellesley College
18. Oberlin College
19. Brown University
20. Barnard College
21. Pomona College
22. University of Pennsylvania
23. University of Wisconsin
24. University of Illinois
25. Wabash College

Source: *Maintaining America's Scientific Productivity: The Necessity of the Liberal Arts College*, Oberlin College

CAREERS

WOMEN IN SCIENCE

Schools with the largest number of female graduates who are members of American Men and Women in Science:

1. California Institute of Technology
2. Massachusetts Institute of Technology
3. Harvey Mudd College
4. Reed College
5. Swarthmore College
6. University of Chicago
7. Haverford College
8. Wabash College
9. Wesleyan University
10. Oberlin College
11. Pomona College
12. Amherst College
13. Carleton College
14. Harvard University
15. Kalamazoo College
16. Princeton University
17. Grinnell College
18. Franklin and Marshall College
19. Earlham College
20. Williams College
21. Cornell University
22. Columbia University
23. Union College
24. Worcester Polytechnic Institute
25. Yale University

Source: *Maintaining America's Scientific Productivity: The Necessity of the Liberal Arts College*, Oberlin College

CAREERS

POPULAR RECRUITING

Schools where at least 600 companies come to recruit:

- Boston University
- Drexel University
- Iowa State University
- North Carolina State University
- Purdue University
- Rochester Institute of Technology
- Rutgers, The State University of New Jersey
- Texas A&M University
- University of California, Berkeley
- University of Florida
- University of Maryland
- University of Michigan
- University of Pennsylvania
- University of Pittsburgh
- University of South Carolina
- University of Virginia
- Virginia Polytechnic Institute and State University
- West Virginia University

CAREERS

JOB BAIT

Schools with the largest number of corporate recruiters per undergrad:

- Babson College
- Carnegie Mellon University
- Claremont McKenna College
- Clarkson University
- Colorado School of Mines
- Colorado State University
- Drexel University
- Harvey Mudd College
- Hood College
- James Madison University
- Lafayette College
- Long Island University, C.W. Post Center
- Rensselaer Polytechnic Institute
- Scripps College
- Spelman College
- Stevens Institute of Technology
- University of Bridgeport
- University of Tulsa
- Webb Institute of Naval Architecture
- Worcester Polytechnic Institute

INDEX

INDEX

The most comprehensive source for more information on schools mentioned in this book is usually the schools themselves. The following lists all schools mentioned that offer four-year degree programs (schools that appear on lists but are not included here do not offer full, four-year degree programs). Application deadlines are provided wherever possible, but this information is subject to change. Please check with the schools to confirm their deadlines.

ABILENE CHRISTIAN UNIVERSITY
Box 6000 ACU Station
Abilene, TX 79699
915-674-2000
Application deadline: Rolling

ACADEMY OF THE NEW CHURCH
Bryn Athyn, PA 19009
215-939-2543

ADELPHI UNIVERSITY
South Avenue
Garden City, NY 11530
516-877-3000
Admissions phone: 516-877-3050
Application deadline: Rolling

AGNES SCOTT COLLEGE
141 East College Avenue
Decatur, GA 30030-4298
404-371-6285
Admissions phone: 404-371-6285
Application deadline: March 1

ALABAMA A&M UNIVERSITY
PO Box 908
Normal, AL 35762
205-851-5000

ALABAMA STATE UNIVERSITY
915 South Jackson Street
Montgomery, AL 36101
205-293-4100
Application deadline: June 1

ALASKA PACIFIC UNIVERSITY
4101 University Drive
Anchorage, AK 99508
907-561-1266
Application deadline: August 15

ALBANY COLLEGE OF PHARMACY
106 New Scotland Avenue
Albany, NY 12208
518-445-7211
Admissions phone: 518-445-7221
Application deadline: None

ALBANY STATE COLLEGE
504 College Drive
Albany, GA 31705
912-430-4600
Application deadline: September 1

ALBION COLLEGE
Albion, MI 49224
517-629-1000
Application deadline: Open

ALBRIGHT COLLEGE
PO Box 15234
Reading, PA 19612-5234
215-921-7512
Admissions phone: 215-921-7512
Application deadline: March 15

ALCORN STATE UNIVERSITY
Lorman, MS 39096
601-877-6100
Application deadline: Open

INDEX

ALDERSON-BROADDUS COLLEGE
Philippi, WV 26416
304-457-1700
Application deadline: September 1

ALFRED UNIVERSITY
Box 765
Alfred, NY 14802
607-871-2115
Admissions phone: 800-541-9229
Application deadline: February 1

ALLEGHENY COLLEGE
Meadville, PA 16335-3901
814-332-3100
Admissions phone: 814-724-4351 or 800-521-5293
Application deadline: February 15

ALMA COLLEGE
Alma, MI 48801-1599
517-463-7111
Admissions phone: 800-321-ALMA
Application deadline: Rolling

AMERICAN INTERNATIONAL COLLEGE
1000 State Street
Springfield, MA 01109
413-737-7000
Application deadline: Open

THE AMERICAN UNIVERSITY
4400 Massachusetts Avenue NW
Washington, DC 20016-8001
202-885-1000
Admissions phone: 202-885-6000
Application deadline: February 1

AMHERST COLLEGE
Amherst, MA 01002
413-542-2000
Admissions phone: 413-542-2328
Application deadline: January 1

ANDERSON UNIVERSITY
Anderson, IN 40612
317-641-4080
Application deadline: September 1

ANDREWS UNIVERSITY
Berrien Springs, MI 49104
616-471-7771
Application deadline: Rolling

ANGELO STATE UNIVERSITY
2601 West Avenue N.
San Angelo, TX 76909
915-942-2041
Application deadline: August 19

ANTIOCH COLLEGE
795 Livermore
Yellow Springs, OH 45387
513-767-7331
Admissions phone: 513-767-7047
Application deadline: August 1

APPALACHIAN STATE UNIVERSITY
Boone, NC 28608
704-262-2000
Application deadline: March 15

ARIZONA STATE UNIVERSITY
Tempe, AZ 85287
602-965-9011
Admissions phone: 602-965-3255
Application deadline: April 15

ARKANSAS COLLEGE
PO Box 2317
Batesville, AR 72501
501-698-4201
Application deadline: August 15

ARKANSAS STATE UNIVERSITY
PO Box 1630
State University, AR 72467
800-643-0080
Application deadline: Open

ARKANSAS TECH UNIVERSITY
Russellville, AR 72801
501-968-0391
Application deadline: Open

ART CENTER COLLEGE OF DESIGN
1700 Lida Street
Pasadena, CA 91103
818-584-5000
Application deadline: Rolling

INDEX

ASBURY COLLEGE
201 N. Lexington Avenue
Wilmore, KY 40390
606-858-3511
Application deadline: Rolling

ASHLAND UNIVERSITY
401 College Avenue
Ashland, OH 44805
419-289-4142
Application deadline: August 25

ATLANTA COLLEGE OF ART
1280 Peachtree Street NE
Atlanta, GA 30309
404-898-1163
Application deadline: Rolling

ATLANTIC UNION COLLEGE
PO Box 1000
South Lancaster, MA 01561
508-368-2000
Application deadline: August 1

AUBURN UNIVERSITY
Auburn University, AL 36849-3501
205-844-4000
Admissions phone: 205-826-4080
Application deadline: September 1

AUGSBURG COLLEGE
731 21st Avenue South
Minneapolis, MN 55454
612-330-1000
Application deadline: August 1

AUGUSTA COLLEGE
Augusta, GA 30910
404-737-1632
Admission deadline: August 18

AUGUSTANA COLLEGE (IL)
639 38th Street
Rock Island, IL 61201-2296
309-794-7000
Admissions phone: 309-794-7341
Application deadline: Rolling, early application is recommended

AUGUSTANA COLLEGE (SD)
29th and Summit
Sioux Falls, SD 57197
605-336-5516 or 800-727-2844
Admissions phone: 605-336-5516 or 800-727-2844
Application deadline: August 1

AUSTIN COLLEGE
900 North Grand Avenue
Sherman, TX 75091
214-813-2000
Admissions phone: 800-442-5363
Application deadline: March 15

AUSTIN PEAY STATE UNIVERSITY
601 College Street
Clarksville, TN 37044
615-648-7011
Application deadline: August 15

AZUSA PACIFIC UNIVERSITY
Azusa, CA 91702
818-969-3434
Application deadline: Rolling

BABSON COLLEGE
Babson Park, MA 02157
617-239-1200
Admissions phone: 800-488-3696
Application deadline: February 1

BALDWIN-WALLACE COLLEGE
275 Eastland Road
Berea, OH 44017
216-826-2222
Application deadline: July 1

BALL STATE UNIVERSITY
2000 University Avenue
Muncie, IN 47306
317-285-8300
Application deadline: March 1

BAPTIST COLLEGE AT CHARLESTON
Charleston, SC 29411
803-794-4326
Application deadline: Open

BARAT COLLEGE
700 E. Westleigh Road
Lake Forest, IL 60045
708-234-3000
Application deadline: None

INDEX

BARCLAY COLLEGE
PO Box 288
Haviland, KS 67059
316-862-5252

BARBER SCOTIA COLLEGE
Concord, NC 28025
704-786-5171
Application deadline: None

BARD COLLEGE
Annandale-on-Hudson, NY 12504
914-758-6822
Admissions phone: 914-758-7472
Application deadline: February 15

BARNARD COLLEGE
3009 Broadway
New York, NY 10027-6598
212-854-5262
Admissions phone: 212-854-2014
Application deadline: February 1

BATES COLLEGE
Lewiston, ME 04240
207-786-6255
Admissions phone: 207-786-6000
Application deadline: February 1

BAYLOR UNIVERSITY
PO Box 97008
Waco, TX 76798-7008
817-755-1011
Admissions phone: 817-755-1811
Application deadline: March 1

BELHAVEN COLLEGE
1500 Peachtree Street
Jackson, MS 39202
601-968-5928
Application deadline: None

BELOIT COLLEGE
700 College Avenue
Beloit, WI 53511
608-363-2000
Application deadline: March 15

BEMIDJI STATE UNIVERSITY
Bemidji, MN 56601
218-755-2040
Application deadline: August 15

BENEDICT COLLEGE
Harden and Blanding Streets
Columbia, SC 29204
803-256-4220
Application deadline: Rolling

BENEDICTINE COLLEGE
1020 North 2nd
Atchison, KS 66002
913-367-5340
Application deadline: August 15

BENNINGTON COLLEGE
Bennington, VT 05201
802-442-5401
Admissions phone: 802-442-6349
Application deadline: February 1

BENTLEY COLLEGE
175 Forest Street
Waltham, MA 02154
617-891-2000
Application deadline: March 10

BEREA COLLEGE
Berea, KY 40404
606-986-9341
Application deadline: April 15

BERRY COLLEGE
Mount Berry Station
P.O. Box 159
Rome, GA 30149
404-235-4494
Application deadline: August 1

BETHANY COLLEGE (WV)
Bethany, WV 26032
304-829-7000
Application deadline: August 15

BETHEL COLLEGE (KS)
300 E. 27th
North Newton, KS 67117
316-283-2500
Application deadline: August 15

BETHEL COLLEGE
St. Paul, MN 55112
612-638-6242
Application deadline: August 15

INDEX

BIOLA UNIVERSITY
13800 Biola Avenue
La Mirada, CA 90639-0001
310-903-6000
Admissions phone: 310-903-4752
Application deadline: June 1

BIRMINGHAM-SOUTHERN COLLEGE
900 Arkadelphia Road
Birmingham, AL 35254
205-226-4686
Admissions phone: 205-266-4686
Application deadline: March 1

BLACKBURN COLLEGE
Nicholas Street
Carlinville, IL 62626
217-854-3231
Application deadline: None

BLOOMSBURG UNIVERSITY OF PENNSYLVANIA
Bloomsburg, PA 17815
717-389-4000
Admissions phone: 717-389-4316
Application deadline: December 31

BOISE STATE UNIVERSITY
Boise, ID 83725
208-385-1156
Application deadline: August 1

BORROMEO COLLEGE OF OHIO
Wickliffe, OH 44092
216-585-5900
Application deadline: August 1

BOSTON COLLEGE
Chestnut Hill, MA 02167
617-552-8000
Admissions phone: 617-552-3100
Application deadline: January 6

BOSTON UNIVERSITY
881 Commonwealth Avenue
Boston, MA 02215
617-353-2300
Admissions phone: 617-353-2300
Application deadline: January 15

BOWDOIN COLLEGE
Brunswick, ME 04011
207-725-3000
Admissions phone: 207-725-3100
Application deadline: January 15

BOWLING GREEN STATE UNIVERSITY
110 McFall Center
Bowling Green, OH 43403
419-372-2086
Admissions phone: 419-372-2086
Application deadline: February 1 (recommended)

BRADLEY UNIVERSITY
1501 W. Bradley Ave.
Peoria, IL 61625
309-676-7611
Admissions phone: 309-677-1000
Application deadline: August 1

BRANDEIS UNIVERSITY
Waltham, MA 02254-9110
617-736-2000
Admissions phone: 617-736-3500
Application deadline: February 1

BRIGHAM YOUNG UNIVERSITY
Provo, UT 84602
801-378-4636
Admissions phone: 801-378-2507
Application deadline: April 15

BROWN UNIVERSITY
Providence, RI 02912
401-863-1000
Admissions phone: 401-863-2378
Application deadline: January 1

BRYANT COLLEGE
1150 Douglas Pike
Smithfield, RI 02917
401-232-6000
Admissions phone: 401-232-6100
Application deadline: December 31

BRYN MAWR COLLEGE
Bryn Mawr, PA 19010-2899
215-526-5000
Admissions phone: 215-526-5152
Application deadline: January 15

INDEX

BUCKNELL UNIVERSITY
Lewisburg, PA 17837
717-524-1101
Admissions phone: 717-524-1101
Application deadline: January 1

BUENA VISTA COLLEGE
4th and College Street
Storm Lake, IA 50588
712-749-2235
Application deadline: April 1

BUTLER UNIVERSITY
4600 Sunset Avenue
Indianapolis, IN 46208
317-283-9255
Application deadline: None

CALIFORNIA INSTITUTE OF THE ARTS
24700 McBean Parkway
Valencia, CA 91355
805-255-1050
Application deadline: February 1

CALIFORNIA INSTITUTE OF TECHNOLOGY
1201 E. California Boulevard
Pasadena, CA 91125
818-356-6811
Admissions phone: 818-356-6341
Application deadline: January 1

CALIFORNIA LUTHERAN UNIVERSITY
60 West Olsen Road
Thousand Oaks, CA 91360
805-492-2411
Application deadline: June 1

CALIFORNIA POLYTECHNIC STATE UNIVERSITY
San Luis Obispo, CA 93407
805-756-2792
Admissions phone: 805-546-2311
Application deadline: November 30

CALIFORNIA STATE POLYTECHNIC UNIVERSITY
3801 W. Temple Avenue
Pomona, CA 91768
714-869-7659
Application deadline: Rolling

CALIFORNIA STATE UNIVERSITY, BAKERSFIELD
9001 Stockdale Highway
Bakersfield, CA 93311
805-664-3138
Application deadline: None

CALIFORNIA STATE UNIVERSITY, CHICO
Chico, CA 95929
916-895-6886
Application deadline: open

CALIFORNIA STATE UNIVERSITY, DOMINGUEZ HILLS
1000 E. Victoria Street
Carson, CA 90747
213-516-3300
Admissions phone: 213-516-3600
Application deadline: November 1

CALIFORNIA STATE UNIVERSITY, FRESNO
5150 N. Maple Avenue
Fresno, CA 93740
209-278-4240
Application deadline: August 1

CALIFORNIA STATE UNIVERSITY, FULLERTON
800 N. State College Boulevard
Fullerton, CA 92634
714-733-2011
Application deadline: None

CALIFORNIA STATE UNIVERSITY, HAYWARD
Hayward, CA 94542
415-881-3000
Application deadline: May 15

CALIFORNIA STATE UNIVERSITY, LONG BEACH
1250 Bellflower Boulevard
Long Beach, CA 90840-0119
213-985-4111
Admissions phone: 213-498-5471
Application deadline: March 15

INDEX

CALIFORNIA STATE UNIVERSITY, LOS ANGELES
5151 State University Drive
Los Angeles, CA 90032
213-343-3000
Application deadline: August 7

CALIFORNIA STATE UNIVERSITY, NORTHRIDGE
Northridge, CA 91330
818-885-3700
Application deadline: November 30

CALIFORNIA STATE UNIVERSITY, SACRAMENTO
Sacramento, CA 95819
916-278-3901
Application deadline: March 1

CALIFORNIA STATE UNIVERSITY, SAN BERNARDINO
5500 University Parkway
San Bernardino, CA 92407
714-880-5000
Application deadline: September 15

CALIFORNIA STATE UNIVERSITY, STANISLAUS
801 West Monte Vista Avenue
Turlock, CA 95380
209-667-3122
Application deadline: August 1

CALIFORNIA UNIVERSITY OF PENNSYLVANIA
California, PA 15419
412-938-4000
Application deadline: August 1

CALVIN COLLEGE
3201 Burton Street, SE
Grand Rapids, MI 49546
616-957-6000
Application deadline: June 1

CAMERON UNIVERSITY
2800 W. Gore Boulevard
Lawton, OK 73505
405-581-2230
Application deadline: None

CAMPBELL UNIVERSITY
Buies Creek, NC 27506
800-334-4111 x2275
Application deadline: Rolling

CANISIUS COLLEGE
2001 Main Street
Buffalo, NY 14208
716-883-7000
Admissions phone: 716-883-7000 or 800-843-1517 (in-state)
Application deadline: Rolling

CAPITAL UNIVERSITY
2199 East Main Street
Columbus, OH 43209
Application deadline: May 1

CARLETON COLLEGE
One North College Street
Northfield, MN 55057
507-663-4000
Admissions phone: 507-663-4190
Application deadline: February 1

CARNEGIE MELLON UNIVERSITY
5000 Forbes Avenue
Pittsburgh, PA 15213-3890
412-268-2000
Admissions phone: 412-268-2082
Application deadline: February 1

CARROLL COLLEGE
Waukesha, WI
414-524-7220
Application deadline: March 15

CARSON-NEWMAN COLLEGE
Jefferson City, TN 37760
615-475-9061
Application deadline: May 15

CASE WESTERN RESERVE UNIVERSITY
10900 Euclid Ave.
Cleveland, OH 44106-7055
216-368-2000
Admissions phone: 216-368-4450
Application deadline: February 15

INDEX

CATHOLIC UNIVERSITY OF AMERICA
Fourth Street and Michigan Avenue NE
Washington, DC 20064
202-319-5000
Admissions phone: 202-319-5305
Application deadline: February 15

CEDAR CREST COLLEGE
100 College Drive
Allentown, PA 18104
215-437-4471
Application deadline: August 1

CEDARVILLE COLLEGE
Box 601
Cedarville, OH 45314
513-766-2211
Application deadline: None

CENTENARY COLLEGE
400 Jefferson Street
Hackettstown, NJ 07840
Application deadline: None

CENTENARY COLLEGE OF LOUISIANA
PO Box 4188
Shreveport, LA 71134
318-869-5131
Application deadline: Rolling

CENTRAL COLLEGE
812 University Avenue
Pella, IA 50219
515-628-9000
Application deadline: None

CENTRAL CONNECTICUT STATE UNIVERSITY
1615 Stanley Street
New Britain, CT 06050
203-827-7000
Application deadline: May 1

CENTRAL MICHIGAN UNIVERSITY
105 Warriner
Mount Pleasant MI 48859
517-774-4000
Admissions phone: 517-774-3076

CENTRAL MISSOURI STATE UNIVERSITY
Warrensburg, MO 64093
816-429-4290
Application deadline: open

CENTRAL STATE UNIVERSITY
1400 Brush Row Road
Wilberforce, OH 45384
513-376-6011
Application deadline: August 1

CENTRE COLLEGE
West Walnut Street
Danville, KY 40422
606-236-5211
Application deadline: March 1

CHAMINADE UNIVERSITY OF HONOLULU
3140 Waialae Avenue
Honolulu, HI 96816
808-735-4711
Application deadline: June 1

CHARLES R. DREW UNIVERSITY OF MEDICINE AND SCIENCE
1621 East 120th Street
Los Angeles, CA 90059
213-563-4974

CHATHAM COLLEGE
Woodland Road
Pittsburgh, PA 15232
412-365-1100
Application deadline: March 1

CHICAGO STATE UNIVERSITY
95th Street at King Drive
Chicago, IL 60628
312-995-2000
Application deadline: None

CHRISTENDOM COLLEGE
Front Royal, VA 22630
703-636-2900
Application deadline: April 1

INDEX

CHRISTIAN BROTHERS UNIVERSITY
650 E. Parkway South
Memphis, TN 38104-5581
901-722-0200
Admissions phone: 901-722-0205
Application deadline: May 1

CHRISTOPHER NEWPORT COLLEGE
Newport News, VA 23606
804-594-7015

THE CITADEL
Charleston, SC 29409
803-792-5000
Admissions phone: 803-792-5230
Application deadline: June 1

CITY UNIVERSITY OF NEW YORK, BARUCH COLLEGE
17 Lexington Avenue
New York, NY 10010
212-280-5262
Application deadline: None

CITY UNIVERSITY OF NEW YORK, BROOKLYN COLLEGE
Avenue H and Bedford Avenue
Brooklyn, NY 11210
718-780-5485
Application deadline: June 15

CITY UNIVERSITY OF NEW YORK, CITY COLLEGE
Convent Avenue and 138th Street
New York, NY 10031
212-650-7000
Admissions phone: 212-650-6977
Application deadline: January 15

CITY UNIVERSITY OF NEW YORK, LEHMAN COLLEGE
250 Bedford Park Boulevard West
Bronx, NY 10468
212-960-8131
Application deadline: None

CITY UNIVERSITY OF NEW YORK, JOHN JAY COLLEGE OF CRIMINAL JUSTICE
New York, NY 10019
212-237-8000
Application deadline: August 31

CITY UNIVERSITY OF NEW YORK, QUEENS COLLEGE
Flushing, NY 11367
718-520-7000
Application deadline: None (suggest early as possible)

CLAREMONT MCKENNA COLLEGE
890 Columbia Avenue
Claremont, CA 91711
714-621-8088
714-621-8088
Application deadline: February 1

CLARION UNIVERSITY OF PENNSYLVANIA
Clarion, PA 16214
814-226-20000
Application deadline: May 1

CLARK UNIVERSITY
950 Main Street
Worcester, MA 01610-1477
508-793-7711
Admissions phone: 508-793-7431
Application deadline: February 15

CLARK ATLANTA UNIVERSITY
James P. Brawley Drive at Fair Street
Atlanta, GA 30314
404-880-8000

CLARKSON UNIVERSITY
Potsdam, NY 13699
315-268-6400
Admissions phone: 315-268-6479
Application deadline: February 1

CLEMSON UNIVERSITY
105 Sikes Hall
Clemson, SC 29634-4024
803-656-2287
Admissions phone: 803-656-2287

CLEVELAND STATE UNIVERSITY
Cleveland, OH 44115
216-687-3755
Application deadline: Open

COE COLLEGE
Cedar Rapids, OH
319-399-8500
Application deadline: Open

COLBY COLLEGE
150 Mayflower Hill Drive
Waterville, ME 04901
207-872-3000
Admissions phone: 207-872-3168
Application deadline: January 15

COLGATE UNIVERSITY
13 Oak Drive
Hamilton, NY 13346-1383
315-824-1000
Admissions phone: 315-824-7401
Application deadline: January 15

COLLEGE OF THE ATLANTIC
105 Eden Street
Bar Harbor, ME 04609
207-288-5015
Admissions phone: 207-288-5015 x230; in state: (800-528-0025)
Application deadline: June 1

COLLEGE OF THE HOLY CROSS
College Street
Worcester, MA 01610
508-793-2011
Admissions phone: 508-793-2443
Application deadline: February 1

THE COLLEGE OF INSURANCE
101 Murray Street
New York, NY 10007
212-962-4111
Admissions phone: 212-962-4111
Application deadline: March 1

COLLEGE OF MOUNT SAINT VINCENT
Riverdale, NY 10471
212-549-8000
Application deadline: Open

COLLEGE OF ST. ELIZABETH
Convent Station, NJ 07961
201-292-6351
Application deadline: Open

COLLEGE OF ST. MARY
Omaha, NE 68124
402-399-2407
Application deadline: August 22

COLLEGE OF THE OZARKS
Point Lookout, MO 65726
(417) 334-6411

COLLEGE OF SANTA FE
Saint Michaels Drive
Santa Fe, NM 87501
505-473-6011

COLLEGE OF STATEN ISLAND
715 Ocean Terrace
Staten Island, NY 10301
718-390-7733

COLLEGE OF WILLIAM AND MARY
Williamsburg, VA 23185
804-221-4000
Admissions phone: 804-221-4223
Application deadline: January 15

COLLEGE OF WOOSTER
Wooster, OH 44691
216-263-2118
Application deadline: February 15

COLORADO COLLEGE
14 E. Cache La Poudre
Colorado Springs, CO 80903-9972
719-389-6000
Admissions phone: 719-389-2344
Application deadline: February 15

COLORADO SCHOOL OF MINES
1500 Illinois Street
Golden, CO 80401
303-273-3300
Application deadline: June 1

COLORADO STATE UNIVERSITY
Fort Collins, CO 80523-0015
303-491-1101
Admissions phone: 303-491-6909

COLUMBIA COLLEGE
10th & Rogers
Columbia, MO 65216
314-875-8700

INDEX

COLUMBIA UNION COLLEGE
Takoma Park, MD 20912
301-891-4230
Application deadline: August 1

COLUMBIA UNIVERSITY
212 Hamilton Hall
New York, NY 10027
212-854-2521
Admissions phone: 212-854-2521
Application deadline: January 10

COLUMBIA UNIVERSITY-SCHOOL OF ENGINEERING
New York, NY 10027
212-280-5000
Admissions phone: 212-280-2931
Application deadline: February 1

CONCORDIA COLLEGE
901 S. 8th Street
Moorhead, MN 56562
218-299-3004
Admissions phone: 218-299-3004
Application deadline: Rolling

CONNECTICUT COLLEGE
270 Mohegan Ave.
New London, CT 06320
203-447-1911
Application deadline: January 15

CONVERSE COLLEGE
Spartanburg, SC 29301-0006
803-596-9040
Application deadline: April 1

COOPER UNION FOR THE ADVANCEMENT OF SCIENCE AND ART
Cooper Square
New York, NY 10003-7183
212-353-4120
Admissions phone: 212-353-4120
Application deadline: January 1

CORNELL COLLEGE
600 First Street West
Mount Vernon, IA 52314
319-895-4215
800-747-1112
Application deadline: March 1

CORNELL UNIVERSITY
410 Thurston Avenue
Ithaca, NY 14850-2488
607-255-2000
Admissions phone: 607-255-5241
Application deadline: January 1

COVENANT COLLEGE
Lookout Mountain, GA 30750
404-820-1560
Application deadline: June 1

CRANBROOK ACADEMY OF ART
500 Lone Pine Road
Bloomfield Hills, MI 48013
313-645-3300

CREIGHTON UNIVERSITY
California Street at 24th
Omaha, NE 68178
402-280-2700
Admissions phone: 402-280-2703
Application deadline: August 1

CUMBERLAND COLLEGE
Williamsburg, KY 40769
606-549-2200
Application deadline: Open

CURRY COLLEGE
Milton, MA 02186
617-333-0500
Application deadline: April 1

DALLAS BAPTIST UNIVERSITY
Dallas, TX 75211
214-333-5360
Application deadline: open

DANIEL WEBSTER COLLEGE
Nashua, NH 03063-1699
603-883-3556
Application deadline: open

DARTMOUTH COLLEGE
Hanover, NH 03755
603-646-1110
Admissions phone: 603-646-2875
Application deadline: January 1

INDEX

DAVID LIPSCOMB UNIVERSITY
3901-4001 Granny White Pike
Nashville, TN 37204
800-333-4358
Application deadline: May 15

DAVIDSON COLLEGE
Davidson, NC 28036
704-892-2000
Admissions phone: 704-892-2230 or 800-768-0380
Application deadline: February 1

DELAWARE VALLEY COLLEGE
Doylestown, PA 18901
215-345-1500
Application deadline: Open

DELTA STATE UNIVERSITY
PO Box 3151
Cleveland, MS 38733
601-846-3000
Application deadline: Open

DENISON UNIVERSITY
Box H
Granville, OH 43023
614-587-0810
Application deadline: February 1

DEPAUL UNIVERSITY
25 E. Jackson Boulevard
Chicago, IL 60604-2287
312-362-8000
Admissions phone: 800-4-DE-PAUL (out-of-state)
Application deadline: August 15

DEPAUW UNIVERSITY
313 S. Locust Street
Greencastle, IN 46135-0037
317-658-4800
Admissions phone: 317-658-4006
Application deadline: February 15

DICKINSON COLLEGE
PO Box 1773
Carlisle, PA 17013-2896
717-243-5121
Admissions phone: 717-245-1231
Application deadline: March 1

DICKINSON STATE UNIVERSITY
Dickinson, ND 58601
701-227-2331
Admissions phone: 701-227-2175
Application deadline: June 15

DORDT COLLEGE
498 4th Avenue NE
Sioux Center, IA 51250
712-722-3771
Application deadline: August 29

DOWLING COLLEGE
Oakdale
Long Island, NY 11769
516-244-3040
Application deadline: Rolling

DRAKE UNIVERSITY
2507 University
Des Moines, IA 50311-4505
515-271-3181
Admissions phone: 515-271-3181
Application deadline: March 1

DREW UNIVERSITY
36 Madison Avenue
Madison, NJ 07940-4063
201-408-3000
Admissions phone: 201-408-DREW (3739)
Application deadline: February 15

DREXEL UNIVERSITY
32nd and Chestnut Streets
Philadelphia, PA 19104
215-895-2000
Admissions phone: 215-895-2400
Application deadline: March 1

DOWLING COLLEGE
Idle Hour Boulevard
Oakdale, NY 11769

DUKE UNIVERSITY
2138 Campus Drive
Durham, NC 27706
919-684-8111
Admissions phone: 919-684-3214
Application deadline: January 15

INDEX

DUQUESNE UNIVERSITY
600 Forbes Avenue
Pittsburgh, PA 15282
412-434-6220
Admissions phone: 412-434-6220
Application deadline: July 1

EARLHAM COLLEGE
National Road West
Richmond, IN 47374
317-983-1600 or 800-EARLHAM
Application deadline: February 15

EAST CAROLINA UNIVERSITY
Fifth Street
Greenville, NC 27858
919-757-6131
Application deadline: December 31

EAST CENTRAL UNIVERSITY
Ada, OK 74820
405-332-8000
Application deadline: August 21

EAST STROUDSBURG UNIVERSITY
East Stroudsburg, PA 18301
717-424-3542
Application Deadline: March 1

EAST TENNESSEE STATE UNIVERSITY
Johnson City, TN 37614
615-929-4112

EASTERN COLLEGE
Fairview Drive
St. Davids, PA 19087
215-341-5810
Application deadline: August 15

EASTERN ILLINOIS UNIVERSITY
Charleston, IL 61920
217-581-5000
217-581-2223 or 800-252-5711
Application deadline: Rolling (contact university for possible early closings)

EASTERN KENTUCKY UNIVERSITY
Lancaster Avenue
Richmond, KY 40475
606-622-2106
Application deadline: Open

EASTERN MENNONITE COLLEGE
1200 Park Road
Harrisonburg, VA 22801
703-433-2771
Application deadline: August 1

EASTERN MICHIGAN UNIVERSITY
Ypsilanti, MI 48197
313-487-1849
Application deadline: June 30

EASTERN MONTANA COLLEGE
1500 N. 30th Street
Billings, MT 59101
406-657-2011
Application deadline: Open

EASTERN NEW MEXICO UNIVERSITY
Portales, NM 88130
505-562-2178
Application Deadline: Open

EASTERN WASHINGTON UNIVERSITY
MS 148
Cheney, WA 99004
509-458-6200
Application deadline: August 1

EASTMAN SCHOOL OF MUSIC
Rochester, NY 14604
716-274-1060
Application deadline: February 1

ECKERD COLLEGE
4200 54th Avenue South
St. Petersburg, FL 33711
813-864-8331
Admissions phone: 813-864-8331
Application deadline: Rolling

EDINBORO UNIVERSITY OF PENNSYLVANIA
Edinboro, PA 16444
814-732-2761
Application deadline: Open

INDEX

ELMHURST COLLEGE
190 Prospect
Elmhurst, IL 60126
312-279-4100
Application deadline: August 15

ELMIRA COLLEGE
Park Place
Elmira, NY 14901
607-734-3911
Application deadline: July 1

EMBRY RIDDLE AERONAUTICAL UNIVERSITY
Daytona Beach, FL 32114
904-239-6000

EMERSON COLLEGE
100 Beacon Street
Boston, MA 02116
617-578-8500
Application deadline: Open

EMMANUEL COLLEGE
400 The Fenway
Boston, MA 02115
617-735-9715
Application deadline: Rolling

EMORY UNIVERSITY
B. Jones Center, Office of Admissions
Atlanta, GA 30322
404-727-6123
Admissions phone: 800-727-6036
Application deadline: February 1

EMPORIA STATE UNIVERSITY
1200 Commercial
Emporia, KS 66801
316-343-1200
Application deadline: Open

EVERGREEN STATE COLLEGE
Olympia, WA 98505
206-866-6000
Application deadline: March 1

FAIRFIELD UNIVERSITY
North Benson Road
Fairfield, CT 06430-7524
203-254-4000
Application deadline: March 1

FAIRLEIGH DICKINSON UNIVERSITY AT RUTHERFORD
West Passaic & Montross Avenue
Rutherford, NJ 07070-2299
201-460-5000
Application deadline: Rolling

FERRIS STATE UNIVERSITY
901 S. Street
Big Rapids, MI 49307
616-592-2000
Application deadline: Open

FISK UNIVERSITY
1000-17th Avenue North
Nashville, TN 37208
615-329-8665
Admissions phone: 615-329-8655
Application deadline: June 15

FITCHBURG STATE COLLEGE
160 Pearl Street
Fitchburg, MA 01420
508-345-2151
Application deadline: March 1

FLAGLER COLLEGE
King Street
PO Box 1027
St. Augustine, FL 32085
904-829-6481
Application deadline: March 1

FLORIDA A&M UNIVERSITY
Tallahassee, FL 32307
904-599-3000
Application deadline: May 15

FLORIDA ATLANTIC UNIVERSITY
PO Box 3091
Boca Raton, FL 33431
407-367-3000
Admissions phone: 407-367-3040
Application deadline: May 1

FLORIDA INSTITUTE OF TECHNOLOGY
150 W. University Boulevard
Melbourne, FL 32901-6988
407-768-8000
Admissions phone: 800-888-4348
Application deadline: Rolling

INDEX

FLORIDA INTERNATIONAL UNIVERSITY
Miami, FL 33199
305-348-2363
Application deadline: Open

FLORIDA STATE UNIVERSITY
Tallahassee, FL 32306
904-644-2525
Admissions phone: 904-644-6200
Application deadline: March 1

FORDHAM UNIVERSITY
East Fordham Road
Bronx, NY 10458
212-599-2000
Admissions phone: 212-579-2133
Application deadline: April 1

FORT HAYS STATE UNIVERSITY
600 Park Street
Hays, KS 67601
913-628-5666
Application deadline: Open

FORT VALLEY STATE COLLEGE
State College Drive
Fort Valley, GA 31030
912-825-6211
Application deadline: September 5

FRANCISCAN UNIVERSITY OF STEUBENVILLE
100 Franciscan Way
PO Box 7200
Steubenville, OH 43952
614-283-3771
Application deadline: August 1

FRANKLIN AND MARSHALL COLLEGE
PO Box 3003
Lancaster, PA 17604-3003
717-291-3911
717-291-3951
Application deadline: February 10

FRANKLIN UNIVERSITY
201 South Grant Avenue
Columbus, OH 43215
614-224-6237
Application deadline: Open

FRESNO PACIFIC COLLEGE
1717 S. Chestnut
Fresno, CA 93702
209-453-2000
Application deadline: July 31

FRIENDS WORLD COLLEGE
Huntington, NY 11743
516-549-1102
Application deadline: Open

FRIENDS UNIVERSITY
2100 University
Wichita, KS 67213
316-261-5800
Application deadline: Open

FROSTBURG STATE UNIVERSITY
Frostburg, MD 21532
301-689-4000
Application deadline: Open

FURMAN UNIVERSITY
Poinsett Highway
Greenville, SC 29613
803-294-2034
Admissions phone: 803-294-2034
Application deadline: February 1

GALLAUDET UNIVERSITY
800 Florida Avenue, NE
Washington, DC 20002
202-651-5000
Admissions phone: 202-651-5000, x5114
Application deadline: March 15

GANNON UNIVERSITY
University Square
Erie, PA 16541
800-458-0871
Application deadline: Open

GARDNER WEBB COLLEGE
Box 817
Boiling Springs, NC 28017
704-434-2361
Application deadline: August 1

INDEX

GENEVA COLLEGE
3200 College Avenue
Beaver Falls, PA 15010
412-846-5100
Application deadline: Rolling

GEORGE FOX COLLEGE
Newberg, OR 97132
503-538-8383
Application deadline: August 1

GEORGE MASON UNIVERSITY
Fairfax, VA 22030
703-323-2000
Application deadline: February 1

THE GEORGE WASHINGTON UNIVERSITY
2121 I Street, NW — Suite 201
Washington, DC 20052
202-994-1000
Admissions phone: 202-994-6040
Application deadline: February 1

GEORGETOWN UNIVERSITY
37th & O Streets
Washington, DC 20057
202-687-3634
Admissions phone: 202-687-3600
Application deadline: January 10

GEORGIA INSTITUTE OF TECHNOLOGY
225 North Ave. NW
Atlanta, GA 30332-0320
404-894-2000
Admissions phone: 404-894-4154
Application deadline: February 1

GEORGIA STATE UNIVERSITY
University Plaza
Atlanta, GA 30303-3083
404-651-2000
Admissions phone: 404-651-2365
Application deadline: August 1

GETTYSBURG COLLEGE
Gettysburg, PA 17325-1486
717-337-6000
Admissions phone: 717-337-6100
Application deadline: February 15

GLASSBORO STATE COLLEGE
U.S. Route 322
Glassboro, NJ 08028
609-863-5000
Application deadline: March 15

GMI ENGINEERING AND MANAGEMENT INSTITUTE
1700 W. Third Avenue
Flint, MI 48504-4898
313-762-9500
Admissions phone: 313-762-7865
Application deadline: December 15 (suggested)

GODDARD COLLEGE
Plainfield, VT 05667
802-454-8311
Application deadline: Open

GOLDEY BEACOM COLLEGE
4701 Limestone Road
Wilmington, DE 19808
302-998-8814
Application deadline: Open

GONZAGA UNIVERSITY
E. 502 Boone Street
Spokane, WA 99258
509-328-4220
Application deadline: April 1

GOSHEN COLLEGE
1700 S. Main
Goshen, IN 46526
219-535-7535
Admissions phone: 800-348-7422
Application deadline: August 1

GOUCHER COLLEGE
Dulaney Road
Baltimore, MD 21204
301-337-6000
Admissions phone: 301-337-6100
Application deadline: February 1

GOVERNORS STATE UNIVERSITY
University Park, IL 60466
312-534-5000

INDEX

GRAMBLING STATE UNIVERSITY
Box 864
Grambling, LA 71245
318-247-3811
318-274-2345
Application deadline: July 15

GRAND CANYON UNIVERSITY
3300 W. Camelback Road
Phoenix, AZ 85017
602-249-3300
Application deadline: August 1

GRAND VALLEY STATE UNIVERSITY
1 Campus Drive
Allendale, MI 49401
616-895-6611
Application deadline: July 19

GREENVILLE COLLEGE
315 East College Avenue
Greenville, IL 62246
618-664-1840
Application deadline: Open

GRINNELL COLLEGE
Grinnell, IA 50112
515-269-4000
Admissions phone: 515-269-3600
Application deadline: February 1

GROVE CITY COLLEGE
100 Campus Drive
Grove City, PA 16127-2104
412-458-2000
Admissions phone: 412-458-2100
Application deadline: February 15

GUILFORD COLLEGE
5800 W. Friendly Ave.
Greensboro, NC 27410
919-316-2100 or 800-992-7759
Admissions phone: 919-316-2100 or 800-992-7759
Application deadline: March 1

GUSTAVUS ADOLPHUS COLLEGE
800 College Avenue
St. Peter, MN 56082
507-933-8000
Admissions phone: 507-933-7676 or 800-GUSTAVUS
Application deadline: April 1

HAHNEMANN UNIVERSITY/ SCHOOL OF HEALTH SCIENCE & HUMANITIES
201 N 15th Street, MS 506
Philadelphia, PA 19102-1192
215-448-8288
Admissions phone: 215-448-8288
Application deadline: March 1 (suggested)

HAMILTON COLLEGE
198 College Hill Road
Clinton, NY 13323-1293
315-859-4011
Admissions phone: 315-859-4421
Application deadline: January 15

HAMLINE UNIVERSITY
1536 Hewitt Avenue
St. Paul, MN 55104-1284
612-641-2800
Admissions phone: 612-641-2207
Application deadline: Rolling

HAMPDEN-SYDNEY COLLEGE
College Road/PO Box 667
Hampden-Sydney, VA 23943
804-223-6000
Admissions phone: 804-223-6120
Application deadline: March 1

HAMPSHIRE COLLEGE
Amherst, MA 01002
413-549-4600
Admissions phone: 413-549-4600 ext. 471
Application deadline: February 1

HAMPTON UNIVERSITY
Hampton, VA 23668
804-727-5000
Application deadline: February 15

HANOVER COLLEGE
Hanover, IN 47243
812-866-7026
Application deadline: March 15

INDEX

HARDING UNIVERSITY
Searcy, AR 72143
501-279-4000
Application deadline: Open

HARTWICK COLLEGE
Oneonta, NY 13820
607-431-4200
Application deadline: March 1

HARVARD UNIVERSITY
8 Garden St.—Byerly Hall
Cambridge, MA 02138
617-495-1000
Admissions phone: 617-495-1551
Application deadline: January 1

HARVEY MUDD COLLEGE
Claremont, CA 91711
714-621-8011
Admissions phone: 714-621-8011
Application deadline: February 1

HAVERFORD COLLEGE
370 Lancaster Avenue
Haverford, PA 19041-1392
215-896-1000
Admissions phone: 215-896-1350
Application deadline: January 15

HAWAII PACIFIC UNIVERSITY
Honolulu, HI 96813
808-544-0200
Admissions phone: 808-544-0248
Application deadline: February 1
(suggested)

HENDERSON STATE
UNIVERSITY
1100 Henderson Street
Arkadelphia, AR 71923
501-246-5511
Application deadline: Open

HENDRIX COLLEGE
Conway, AR 72032
501-329-6811
Application deadline: Open

HILLSDALE COLLEGE
33 East College Street
Hillsdale, MI 49242
517-437-7341
Admissions phone: 517-437-7341
x327
Application deadline: July 1

HIRAM COLLEGE
Hiram, OH 44234
216-569-3211
Application deadline: April 15

HOBART AND WILLIAM
SMITH COLLEGES
Geneva, NY 14456
315-789-5500
Admissions phone: 315-781-3622 or
800-852-2256 (H)
315-781-3472 (WS)
Application deadline: February 15

HOFSTRA UNIVERSITY
Hempstead, NY 11550
516-463-6600
Admissions phone: 516-560-6700
Application deadline: February 15
(suggested)

HOLLINS COLLEGE
PO Box 9707
Roanoke, VA 24020
703-362-6400
Admissions phone: 703-362-6401
Application deadline: February 15

HOOD COLLEGE
Frederick, MD 21701-9988
301-663-3131
Admissions phone: 301-663-3131
Application deadline: March 31

HOPE COLLEGE
69 E. 10th Street, Box 9000
Holland, MI 49422-9000
800-654-HOPE (out of state)
800-822-HOPE (Michigan)
Admissions phone: 800-654-HOPE
(out of state)
800-822-HOPE (Michigan)
Application deadline: Rolling

HOUGHTON COLLEGE
Houghton, NY 14744
716-567-9200
Application deadline: Open

INDEX

HOWARD UNIVERSITY
Washington, DC 20059
202-806-6100
Admissions phone: 202-806-2750
Application deadline: April 1

HOWARD PAYNE UNIVERSITY
1000 Fisk Avenue
Brownwood, TX 76801
915-646-2502
Application deadline: August 16

HUMBOLDT STATE
UNIVERSITY
Arcata, CA 95521
707-826-3011
Application deadline: December 15

IDAHO STATE UNIVERSITY
Pocatello, ID 83209
208-236-0211
Application deadline: August 24

ILLINOIS INSTITUTE OF
TECHNOLOGY
Chicago, IL 60616
312-567-3000
Admissions phone: 312-567-3025
Application deadline: Rolling

ILLINOIS STATE UNIVERSITY
Normal, IL 61761
309-438-2181
Admissions phone: 800-366-2478
Application deadline: Rolling

ILLINOIS WESLEYAN
UNIVERSITY
Box 2900
Bloomington, IL 61702
309-556-3034
Admissions phone: 309-556-3031
Application deadline: February 1

INDIANA STATE UNIVERSITY
Terre Haute, IN 47809
812-237-6311
Admissions phone: 812-237-2121
Application deadline: August 15

INDIANA UNIVERSITY
300 North Jordanna
Bloomington, IN 47405
812-855-4848
Admissions phone: 812-335-0661
Application deadline: July 15
(suggested December 15)

INDIANA UNIVERSITY—
PURDUE UNIVERSITY,
FORT WAYNE
2101 Coliseum Boulevard East
Fort Wayne, IN 46805
219-481-6100
Application deadline: August 1

INDIANA UNIVERSITY—
PURDUE UNIVERSITY,
INDIANAPOLIS
425 University Boulevard
Indianapolis, IN 46202
317-274-5555
Application deadline: June 15

INDIANA UNIVERSITY OF
PENNSYLVANIA
216 Pratt Hall
Indiana, PA 15705
412-357-2100
Admissions phone: 412-357-2230
Application deadline: December 31

IONA COLLEGE
715 North Avenue
New Rochelle, NY 10801
914-633-2000
Application deadline: Rolling

IOWA STATE UNIVERSITY
Ames, IA 50011
515-294-4111
Admissions phone: 515-294-5836
Application deadline: None
(suggested January 1)

ITHACA COLLEGE
947 Danby Road
Ithaca, NY 14850
607-274-3124
Application deadline: March 1

JACKSONVILLE STATE
UNIVERSITY
Jacksonville, AL 36265
205-782-5781
Application deadline: Rolling

JACKSONVILLE UNIVERSITY
2800 University Boulevard North
Jacksonville, FL 32211
904-744-3950
Application deadline: Open

JAMES MADISON UNIVERSITY
Harrisonburg, VA 22807
703-568-6211
Admissions phone: 703-568-6147
Application deadline: February 1

JOHN BROWN UNIVERSITY
Siloam Springs, AR 72761
501-524-3131
Application deadline: July 15

JOHN CARROLL UNIVERSITY
20700 North Parks Boulevard
University Heights, OH 44118
216-397-1886
Application deadline: June 1

JOHNS HOPKINS UNIVERSITY
Baltimore, MD 21218
301-338-8000
Admissions phone: 301-338-8171
Application deadline: January 1

JUILLIARD SCHOOL
60 Lincoln Center Plaza
New York, NY 10023-6590
212-799-5000
Admissions phone: 212-799-5000 x223
Application deadline: January 8 (Drama auditions & March Dance, Music auditions)
Application deadline: March 15 (May Dance, Music auditions)

JUNIATA COLLEGE
1700 Moore Street
Huntingdon, PA 16652
814-643-4310
Application deadline: March 1

KALAMAZOO COLLEGE
1200 Academy Street
Kalamazoo, MI 49006-3295
800-253-3602
Admissions phone: 616-383-8408
Application deadline: March 1 (suggested)

KANSAS STATE UNIVERSITY
Manhattan, KS 66506-0110
913-532-6011
Admissions phone: 913-532-6250
Application deadline: None (suggest December)

KEAN COLLEGE OF NEW JERSEY
Morris Avenue
Union, NJ 07083
908-527-2195
Application deadline: June 30

KEARNEY STATE COLLEGE
Kearney, NE 68849
308-234-8526
Application deadline: Rolling

KEENE STATE COLLEGE
229 Main Street
Keene, NH 03431
603-352-1909
Application deadline: May 1

KENT STATE UNIVERSITY
Kent, OH 44242-0001
216-672-2121
Admissions phone: 216-672-2444
Application deadline: March 15

KENYON COLLEGE
Admissions Office - Ransom Hall
Gambier, OH 43022
614-427-5776 or 800-848-2468
Admissions phone: 614-427-5776 or 800-848-2468
Application deadline: February 15

KEUKA COLLEGE
Keuka Park, NY 14478
315-536-4411
Application deadline: Open

KING COLLEGE
1350 King College Road
Bristol, TN 37620
800-362-0014
Admissions phone: 800-362-0014
Application deadline: August 15

INDEX

KING'S COLLEGE
133 North River Street
Wilkes Barre, PA 18711
717-826-5900
Application deadline: August 15

KNOX COLLEGE
Galesburg, IL 61401-4999
309-343-0112 x123
Admissions phone: 800-678-5669
Application deadline: February 15

KUTZTOWN UNIVERSITY
Kutztown, PA 19530
215-683-4000

LAFAYETTE COLLEGE
High Street
Easton, PA 18042-1770
215-250-5000
Admissions phone: 215-250-5100
Application deadline: February 1

LA SALLE UNIVERSITY
Olney Avenue at 20th Street
Philadelphia, PA 19141
215-951-1000
Application deadline: August 1

LAKE FOREST COLLEGE
Sheridan and College Road
Lake Forest, IL 60045
312-234-3100
Application deadline: February 15

LAKE SUPERIOR STATE UNIVERSITY
Sault Ste. Marie, MI 49783
906-635-6841
Application deadline: September 1

LAMAR UNIVERSITY
Lamar Station
Box 10001
Beaumont, TX 77710
409-880-7011
Application deadline: August 1

LAWRENCE UNIVERSITY
PO Box 599
Appleton, WI 54912
414-832-7000
Application deadline: February 15

LETOURNEAU UNIVERSITY
PO Box 7001
Longview, TX 75607
903-753-0231
Application deadline: Open

LEBANON VALLEY COLLEGE
101 N. College Avenue
Annville, PA 17003
717-867-6100
Application deadline: Open

LEE COLLEGE
North Ocoee Street
Cleveland, TN 37311
615-472-2111
Application deadline: Open

LEMOYNE-OWEN COLLEGE
807 Walker Avenue
Memphis, TN 38126
901-774-9090
Application deadline: July 15

LENOIR-RHYNE COLLEGE
Hickory, NC 28603
703-328-1741
Application deadline: Rolling

LEHIGH UNIVERSITY
Bethlehem, PA 18015
215-758-3000
Admissions phone: 215-758-3100
Application deadline: March 1
(suggest January 1)

LEWIS AND CLARK COLLEGE
Portland, OR 97219
503-768-7188
Admissions phone: 503-768-7040 or 800-444-4111
Application deadline: February 1

LIMESTONE COLLEGE
Gaffney, SC 29340
803-489-7151
Application deadline: open

LINCOLN UNIVERSITY
Lincoln University, PA 19352
215-932-8300
Application deadline: Open

INDEX

LINFIELD COLLEGE
900 So. Baker Street
McMinnville, OR 97128
503-472-4121
Application deadline: Rolling

LIVINGSTONE COLLEGE
701 West Monroe Street
Salisbury, NC 28144
Application deadline: Open

LOCK HAVEN UNIVERSITY OF PENNSYLVANIA
North Fairview Street
Lock Haven, PA 17745
717-893-2027
Application deadline: Rolling

LOMA LINDA UNIVERSITY
Loma Linda, CA 92350
800-422-4558
Application deadline: Open

LONG ISLAND UNIVERSITY, C.W. POST CENTER
Brookville, NY 11548
516-299-0200
Admissions phone: 516-299-2413
Application deadline: None (suggest early as possible)

LONGWOOD COLLEGE
Farmville, VA 23901
804-395-2000
Application deadline: Rolling

LOUISIANA STATE UNIVERSITY AND A & M COLLEGE
110 Thomas Boyd Hall
Baton Rouge, LA 70803-2802
504-388-3202
Admissions phone: 504-388-1175
Application deadline: July 1

LOUISIANA TECH UNIVERSITY
Box 3178 Tech Station
Ruston, LA 71272
318-257-3036

LOYOLA COLLEGE
4501 N. Charles Street
Baltimore, MD 21210
410-323-1010
Admissions phone: 410-617-2252
Application deadline: February 1

LOYOLA MARYMOUNT UNIVERSITY
Loyola Boulevard at W. 80th Street
Los Angeles, CA 90045
213-338-2775
Application deadline: February 1

LOYOLA UNIVERSITY
New Orleans, LA 70118
504-865-2011
Admissions phone: 504-865-3240
Application deadlines: August 1 and January 5

LUTHER COLLEGE
700 College Drive
Decorah, IA 52101
319-387-2000
Application deadline: March 1

LYNCHBURG COLLEGE
1501 Lakeside Drive
Lynchburg, VA 24503
804-522-8100
800-426-8101
Application deadline: Open

MACALESTER COLLEGE
1600 Grand Avenue
St. Paul, MN 55105-1899
612-696-6000
Admissions phone: 612-696-6357
Application deadline: February 1

MACMURRAY COLLEGE
447 E. College
Jacksonville, IL 62650
217-479-7000
217-479-7056 (or i.s: 800-252-7485)
Application deadline: June 1

MADONNA UNIVERSITY
36600 Schoolcraft Road
Livonia, MI 48150
313-591-5000
August 1

MAGDALEN COLLEGE
270 D.W. Highway South
Bedford, NH 03102
603-669-7735

INDEX

MALONE COLLEGE
515 25th Street N.W.
Canton, OH 44709
216-489-0800
Application deadline: Rolling

MANHATTAN COLLEGE
Riverdale, NY 10471
212-920-0100
Admissions phone: 212-920-0200
Application deadline: March 1

MANHATTAN SCHOOL OF MUSIC
120 Claremont Avenue
New York, NY 10027
212-749-2802
Application deadline: July 15

MANHATTANVILLE COLLEGE
125 Purchase Street
Purchase, NY 10577
914-694-2200
Application deadline: March 1

MANKATO STATE UNIVERSITY
Mankato, MN 56002
507-389-2463
Application deadline: Open

MANSFIELD UNIVERSITY
Beecher House
Mansfield, PA 16933
717-662-4243
Application deadline: July 15

MARIETTA COLLEGE
5th Street
Marietta, OH 45750
614-374-4643
Application deadline: May 1

MARIST COLLEGE
North Road
Poughkeepsie, NY 12601
914-575-3000
Application deadline: March 1

MARLBORO COLLEGE
Marlboro, VT 05344
802-257-4333
Admissions phone: 802-257-4333
Application deadline: February 1

MARQUETTE UNIVERSITY
517 N 14th Street
Milwaukee, WI 53233
414-288-7700
Admissions phone: 414-224-7302
Application deadline: None (suggest fall of senior year)

MARSHALL UNIVERSITY
400 Hal Greer Boulevard
Huntington, WV 25755
304-696-3170
Application deadline: August 15

MARY WASHINGTON COLLEGE
Fredericksburg, VA 22401
703-899-4100
Application deadline: February 1

MARYGROVE COLLEGE
8425 West McNichols Road
Detroit, MI 48221
313-862-8000
Application deadline: Open

MARYMOUNT COLLEGE TARRYTOWN
100 Marymount Avenue
Tarrytown, NY 10591
914-631-3200
Admissions phone: 914-631-3200 x 295
Application deadline: August 15

MARYMOUNT MANHATTAN COLLEGE
221 East 71st Street
New York, NY 10021
212-517-0400
Application deadline: March 15

MASSACHUSETTS COLLEGE OF PHARMACY
Boston, MA 02115
617-732-2850
Application deadline: July 1

MASSACHUSETTS INSTITUTE OF TECHNOLOGY
Cambridge, MA 02139-4301
617-253-1000
Admissions phone: 617-253-4791
Application deadline: January 1

INDEX

MEDICAL COLLEGE OF GEORGIA
Augusta, GA 30912
404-721-2725

MEMPHIS STATE UNIVERSITY
Memphis, TN 38152
901-678-2000
Application deadline: August 1

MERCER UNIVERSITY
1400 Coleman Avenue
Macon, GA 31207
912-752-2650
Application deadline: Rolling

MERCY COLLEGE
555 Broadway
Dobbs Ferry, NY 10522
914-693-4500

MERCY COLLEGE OF DETROIT
Detroit, MI 48219
313-592-6030
Application deadline: August 15

MESSIAH COLLEGE
Grantham, PA 17027
717-766-2511
Admissions phone: 717-691-6000
Application deadline: April 1

METHODIST COLLEGE
5400 Ramsey Street
Fayetteville, NC 28311
919-488-7110
Application deadline: Open

METROPOLITAN STATE COLLEGE
1006 11th Street, Box 16
Denver, CO 80217
303-556-3058
Application deadline: August 1

MIAMI UNIVERSITY
Oxford, OH 45056
513-529-1809
Application deadline: March 1
(commuters August 1)

MICHIGAN STATE UNIVERSITY
East Lansing, MI 48824-1046
517-355-1855
Admissions phone: 517-355-8332
Application deadline: 30 days prior to start of term

MICHIGAN TECHNOLOGICAL UNIVERSITY
1400 Townsend Drive
Houghton, MI 49931
906-487-1885
Application deadline: August 1

MIDDLEBURY COLLEGE
Middlebury, VT 05753-6002
802-388-3711
Admissions phone: 802-388-3711, x5153
Application deadline: January 15

MILLERSVILLE UNIVERSITY
Millersville, PA 17551
717-872-3024
Application deadline: Rolling

MILLIKIN UNIVERSITY
1184 W. Main Street
Decatur, IL 62522
217-424-6210
Application deadline: Open

MILLS COLLEGE
Oakland, CA 94613
415-430-2149
Admissions phone: 415-430-2135
Application deadline: February 1

MILLSAPS COLLEGE
1701 North State Street
Jackson, MS 39210
601-974-1000
Application deadline: April 1

MILWAUKEE SCHOOL OF ENGINEERING
Milwaukee, WI 53201-0644
414-277-7300
Admissions phone: 414-277-7200
Application deadline: None

MISSISSIPPI COLLEGE
Clinton, MS 39058
601-925-3240
Application deadline: rolling

MISSISSIPPI STATE
UNIVERSITY
Mississippi State, MS 39762
601-325-2131
Application deadline: Open

MISSOURI SOUTHERN
STATE COLLEGE
Newman and Duquesne Road
Joplin, MO 64801
417-625-9300
Application deadline: August 1

MISSOURI WESTERN STATE
COLLEGE
4525 Downs Drive
St. Joseph, MO 64507
816-271-4200
Application deadline: August 1

MONTANA COLLEGE OF
MINERAL SCIENCE AND
TECHNOLOGY
West Park Street
Butte, MT 59701
406-496-4101
Application deadline: July 1

MONTANA STATE
UNIVERSITY
Bozeman, Montana 59717
406-994-0211
Admissions phone: 406-994-2452
Application deadline: 30 days prior to registration

MONTCLAIR STATE COLLEGE
Valley Road & Normal Avenue
Upper Montclair, NJ 07043
201-893-4000
Application deadline: March 1

MORAVIAN COLLEGE
1200 Main Street
Bethlehem, PA 18018
215-861-1300
Application deadline: March 1

MOORHEAD STATE
UNIVERSITY
Moorhead, MN 56563
218-236-2161
Application deadline: August 15

MOREHOUSE COLLEGE
830 Westview Drive SW
Atlanta, GA 30314
404-681-2800
Application deadline: February 15

MOUNT HOLYOKE COLLEGE
South Hadley, MA 01075
413-538-2000
Admissions phone: 413-538-2023
Application deadline: February 1

MOUNT ST. MARY'S COLLEGE
Emmitsburg, MD 21727
301-447-5214
Application deadline: March 1

MOUNT UNION COLLEGE
1972 Clark Avenue
Alliance, OH 44601
216-821-5320
Application deadline: Rolling

MUHLENBERG COLLEGE
2400 W. Chew Street
Allentown, PA 18104-5586
215-821-3200
Admissions phone: 215-821-3200
Application deadline: February 15

MURRAY STATE UNIVERSITY
15th and Main Street
Murray, KY 42071
502-762-3741
Application deadline: August 1

MUSKINGUM COLLEGE
New Concord, OH 43762
614-826-8211
Application deadline: August 1

NEBRASKA WESLEYAN
UNIVERSITY
500 St. Paul Avenue
Lincoln, NE 68504
412-466-2371
Application deadline: August 15

INDEX

NEUMANN COLLEGE
Concord Road
Aston, PA 19014
215-459-0905
Application deadline: Open

NEW COLLEGE OF THE UNIVERSITY OF SOUTH FLORIDA
Sarasota, FL 34243-2197
813-355-2693
Admissions phone: 813-355-2963
Application deadline: July 15

NEW JERSEY INSTITUTE OF TECHNOLOGY
Newark, NJ 07102-9938
201-596-3000
Admissions phone: 201-596-3300
Application deadline: April 1

NEW MEXICO INSTITUTE OF MINING AND TECHNOLOGY
Socorro, NM 87801
505-835-5425
Admissions phone: 505-835-5424
Application deadline: August 15

NEW MEXICO STATE UNIVERSITY
Las Cruces, NM 88003-0001
505-646-0111
Admissions phone: 505-646-3121
Application deadline: None

NEW SCHOOL FOR SOCIAL RESEARCH, EUGENE LANG COLLEGE
66 West 12th Street
New York, NY 10011
212-229-5600
Admissions phone: 212-229-5665
Application deadline: February 1

NEW YORK INSTITUTE OF TECHNOLOGY
Wheatley Road
Old Westbury, NY 11568
516-686-7516
Application deadline: Open

NEW YORK UNIVERSITY
22 Washington Square North
New York, NY 10011
212-998-4500
212-998-4500
Application deadline: February 1

NICHOLLS STATE UNIVERSITY
PO Box 2004 University Station
Thibodaux, LA 70310
504-446-8111
Application Deadline: August 15

NORFOLK STATE UNIVERSITY
2401 Corprew Avenue
Norfolk, VA 23504
804-683-8600
Application deadline: Rolling

NORTHEAST LOUISIANA UNIVERSITY
700 University Avenue
Monroe, LA 71209
318-342-1000
Application deadline: August 17

NORTHEAST MISSOURI STATE UNIVERSITY
205 McClain Hall
Kirksville, MO 63501
816-785-4000
Admissions phone: 816-785-4114
Application deadline: March 1 (suggested)

NORTHEASTERN STATE UNIVERSITY
Tahlequah, OK 74464
918-456-5511
Application deadline: August 1

NORTH CAROLINA CENTRAL UNIVERSITY
Fayetteville Street
Durhman, NC 27707
919-560-6100

NORTH CAROLINA STATE UNIVERSITY
Raleigh, NC 27695-7103
919-737-2011
Admissions phone: 919-737-2434
Application deadline: May 1

INDEX

NORTH CENTRAL COLLEGE
30 North Brainard Street
PO Box 3063
Naperville, IL 60540
708-420-3400
Application deadline: Open

NORTH DAKOTA STATE UNIVERSITY
Fargo, ND 58105
701-237-8643
Application deadline: Open

NORTH PARK COLLEGE
3225 W. Foster Avenue
Chicago, IL 60625
312-583-2700
Application deadline: Open

NORTHEASTERN UNIVERSITY
Boston, MA 02115-9056
617-437-2000
Admissions phone: 617-437-2200
Application deadline: None (suggest January 15)

NORTHERN ARIZONA UNIVERSITY
PO Box 4132
Flagstaff, AZ 86011
602-523-9011
Application deadline: April 1

NORTHERN ILLINOIS UNIVERSITY
DeKalb, IL 60115
815-753-0446
Admissions phone: 815-753-0446
Application deadline: 30 days prior to start of term

NORTHERN MICHIGAN UNIVERSITY
Marquette, MI 49855
906-227-2650
Application deadline: August 1

NORTHLAND COLLEGE
Ashland, WI 54806
715-682-1699
Application deadline: Open

NORTHWEST NAZARENE COLLEGE
623 Holly Street
Nampa, ID 86351
208-467-8496
Application deadline: Open

NORTHWESTERN COLLEGE
101 College Lane
Orange City, IA 51041
712-737-4821
Application deadline: Open

NORTHWESTERN COLLEGE
3003 North Snelling Avenue
St. Paul, MN 55113
612-631-5100
Application deadline: August 15

NORTHWESTERN STATE UNIVERSITY OF LOUISIANA
Natchitoches, LA 71497
318-357-6011
Application deadline: August 1

NORTHWESTERN UNIVERSITY
1801 Hinman Avenue
Evanston, IL 60204-3060
708-491-7271
Admissions phone: 312-491-7271
Application deadline: January 1

NORWICH UNIVERSITY
Northfield, VT 05663
802-485-2000
Application deadline: Rolling

OAKLAND UNIVERSITY
205 Wilson Hall
Rochester, MI 48309
313-370-3360
Application deadline: July 15

OAKWOOD COLLEGE
Huntsville, AL 35896
205-726-7000
Application deadline: Open

OBERLIN COLLEGE
Oberlin, OH 44074
216-775-8121
Admissions phone: 216-775-8411
Application deadline: February 1 (music conservatory March 15)

OCCIDENTAL COLLEGE
1600 Campus Road
Los Angeles, CA 90041
213-259-2500
Admissions phone: 213-259-2700
Application deadline: February 1

OGLETHORPE UNIVERSITY
Atlanta, GA 30319-2797
404-261-1441
Admissions phone: 404-233-6864
Application deadline: August 1

OHIO NORTHERN UNIVERSITY
Ada, OH 45810
419-772-2000
Application deadline: August 1

OHIO STATE UNIVERSITY
3rd Floor Lincoln Tower
1800 Cannon Drive
Columbus, OH 43210-1200
614-292-3980
Admissions phone: 614-292-3980
Application deadline: February 15

OHIO UNIVERSITY
120 Chubb Hall
Athens, OH 45701-2979
614-593-1000
Admissions phone: 614-593-4100
Application deadline: March 1

OHIO WESLEYAN UNIVERSITY
Delaware, OH 43015
614-369-4431
Admissions phone: 614-368-3020 (or 800-922-8953 out-of-state; 800-862-0612 Ohio)
Application deadline: March 1

OKLAHOMA STATE UNIVERSITY
Stillwater, OK 74078
800-522-6809
Admissions phone: 405-744-6876
Application deadline: August 20

OLD DOMINION UNIVERSITY
Norfolk, VA 23529
804-683-3000
Application deadline: May 1

ORAL ROBERTS UNIVERSITY
Tulsa, OK 74171
918-495-6161
Admissions phone: 918-495-6161 ext. 6500
Application deadline: None (suggest by end of 11th year)

OREGON STATE UNIVERSITY
Corvalis, OR 97331
503-737-0123
Admissions phone: 503-754-4411
Application deadline: 30 days prior to entrance

OTIS/PARSONS SCHOOL OF ART AND DESIGN
2401 Wilshire Blvd.
Los Angeles, CA 90057
213-251-0501
Admissions phone: 213-251-0505 or 800-527-OTIS
Application deadline: None (suggest March 1)

OUACHITA BAPTIST UNIVERSITY
410 Ouachita
Arkadelphia, AR 71923
501-246-4531
Application deadline: Open

PACE UNIVERSITY
New York, NY 10038-1502
212-346-1200
Admissions phone: 212-488-1323
Application deadline: August 15

PACIFIC LUTHERAN UNIVERSITY
Tacoma, WA 98447
206-535-7151
Admissions phone: 206-535-7151
Application deadline: May 1

PACIFIC UNION COLLEGE
Angwin, CA 94508
707-965-6336
Application deadline: Open

PACIFIC UNIVERSITY
2043 College Way
Forest Grove, OR 97116
503-357-6151
Application deadline: August 1

PALM BEACH ATLANTIC
COLLEGE
901 S. Flagler Avenue
PO Box 3353
W. Palm Beach, FL 33401
407-650-7700
Application deadline: August 1

PARSONS SCHOOL OF DESIGN
66 Fifth Avenue
New York, NY 10011
212-229-8900
Application deadline: Open

PEMBROKE STATE
UNIVERSITY
Pembroke, NC 28372
919-521-4214
Application deadline: July 15

PENNSYLVANIA STATE
UNIVERSITY
University Park, PA 16802
814-865-4700
Admissions phone: 814-865-5471
Application deadline: November 30
(suggested)

PENNSYLVANIA STATE
UNIVERSITY, OGONTZ
1600 Woodland Road
Abington, PA 19001
215-886-9400

PEPPERDINE UNIVERSITY
Malibu, CA 90263
213-456-4000
Admissions phone: 213-456-4392
Application deadline: February 15

PHILADELPHIA COLLEGE OF
PHARMACY AND SCIENCE
600 South Forty-third Street
Philadelphia, PA 19104
215-596-8810
Application deadline: Rolling

PHILLIPS UNIVERSITY
100 S. University Avenue
Enid, OK 73701
405-237-4433
Application deadline: August 15

PITTSBURG STATE
UNIVERSITY
1701 S. Broadway
Pittsburg, KS 66762
316-231-7000
Application deadline: Open

PITZER COLLEGE
1050 North Mills Avenue
Claremont, CA 91711
714-621-8000
Application deadline: February 1

POINT LOMA NAZARENE
COLLEGE
3900 Lomaland Drive
San Diego, CA 92106
619-221-2200
Application deadline: Open

POMONA COLLEGE
Claremont, CA 91711-6312
714-621-8000
Admissions phone: 714-621-8134
Application deadline: January 15

PORTLAND STATE
UNIVERSITY
PO Box 751
Portland, OR 97207
503-725-4433
Application deadline: July 1

PRATT INSTITUTE
Brooklyn, NY 11205
718-636-3600
Admissions phone: 718-636-3669
Application deadline: April 1

PRESBYTERIAN COLLEGE
South Broad Street
Clinton, SC 29325
800-476-7272
803-833-2820
Application deadline: May 1

INDEX

PRESCOTT COLLEGE
220-M Grove Avenue
Prescott, AZ 86301
602-778-2090
Application deadline: May 15

PRINCETON UNIVERSITY
Princeton, NJ 08544
609-258-3000
Admissions phone: 609-452-3060
Application deadline: January 1

PRINCIPIA COLLEGE
Elsah, IL 62028
618-374-5176
Application deadline: August 15

PROVIDENCE COLLEGE
Providence, RI 02918-0001
401-865-2141
Admissions phone: 401-865-2535
Application deadline: February 1

PURDUE UNIVERSITY
Office of Admissions, 1080
Schleman Hall
West Lafayette, IN 47907
317-494-4600
Admissions phone: 317-494-1776
Application deadline: None
(engineering, nursing, flight
technology: November 15)

QUINNIPIAC COLLEGE
Mt. Carmel Avenue
Hamden, CT 06518
203-288-5251
Application deadline: Open

RADFORD UNIVERSITY
PO Box 5430
Radford, VA 24142
703-831-5000
Application deadline: April 1

RAMAPO COLLEGE
Mahwah, NJ 07430
201-529-7600
Deadline: March 15

RANDOLPH-MACON COLLEGE
Admissions Office
Ashland, VA 23005
804-798-8372
Admissions phone: 804-752-7305 or
800-888-1762
Application deadline: March 1
(suggested)

RANDOLPH-MACON WOMAN'S
COLLEGE
Lynchburg, VA 24503
804-846-7392
Admissions phone: 804-846-9680
Application deadline: February 15

REED COLLEGE
Portland, OR 97202-8199
503-771-1112
Admissions phone: 503-777-7511 or
800-547-4750
Application deadline: February 1

REGIS COLLEGE
235 Wellesley Street
Weston, MA 02193
617-893-1820
Application deadline: Open

RENSSELAER POLYTECHNIC
INSTITUTE
Troy, NY 12180-3590
518-276-6000
Admissions phone: 518-276-6216
Application deadline: January 15

RHODE ISLAND SCHOOL
OF DESIGN
Providence, RI 02903
401-331-3511
Admissions phone: 401-331-3511
Application deadline: January 21

RHODES COLLEGE
2000 N. Parkway
Memphis, TN 38112
800-844-5969
Admissions phone: 901-726-3700 or
800-844-5969
Application deadline: February 1

RICE UNIVERSITY
Houston, TX 77251
713-527-8101
713-527-OWLS
Application deadline: January 15

INDEX

RIPON COLLEGE
PO Box 248
Ripon, WI 54971
414-748-8118
Application deadline: March 15

ROBERTS WESLEYAN
COLLEGE
2301 Westside Drive
Rochester, NY 14624
716-594-9471
Application deadline: Open

ROCHESTER INSTITUTE OF
TECHNOLOGY
Rochester, NY 14623-0887
716-475-2400
Admissions phone: 716-475-6631
Application deadline: None

ROLLINS COLLEGE
Winter Park, FL 32789
407-646-2000
Admissions phone: 407-646-2161
Application deadline: February 15

ROOSEVELT UNIVERSITY
430 South Michigan Avenue
Chicago, IL 60605
312-341-3515
Application deadline: Open

ROSE-HULMAN INSTITUTE
OF TECHNOLOGY
5500 Wabash Avenue
Terre Haute, IN 47803
812-877-1511
Admissions phone: 812-877-1511
Application deadline: March 1

ROSEMONT COLLEGE
Rosemont, PA 19010
215-527-0200
Admissions phone: 215-525-6420
Application deadline: Rolling

RUSH UNIVERSITY
1753 West Congress Parkway
Chicago, IL 60612
312-942-5000

RUTGERS, THE STATE
UNIVERSITY OF NEW JERSEY
New Brunswick, NJ 08903
201-932-1766
Admissions phone: 201-932-3770
Application deadline: January 15

RUTGERS, THE STATE
UNIVERSITY OF NEW JERSEY
PO Box 93740
Camden, NJ 08101
609-757-1766
Application deadline: May 1

SACRED HEART UNIVERSITY
Fairfield, CT 06432-1000
203-371-7999
Admissions phone: 203-371-7880
Application deadline: None (suggest early as possible)

SAGINAW VALLEY STATE
UNIVERSITY
University Center, MI 48710
517-790-4200
Application deadline: Open

ST. ANDREWS PRESBYTE-
RIAN COLLEGE
Laurinburg, NC 28352
919-276-3652
Application deadline: open

ST. ANSELM COLLEGE
Saint Anselm Drive
Manchester, New Hampshire 03102
603-641-7500
Admissions phone: 603-641-7500
Application deadline: Rolling

ST. AUGUSTINE'S COLLEGE
1315 Oakwood Avenue
Raleigh, NC 27610
919-828-4451
Application deadline: Open

ST. CLOUD STATE
UNIVERSITY
720 S. 4 Avenue
St. Cloud, MN 56301
612-255-2243
Application deadline: May 1

INDEX

ST. FRANCIS COLLEGE
Loretto, PA 15940
814-472-3131

ST. JOHN'S COLLEGE
PO Box 2800
Annapolis, MD 21404
410-263-2371
Admissions phone: 410-626-2522 or 800-727-9238
Application deadline: March 1 (suggested)
St. John's of Maryland and New Mexico are affiliated. Students apply jointly to both schools, and then decide where to enroll. When St. John's College appears in this book without a state name, the listing applies to both campuses.

ST. JOHN'S COLLEGE
Santa Fe, NM 87501-4599
505-982-3691
Admissions phone: 505-982-3691
Application deadline: March 1 (suggested)
St. John's of Maryland and New Mexico are affiliated. Students apply jointly to both schools, and then decide where to enroll. When St. John's College appears in this book without a state name, the listing applies to both campuses.

ST. JOHN'S UNIVERSITY
Jamaica, NY 11439
718-990-6161
Admissions phone: 718-990-6161
Application deadline: None (suggest March 1)

ST. JOHN'S UNIVERSITY
Collegeville, MN 56321
612-363-2011
Application deadline: Open

ST. JOSEPH COLLEGE
1678 Asylum Avenue
West Hartford, CT 06117
203-232-4571
Application deadline: May 1

ST. JOSEPH'S COLLEGE
5600 City Avenue
Philadelphia, PA 19131
215-660-1000
Application deadline: March 1

ST. LAWRENCE UNIVERSITY
Canton, NY 13617
315-379-5011
Application deadline: February 1

ST. LOUIS UNIVERSITY
221 N. Grand Blvd.
St. Louis, MO 63103
800-325-6666
Admissions phone: 314-658-2500
Application deadline: Rolling

ST. MARY'S COLLEGE OF CALIFORNIA
Moraga, CA 94575
510-631-4000
Application deadline: March 1

ST. MARY'S COLLEGE
Notre Dame, IN 46556
219-284-4000
Application deadline: March 1

ST. MARY'S COLLEGE OF MARYLAND
St. Mary's City, MD 20686
301-862-0200
Application deadline: January 15

ST. MARY'S UNIVERSITY OF SAN ANTONIO
One Camino Santa Maria
San Antonio, TX 78228
512-436-3011
Application deadline: August 15

ST. MICHAEL'S COLLEGE
Winooski Park
Colchester, VT 05439
802-654-2000
Admissions phone: 802-654-3000
Application deadline: (suggest February 1)

ST. NORBERT COLLEGE
De Pere, WI 54115
414-337-3005
Application deadline: June 1

ST. OLAF COLLEGE
Northfield, MN 55057-1098
507-663-2222
Admissions phone: 507-663-3025
Application deadline: February 1

ST. PETER'S COLLEGE
2641 Kennedy Boulevard
Jersey City, NJ 07306
201-915-9000
Application deadline: April 1

ST. THOMAS AQUINAS COLLEGE
Route 340
Sparkill, NY 10976
914-359-9500
Application deadline: Open

ST. VINCENT COLLEGE
Latrobe, PA 15650
412-539-9761
Application deadline: May 1

SALEM COLLEGE
PO Box 10548
Winston-Salem, NC 27108
919-721-2621
Application deadline: Rolling

SALEM STATE COLLEGE
352 Lafayette Street
Salem, MA 01970
508-741-6000
Application deadline: March 1

SALISBURY STATE UNIVERSITY
Camden Avenue
Salisbury, MD 21801
301-543-6000
Application deadline: March 1

SAM HOUSTON STATE UNIVERSITY
Huntsville, TX 77341
409-294-1111
Application deadline: Open

SAMFORD UNIVERSITY
800 Lakeshore Drive
Birmingham, AL 35229
205-870-2011
Application deadline: July 1

SAN DIEGO STATE UNIVERSITY
San Diego, CA 92182
619-594-5200
Application deadline: November 30

SAN FRANCISCO STATE UNIVERSITY
1600 Holloway Avenue
San Francisco, CA 94132
415-338-1111
Application deadline: November 30

SAN JOSE STATE UNIVERSITY
1 Washington Square
San Jose, CA 95192
408-924-1000
Application deadline: Open

SAN FRANCISCO CONSERVATORY OF MUSIC
San Francisco, CA 94122
415-564-8086
Admissions phone: 415-759-3431
Application deadline: July 1

SANGAMON STATE UNIVERSITY
Shepherd Road
Springfield, IL 62794
217-786-6600

SANTA CLARA UNIVERSITY
Santa Clara, CA 95053
408-554-4764
Admissions phone: 408-554-4700
February 1

SARAH LAWRENCE COLLEGE
Bronxville, NY 10708
914-337-0700
Admissions phone: 914-395-2510
Application deadline: February 1

INDEX

SCHOOL FOR
INTERNATIONAL TRAINING
Brattleboro, VT 05301
802-257-7751
Application deadline: Open

SCHOOL OF VISUAL ARTS
New York, NY 10010
212-679-7350
Application deadline: Open

SCRIPPS COLLEGE
1030 Columbia Avenue
Claremont, CA 91711
714-621-8000
Admissions phone: 714-621-8149
Application deadline: February 1

SEATTLE PACIFIC
UNIVERSITY
Seattle, WA 98119
206-281-2021
Application deadline: September 1

SEATTLE UNIVERSITY
Broadway and Madison
Seattle, WA 98122
206-296-6000
Application deadline: August 25

SETON HALL UNIVERSITY
South Orange Avenue
South Orange, NJ 07079
201-761-9000
Application deadline: March 1

SHIMER COLLEGE
Waukegam, IL 60079
708-623-8400
Application deadline: Open

SHIPPENSBURG UNIVERSITY
Shippensburg, PA 17257
717-532-9121
Application deadline: March 1

SIMMONS COLLEGE
300 The Fenway
Boston, MA 02115
617-738-2000
Application deadline: February 1

SIMON'S ROCK COLLEGE OF
BARD
84 Alford Road
Great Barrington, MA 01230
413-528-0771
Application deadline: July 1

SIMPSON COLLEGE
701 "C" Street
Indianola, IA 50125
515-961-1624
Application deadline: Open

SIOUX FALLS COLLEGE
1501 South Prairie
Sioux Falls, SD 57105
605-331-5000
Application deadline: Rolling

SKIDMORE COLLEGE
Saratoga Springs, NY 12866-1632
518-584-5000
Admissions phone: 518-587-7569
Application deadline: February 1

SLIPPERY ROCK UNIVERSITY
Maltby Center
Slippery Rock, PA 16057
412-738-2015
Application deadline: May 1

SMITH COLLEGE
Northampton, MA 01063
413-584-2700
Admissions phone: 413-584-0515
Application deadline: January 15

SONOMA STATE UNIVERSITY
Rohnert Park, CA 94928
707-664-2778
Application deadline: Open

SOUTH CAROLINA STATE
COLLEGE
Orangeburg, SC 29117
803-536-7185
Application deadline: July 31

INDEX

SOUTH DAKOTA SCHOOL OF MINES AND TECHNOLOGY
Rapid City, SD 57701-3995
605-394-2511
Admissions phone: 605-394-2400
Application deadline: Open (suggest January)

SOUTH DAKOTA STATE UNIVERSITY
Box 2201
Brookings, SD 57007
605-688-4121
Application deadline: Open

SOUTHEAST MISSOURI STATE UNIVERSITY
One University Plaza
Cape Girardeau, MO 63701
314-651-2255
Application deadline: June 15

SOUTHEASTERN LOUISIANA UNIVERSITY
University Station
PO Box 752
Hammond, LA 70402
504-549-2123
Application deadline: July 15

SOUTHEASTERN MASSACHUSETTS UNIVERSITY
Old Westport Road
North Dartmouth, MA 02747
508-999-8000
Application deadline: Open

SOUTHEASTERN OKLAHOMA STATE UNIVERSITY
Station A
Durant, OK 74701
405-924-0121
Application deadline: August 15

SOUTHERN ARKANSAS UNIVERSITY
Box 1382
Magnolia, AR 71753
501-235-4000
Application deadline: August 15

SOUTHERN CALIFORNIA COLLEGE
55 Fair Drive
Costa Mesa, CA 92626
714-556-3610
Application deadline: July 31

SOUTHERN CONNECTICUT STATE UNIVERSITY
501 Crescent Street
New Haven, CT 06515
203-397-4000
Application deadline: July 1

SOUTHERN UNIVERSITY AND A&M COLLEGE
Baton Rouge, LA 70813
504-771-2430
Application deadline: July 1

SOUTHERN UTAH UNIVERSITY
351 West Center
Cedar City. UT 84720
801-586-7700
Application deadline: September 1

SOUTHERN ILLINOIS UNIVERSITY
Carbondale, IL 62901
618-453-2121
Admissions phone: 618-453-4381
Application deadline: 8-10 months prior to entrance

SOUTHERN ILLINOIS UNIVERSITY, EDWARDSVILLE
Edwardsville, IL 62026
618-692-2000

SOUTHERN METHODIST UNIVERSITY
Dallas, TX 75275
214-692-2000
Admissions phone: 214-692-2058
Application deadline: January 15

SOUTHERN OREGON STATE COLLEGE
Ashland, OR 97520
503-482-6111
Application deadline: Open

SOUTHWEST BAPTIST
UNIVERSITY
Bolivar, MO 65613
417-326-5281
Application deadline: September 15

SOUTHWEST TEXAS STATE
UNIVERSITY
San Marcos, TX 78666
512-245-2111
Application deadline: August 1

SOUTHWESTERN OKLAHOMA
STATE UNIVERSITY
100 Campus Drive
Weatherford, OK 73096
405-772-6611
Application deadline: August 1

SOUTHWESTERN UNIVERSITY
University at Maple
Georgetown, TX 78626
512-863-6511
Application deadline: February 15

SPELMAN COLLEGE
Atlanta, GA 30314-3643
404-681-3643
Admissions phone: 800-241-3421
Application deadline: February 1

SPRING HILL COLLEGE
4000 Dauphin Street
Mobile, AL 36608
205-460-2121
Application deadline: August 1

SPRINGFIELD COLLEGE
263 Alden Street
Springfield, MA 01109
413-788-3100

STANFORD UNIVERSITY
Stanford, CA 94305-3005
415-723-2300
Admissions phone: 415-723-2091
Application deadline: December 15
(subject to change)

STATE UNIVERSITY OF NEW
YORK, ALBANY
Albany, NY 12222
518-442-3300
Admissions phone: 518-442-5435
Application deadline: January 15

STATE UNIVERSITY OF NEW
YORK, BINGHAMTON
Binghamton, NY 13902-6000
607-777-2171
Admissions phone: 607-777-2171
Application deadline: February 15
(suggest January 1)

STATE UNIVERSITY OF NEW
YORK, BUFFALO
Buffalo, NY 14260
716-636-2000
Admissions phone: 716-831-2111
Application deadline: Open (suggest
January 5)

STATE UNIVERSITY OF NEW
YORK, FARMINGDALE
Melville Road
Farmingdale, NY 11735
516-420-2000

STATE UNIVERSITY OF NEW
YORK, GENESEO
Geneseo, NY 14454-1471
716-245-5571
Admissions phone: 716-245-5571
Application deadline: January 15

STATE UNIVERSITY OF NEW
YORK, MORRISVILLE
Morrisville, NY 13408
315-684-6000

STATE UNIVERSITY OF NEW
YORK, ONEONTA
Oneonta, NY 13820
607-431-2500
Application deadline: Rolling

STATE UNIVERSITY OF NEW
YORK, POTSDAM
Potsdam, NY 13676
315-267-2180
Application deadline: Open

INDEX

STATE UNIVERSITY OF NEW YORK, STONY BROOK
Stony Brook, NY 11794
516-632-6000
Admissions phone: 516-632-6868
Application deadline: July 31 (suggest fall of senior year)

STATE UNIVERSITY OF NEW YORK COLLEGE, CORTLAND
PO Box 2000
Cortland, NY 13045
607-753-2011
Application deadline: February 1

STATE UNIVERSITY OF NEW YORK COLLEGE OF ARTS AND SCIENCES, BROCKPORT
Brockport, NY 14420
716-395-2751
Application deadline: January 15

STATE UNIVERSITY OF NEW YORK COLLEGE OF ARTS AND SCIENCES, NEW PALTZ
75 So. Manheim Boulevard
New Paltz, NY 12561
914-257-2121
Application deadline: May 1

STATE UNIVERSITY OF NEW YORK COLLEGE OF ARTS AND SCIENCES, OSWEGO
Oswego, NY 13126
315-341-2250
Application deadline: March 15

STATE UNIVERSITY OF NEW YORK COLLEGE OF ARTS AND SCIENCES, PURCHASE
Lincoln Avenue
Purchase, NY 10577
914-251-6000
Application deadline: August 1

STATE UNIVERSITY OF NEW YORK HEALTH SCIENCE CENTER, SYRACUSE
Syracuse, NY 13210
315-473-4570
Admissions phone: 315-473-4570
Application deadline: Varies (suggest January 1)

STEPHEN F. AUSTIN STATE UNIVERSITY
Box 13051, SFA Station
Nacogdoches, TX 75962
409-568-2011
Admissions phone: 409-568-2504
Application deadline: April 1 (suggested)

STEPHENS COLLEGE
1200 East Broadway
Columbia, MO 65215
314-442-2211
Admissions phone: 314-876-7207
Application deadline: None

STETSON UNIVERSITY
Deland, FL 32720
904-822-7000
Application deadline: March 1

STEVENS INSTITUTE OF TECHNOLOGY
Castle Point on the Hudson
Hoboken, NJ 07030
201-216-5100
Admissions phone: 201-216-5194
Application deadline: March 1

STOCKTON STATE COLLEGE
Pomona, NJ 08240
609-652-4261
Application deadline: May 1

STONEHILL COLLEGE
320 Washington Street
North Easton, MA 02357
508-238-1081
Admissions phone: 508-230-1373
Application deadline: February 15

SUL ROSS STATE UNIVERSITY
Box 0112
Alpine, TX 79832
915-837-8011
Application deadline: Open

SUSQUEHANNA UNIVERSITY
University Avenue
Selinsgrove, PA 17870
717-374-0101
Application deadline: March 15

SWARTHMORE COLLEGE
Swarthmore, PA 19081
215-328-8000
Admissions phone: 215-328-8300
Application deadline: February 15

SWEET BRIAR COLLEGE
Box B
Sweet Briar, VA 24595
804-381-6100
Application deadline: February 15

SYRACUSE UNIVERSITY
Syracuse, NY 13244-1120
315-443-1870
Admissions phone: 315-423-3611
Application deadline: February 1

TABOR COLLEGE
Hillsboro, KS 67063
316-947-3121

TAYLOR UNIVERSITY
Upland, IN 46989
317-998-2751
Application deadline: Open

TEIKYO MARYCREST UNIVERSITY
1607 West 12th Street
Davenport, IA 52804
319-326-9512
Application deadline: Open

TEMPLE UNIVERSITY
Philadelphia, PA 19122-1803
215-787-7200
Admissions phone: 215-787-7200
Application deadline: June 15

TENNESSEE STATE UNIVERSITY
Nashville, TN 37209-1561
615-320-3131
Admissions phone: 615-320-3420
Application deadline: August 1

TENNESSEE TECHNOLOGICAL UNIVERSITY
Campus Box 5006
USPS 077-460
Cookeville, TN 38505
615-372-3888
Application deadline: July 20

TENNESSEE TEMPLE UNIVERSITY
1815 Union Avenue
Chattanooga, TN 37404
615-493-4262

TEXAS A&I UNIVERSITY
Kingsville, TX 78363
512-595-3907
Application deadline: Open

TEXAS A&M UNIVERSITY
College Station, TX 77843-0100
409-845-1031
Admissions phone: 409-845-1031
Application deadline: March 1

TEXAS A&M UNIVERSITY, GALVESTON
Pelican Island
Galveston, TX 77553-1675
409-740-4400
Admissions phone: 409-740-4415
Application deadline: September 1

TEXAS CHRISTIAN UNIVERSITY
Forth Worth, TX 76129
817-921-7000
Admissions phone: 817-921-7490
Application deadline: May 1

TEXAS LUTHERAN COLLEGE
1000 West Court
Seguin, TX 78155
512-312-8000
Application deadline: August 1

TEXAS TECH UNIVERSITY
Lubbock, TX 79409
806-742-2011
Admissions phone: 806-742-3661
Application deadline: August 15

TEXAS WOMAN'S UNIVERSITY
Box 22909
Denton, TX 76204
817-898-2000
Application deadline: Open

INDEX

THOMAS AQUINAS COLLEGE
10000 North Ojai Road
Santa Paula, CA 93060
805-525-4417
Admissions phone: 805-525-4417
Application deadline: Rolling

THOMAS MORE COLLEGE
333 Thomas More Parkway
Crestview Hills, KY 41017
606-344-3332
Admissions phone: 606-344-3332
Application deadline: Rolling

TOWSON STATE UNIVERSITY
Towson, MD 21204
301 830-2000
Application deadline: March 1

TRANSYLVANIA UNIVERSITY
300 North Broadway
Lexington, KY 40508
606-233-8300
Application deadline: June 1

TRENTON STATE COLLEGE
Hillwood Lakes, NJ 08650-4700
609-771-1855
Admissions phone: 609-771-2131
Application deadline: March 1

TREVECCA NAZARENE COLLEGE
333 Murfreesboro Road
Nashville, TN 37210
615-248-1200
Application deadline: Open

TRINITY COLLEGE
300 Summit Street
Hartford, CT 06106
203-297-2000
Admissions phone: 203-297-2180
Application deadline: January 15

TRINITY COLLEGE
Franklin Street and Michigan Avenue, NE
Washington, DC 20017
202-939-5000
Application deadline: February 1

TRINITY COLLEGE
2077 Half Day Road
Deerfield, IL 60015
312-948-8980
Application deadline: Open

TRINITY UNIVERSITY
715 Stadium Drive
San Antonio, TX 78212
512-736-7011
Admissions phone: 512-736-7207
Application deadline: February 1

TROY STATE UNIVERSITY
University Avenue
Troy, AL 36082
205-566-8112
Application deadline: August 1

TUFTS UNIVERSITY
Medford, MA 02155
617-381-3170
Admissions phone: 617-381-3170
Application deadline: January 1

TULANE UNIVERSITY
New Orleans, LA 70118
504-865-5000
Admissions phone: 504-865-5731
Application deadline: January 15

TUSKEGEE UNIVERSITY
Tuskegee, AL 36088
205-727-8011
Admissions phone: 205-727-8500
Application deadline: April 15

UNION COLLEGE
Becker Hall
Schenectady, NY 12308
518-370-6112
Admissions phone: 518-370-6112
Application deadline: February 1

UNION UNIVERSITY
2447 Highway 45-Bypass
Jackson, TN 38305
901-668-1818
Application deadline: Open

INDEX

UNITED STATES AIR FORCE ACADEMY
Colorado Springs, CO 80840-5000
719-472-1818
Application deadline: January 31

UNITED STATES COAST GUARD ACADEMY
New London, CT 06320-4195
203-444-8501
Admissions phone: 203-444-8501
Application deadline: December 15

UNITED STATES MERCHANT MARINE ACADEMY
Kings Point, NY 11024
516-773-5000
Admissions phone: 516-773-5391
Application deadline: March 1

UNITED STATES MILITARY ACADEMY
West Point, NY 10996-1797
914-938-4011
Admissions phone: 914-938-4041
Application deadline: March 21 (suggest September)

UNITED STATES NAVAL ACADEMY
Annapolis, MD 21402-5018
301-267-4361
Admissions phone: 800-638-9156
Application deadline: March 1

UNIVERSITY OF AKRON
302 Buchtel Common
Akron, OH 44325
216-972-7111
Application deadline: August 10

UNIVERSITY OF ALABAMA, BIRMINGHAM
UAB Station
Birmingham, AL 35294
205-934-4011
Application deadline: Open

UNIVERSITY OF ALABAMA, HUNTSVILLE
Huntsville, AL 35899
205-895-6070
Application deadline: August 15

UNIVERSITY OF ALABAMA
Tuscaloosa, AL 35487-0132
205-348-6010
Admissions phone: 205-348-5666
Application deadline: August 1

UNIVERSITY OF ALASKA, ANCHORAGE
3211 Providence Drive
Anchorage, AK 99508
907-786-1525
Application deadline: July 1

UNIVERSITY OF ALASKA, FAIRBANKS
Fairbanks, AK 99775
907-474-7521
Admissions phone: 907-474-7521
Application deadline: August 1

UNIVERSITY OF ARIZONA
Tucson, AZ 85721
602-621-3237
Admissions phone: 602-621-3237
Application deadline: April 1 (suggest October 1)

UNIVERSITY OF ARKANSAS
22 Administration Building
Fayetteville, AR 72701
501-575-2000
Admissions phone: 501-575-5346 or 800-632-0035
Application deadline: 1 week prior to entrance

UNIVERSITY OF ARKANSAS, LITTLE ROCK
2801 S. University Avenue
Little Rock, AR 72204
501-569-3000
Application deadline: August 1

UNIVERSITY OF THE ARTS
Philadelphia, PA 19102
215-875-4808
Application deadline: April 1

UNIVERSITY OF BRIDGEPORT
Bridgeport, CT 06601
203-576-4552
Admissions phone: 203-576-4552
Application deadline: August 1

UNIVERSITY OF CALIFORNIA,
BERKELEY
Berkeley, CA 94720
510-642-6000
Admissions phone: 415-642-0569
Application deadline: November 30

UNIVERSITY OF CALIFORNIA,
DAVIS
Davis, CA 95616
916-752-1011
Admissions phone: 916-752-2971
Application deadline: November 30

UNIVERSITY OF CALIFORNIA,
IRVINE
Irvine, CA 92717
714-856-6345
Admissions phone: 714-856-6703
Application deadline: November 30

UNIVERSITY OF CALIFORNIA,
LOS ANGELES
Los Angeles, CA 90024
213-825-4321
Admissions phone: 213-825-3101
Application deadline: November 30

UNIVERSITY OF CALIFORNIA,
RIVERSIDE
900 University Ave.
Riverside, CA 92521-0118
714-787-1012
Admissions phone: 714-787-3411
Application deadline: November 30

UNIVERSITY OF CALIFORNIA,
SAN DIEGO
La Jolla, CA 92093
619-534-4831
Admissions phone: 619-534-3160
Application deadline: November 30

UNIVERSITY OF CALIFORNIA,
SAN FRANCISCO
500 Parnassus Avenue
San Francisco, CA 94143
415-476-9000

UNIVERSITY OF CALIFORNIA,
SANTA BARBARA
Santa Barbara, CA 93106
805-893-2327
Admissions phone: 805-961-2881
Application deadline: November 30

UNIVERSITY OF CALIFORNIA,
SANTA CRUZ
Santa Cruz, CA 95064
408-459-0111
Admissions phone: 408-459-4008
Application deadline: November 30

UNIVERSITY OF CENTRAL
ARKANSAS
Conway, AR 72032
501-329-2931
Application deadline: Open

UNIVERSITY OF CENTRAL
FLORIDA
400 Central Florida Boulevard
Orlando, FL 32816
407-823-2000
Application deadline: March 15

UNIVERSITY OF CHICAGO
1116 E. 59th Street
Chicago, IL 60637
312-702-8650
Admissions phone: 312-702-8650
Application deadline: January 15

UNIVERSITY OF CINCINNATI
Cincinnati, OH 45221
513-556-6000
Admissions phone: 513-556-1100
Application deadline: December 15
(suggested for assured consideration)

UNIVERSITY OF COLORADO
Boulder, CO 80309
303-492-1411
Admissions phone: 303-492-6301
Application deadline: February 15

UNIVERSITY OF COLORADO,
COLORADO SPRINGS
PO Box 7150
Colorado Springs, CO 80933
719-593-3000
Application deadline: July 1

INDEX

UNIVERSITY OF COLORADO, DENVER
1200 Larmimer Street
Denver, CO 80204
303-556-2660
Application deadline: July 22

UNIVERSITY OF CONNECTICUT
Storrs, CT 06269
203-486-2000
Admissions phone: 203-486-3137
Application deadline: April 1

UNIVERSITY OF DALLAS
Irving, TX 75062
214-721-5266
Application deadline: February 15 for fall entry; April 1 for spring entry

UNIVERSITY OF DAYTON
300 College Park
Dayton, OH 45469
513-229-1000
Admissions phone: 513-229-4411 or 800-837-7433
Application deadline: Varies (suggest 1st semester of senior year)

UNIVERSITY OF DELAWARE
Newark, DE 077580
302-451-2000
Admissions phone: 302-451-8123
Application deadline: March 1

UNIVERSITY OF DENVER
Denver, CO 80208-0132
303-871-2000
Admissions phone: 303-871-2036
Application deadline: September 1

UNIVERSITY OF THE DISTRICT OF COLUMBIA
Van Ness Campus
4200 Connecticut Avenue, NW
Washington, DC 20008
202-282-7300
Application deadline: August 1

UNIVERSITY OF EVANSVILLE
1800 Lincoln Avenue
Evansville, IN 47722
812-479-2000
Application deadline: February 15

UNIVERSITY OF FINDLAY
1000 North Main Street
Findlay, OH 45840
419-422-8313
Application deadline: August 15

UNIVERSITY OF FLORIDA
Gainesville, FL 32611
904-392-3261
Admissions phone: 904-392-1365
Application deadline: February 1

UNIVERSITY OF GEORGIA
Athens, GA 30602
404-542-3000
Admissions phone: 404-542-8776
Application deadline: 20 days prior to entrance

UNIVERSITY OF HARTFORD
200 Bloomfield Avenue
West Hartford, CT 06117
203-243-4296
Application deadline: February 1

UNIVERSITY OF HAWAII
Honolulu, HI 96822
808-956-8111
Admissions phone: 808-956-8975
Application deadline: June 1 (suggested)

UNIVERSITY OF HOUSTON
Houston, TX 77204-2161
713-749-1201
Admissions phone: 713-749-2321
Application deadline: June 15

UNIVERSITY OF IDAHO
Moscow, ID 83843
208-885-6111
Admissions phone: 208-885-6326
Application deadline: August 1

UNIVERSITY OF ILLINOIS
Urbana, IL 61801
217-333-1000
Admissions phone: 217-333-0302
Application deadline: January 1

INDEX

UNIVERSITY OF ILLINOIS, CHICAGO
601 S. Morgan
Chicago, IL 60680
312-996-7000
Application deadline: February 28

UNIVERSITY OF IOWA
Iowa City, IO 52242
319-335-3847
Admissions phone: 319-335-3847
Application deadline: May 15

UNIVERSITY OF JUDAISM, LEE COLLEGE
Los Angeles, CA 90077
213-476-9777
Admissions phone: 213-476-9777
Application deadline: January 31

UNIVERSITY OF KANSAS
Lawrence, KS 66045-1910
913-864-2700
Admissions phone: 913-864-3911
Application deadline: February 1

UNIVERSITY OF KENTUCKY
Lexington, KY 40506
606-257-9000
Admissions phone: 606-257-2000
Application deadline: June 1

UNIVERSITY OF LOUISVILLE
Louisville, KY 40292
502-588-6555
Admissions phone: 502-588-6525
Application deadline: July 30

UNIVERSITY OF LOWELL
One University Avenue
Lowell, MA 01854
508-934-4000
Application deadline: April 1

UNIVERSITY OF MAINE
Orono, ME 04469
207-581-1110
Admissions phone: 207-581-1561
Application deadline: February 1

UNIVERSITY OF MARYLAND
Office of Undergraduate Admission,
Mitchell Building
College Park, MD 20742-1672
301-405-1000
Admissions phone: 301-314-8385
Application deadline: February 15

UNIVERSITY OF MARYLAND, EASTERN SHORE
Princess Anne, MD 21853
301-651-2200
Application deadline: July 9

UNIVERSITY OF MASSACHUSETTS
Amherst, MA 01003
413-545-0111
Admissions phone: 413-545-0222
Application deadline: February 15

UNIVERSITY OF MASSACHUSETTS, BOSTON
Harbor Campus
Boston, MA 02125
617-287-5000
Application deadline: June 15

UNIVERSITY OF MEDICINE & DENTISTRY OF NEW JERSEY
100 Bergen Street
Newark, NJ 07103
201-456-5000

UNIVERSITY OF MIAMI
Coral Gables, FL 33124
305-284-2211
Admissions phone: 305-284-4323
Application deadline: March 1

UNIVERSITY OF MICHIGAN
Ann Arbor, MI 48109-1316
313-764-7433
Admissions phone: 313-764-7433

UNIVERSITY OF MICHIGAN, DEARBORN
4901 Evergreen
Dearborn, MI 48128
313-593-5000
Application deadline: Open

UNIVERSITY OF MICHIGAN, FLINT
303 E. Kearsley
Flint, MI 48502
313-762-3000
Application deadline: August 21

UNIVERSITY OF MINNESOTA, DULUTH
10 University Drive
Duluth, MN 55812
218-726-8000
Application deadline: February 1

UNIVERSITY OF MINNESOTA, MORRIS
Morris, MN 56267
612-589-6035
Application deadline: March 15

UNIVERSITY OF MINNESOTA
231 Pillsbury Drive
Minneapolis, MN 55455
612-625-5000
Admissions phone: 612-625-2008
Application deadline: Open (suggest fall prior to admission)

UNIVERSITY OF MISSISSIPPI
Oxford, MS 38677
601-232-7226
Admissions phone: 601-232-7226
Application deadline: 20 days prior to entrance

UNIVERSITY OF MISSOURI
130 Jesse Hall
Columbia, MO 65211
Admissions phone: 314-882-7786
314-882-7786
Application deadline: May 15

UNIVERSITY OF MISSOURI, KANSAS CITY
5100 Rockhill Road
Kansas City, MO 64110
816-235-1000
Application deadline: July 1

UNIVERSITY OF MISSOURI, ST. LOUIS
8001 Natural Bridge Road
St. Louis, MO 63121
314-553-5451
Application deadline: July 1

UNIVERSITY OF MONTANA
Missoula, MT 59812
406-243-0211
Admissions phone: 406-243-4277
Application deadline: July 1

UNIVERSITY OF MONTEVALLO
Station 6001
Montevallo, AL 35115
205-665-6000
Application deadline: July 31

UNIVERSITY OF NEBRASKA, LINCOLN
Lincoln, NE 68588-0415
402-472-3601
Admissions phone: 402-472-3620
Application deadline: August 1

UNIVERSITY OF NEBRASKA, OMAHA
Omaha, NE 68182
412-554-2393
Application deadline: August 1

UNIVERSITY OF NEVADA
Las Vegas, NV 89154
702-739-3443
Admissions phone: 702-739-3443
Application deadline: August 17

UNIVERSITY OF NEVADA, RENO
Reno, NV 89557
702-784-4636
Application deadline: June 15

UNIVERSITY OF NEW HAMPSHIRE
Durham, NH 03824
603-862-1234
Admissions phone: 603-862-1360
Application deadline: February 1

UNIVERSITY OF NEW MEXICO
Albuquerque, NM 87131
505-277-2446
Admissions phone: 505-277-7575
Application deadline: August 1 (April 1 medical technology)

UNIVERSITY OF NORTH ALABAMA
Wesleyan Avenue
Florence, AL 35632
205-760-4100
Application deadline: August 9

INDEX

UNIVERSITY OF NORTH CAROLINA, ASHEVILLE
One University Heights
Asheville, NC 28804
704-251-6600
Application deadline: July 1

UNIVERSITY OF NORTH CAROLINA
Chapel Hill, NC 27599-2200
919-962-2211
Admissions phone: 919-966-3621
Application deadline: January 15

UNIVERSITY OF NORTH CAROLINA
Monogram Building CB# 2200
Chapel Hill, NC 27599
919-962-2211
Application deadline: January 15

UNIVERSITY OF NORTH CAROLINA, WILMINGTON
601 S. College Road
Wilmington, NC 28403
919-395-3000
Application deadline: February 15

UNIVERSITY OF NORTH DAKOTA
Grand Forks, ND 58202
701-777-2011
Admissions phone: 701-777-3821
Application deadline: July 1

UNIVERSITY OF NORTH FLORIDA
4567 St. Johns Bluff Road, S.
Jacksonville, FL 32216
904-646-2624
Application deadline: July 15

UNIVERSITY OF NORTH TEXAS
PO Box 13797
Denton, TX 76203-3797
817-565-2000
Admissions phone: 817-565-2681
Application deadline: June 15

UNIVERSITY OF NORTHERN COLORADO
Greeley, CO 80639
303-351-1890
Application deadline: August 15

UNIVERSITY OF NORTHERN IOWA
1222 West 27th Street
Cedar Falls, IA 50614
319-273-2281
Application deadline: August 15

UNIVERSITY OF NOTRE DAME
113 Main Building
Notre Dame, IN 46556
219-239-5000
Admissions phone: 219-239-7505
Application deadline: January 8

UNIVERSITY OF OKLAHOMA
Norman, OK 73019-0430
405-325-2151
Admissions phone: 405-325-2251
Application deadline: June 1 (suggested)

UNIVERSITY OF OKLAHOMA HEALTH SCIENCE CENTER
P.O. Box 26901
Oklahoma City, OK 73190
405-271-2376

UNIVERSITY OF OREGON
Eugene, OR 97403-1217
503-346-3111
Admissions phone: 503-346-3201
Application deadline: March 1

UNIVERSITY OF OSTEOPATHIC MEDICINE AND HEALTH SCIENCES
3200 Grand Avenue
Des Moines, IA 50312
515-271-1400

UNIVERSITY OF THE PACIFIC
Stockton, CA 95211
209-946-2211
Admissions phone: 209-946-2211
Application deadline: Open

UNIVERSITY OF PENNSYLVANIA
Philadelphia, PA 19104
215-898-5000
Admissions phone: 215-898-7507
Application deadline: January 1

UNIVERSITY OF PITTSBURGH
Pittsburgh, PA 15260
412-624-4144
Admissions phone: 412-624-PITT
Application deadline: Open (March 1 if housing is desired)

UNIVERSITY OF PITTSBURGH, JOHNSTOWN
Johnstown, PA 15904
814-269-7000

UNIVERSITY OF PORTLAND
5000 North Willamette Road
Portland, OR 97203
503-283-7147
Application deadline: Open

UNIVERSITY OF PUERTO RICO
Rio Piedras, PR 00931
809-764-7260
Application deadline: December 15

UNIVERSITY OF PUGET SOUND
1500 N. Warren
Tacoma, WA 98416
206-756-3100
Admissions phone: 206-756-3211
Application deadline: March 1

UNIVERSITY OF REDLANDS
PO Box 3080
1200 East Colton Avenue
Redlands, CA 92373
714-793-2121
Application deadline: March 1

UNIVERSITY OF RHODE ISLAND
Kingston, RI 02881
401-792-1000
Admissions phone: 401-792-9800
Application deadline: March 1

UNIVERSITY OF RICHMOND
Richmond, VA 23173
804-289-8000
Admissions phone: 804-289-8640
Application deadline: February 1

UNIVERSITY OF ROCHESTER
Wilson Boulevard
Rochester, NY 14627
716-275-2121
Admissions phone: 716-275-3221
Application deadline: January 15

UNIVERSITY OF ST. THOMAS
3812 Montrose Boulevard
Houston, TX 77006
713-522-7911
Application deadline: Open

UNIVERSITY OF ST. THOMAS
2115 Summit Avenue
St. Paul, MN 55105
612-647-5265

UNIVERSITY OF SAN DIEGO
Alcala Park
San Diego, CA 92110
619-260-4600
Admissions phone: 619-260-4506
Application deadline: February 7

UNIVERSITY OF SAN FRANCISCO
Ignatian Heights
San Francisco, CA 94117
415-666-6292
Application deadline: February 15

UNIVERSITY OF SCRANTON
Scranton, PA 18510-2192
717-941-7400
Admissions phone: 717-961-7540
Application deadline: July 1

UNIVERSITY OF THE SOUTH
Sewanee, TN 37375-4004
615-598-1000
Admissions phone: 615-598-1238
Application deadline: February 15

UNIVERSITY OF SOUTH ALABAMA
307 University Boulevard
Mobile, AL 36688
205-460-6141
Application deadline: September 10

UNIVERSITY OF SOUTH CAROLINA
Columbia, SC 29208
803-777-7000
Admissions phone: 803-777-7700
Application deadline: March 1

INDEX

UNIVERSITY OF SOUTH DAKOTA
414 East Clark
Vermillion, SD 57069
605-677-5011
Application deadline: September 6

UNIVERSITY OF SOUTH FLORIDA
4202 East Fowler Avenue
Tampa, FL 33620
813-974-2011
Application deadline: June 1

UNIVERSITY OF SOUTHERN CALIFORNIA
700 Childs Way
Los Angeles, CA 90089-0911
213-740-1111
Application deadline: February 1 (December 15 if competing for scholarships)

UNIVERSITY OF SOUTHERN COLORADO
2200 Bonforte Boulevard
Pueblo, CO 81001
719-549-2100
Application deadline: July 22

UNIVERSITY OF SOUTHERN INDIANA
8600 University Boulevard
Evansville, IN 47712
812-464-8600
Application deadline: August 15

UNIVERSITY OF SOUTHERN MAINE
96 Falmouth Street
Portland, ME 04103
207-780-4141
Application deadline: July 15

UNIVERSITY OF SOUTHERN MISSISSIPPI
Box 5011 Southern Station
Hattiesburg, MS 39406
601-266-4111
Application deadline: August 10

UNIVERSITY OF TENNESSEE
320 Student Services Building
Knoxville, TN 37996-0230
615-974-2184
Admissions phone: 615-974-2184
Application deadline: July 1 (February 1 if applying for scholarship or financial aid)

UNIVERSITY OF TENNESSEE, MARTIN
Martin, TN 38238
901-587-7020
Application deadline: August 1

UNIVERSITY OF TEXAS, ARLINGTON
Arlington, TX 76019
817-273-2011
Admissions phone: 817-273-2118
Application deadline: 3 months prior to entrance

UNIVERSITY OF TEXAS
Austin, TX 78712
512-471-3434
Admissions phone: 512-471-1711
Application deadline: March 1

UNIVERSITY OF TEXAS, EL PASO
El Paso, TX 79968
915-747-5000
Admissions phone: 915-747-5576
Application deadline: 60 days prior to entrance (suggested)

UNIVERSITY OF TEXAS, GALVESTON
301 University Boulevard
Galveston, TX 77550
409-761-1011

UNIVERSITY OF TEXAS HEALTH SCIENCE CENTER
PO Box 20036
Houston, TX 77225
713-792-4975

UNIVERSITY OF TEXAS, SAN ANTONIO
San Antonio, TX 78285
512-691-4011
Application deadline: July 1

INDEX

UNIVERSITY OF TEXAS
SOUTHWESTERN MEDICAL
CENTER, DALLAS
5 Harry Hines Boulevard
Dallas, TX 75235
214-688-3404

UNIVERSITY OF TOLEDO
2801 Bancroft
Toledo, OH 43606
419-537-4242
Application deadline: Rolling

UNIVERSITY OF TULSA
600 S. College Ave.
Tulsa, OK 74104
918-631-2307 or 800-331-3050
Admissions phone: 918-631-2307
Application deadline: Open (suggest early as possible)

UNIVERSITY OF UTAH
Salt Lake City, UT 84112
801-581-7281
Admissions phone: 801-581-7281
Application deadline: July 1

UNIVERSITY OF VERMONT
Burlington, VT 05401-0160
802-656-3480
Admissions phone: 802-656-3370
Application deadline: February 1

UNIVERSITY OF VIRGINIA
Charlottesville, VA 22906
804-982-3200
Admissions phone: 804-924-7751
Application deadline: January 2

UNIVERSITY OF
WASHINGTON
1410 NE Campus Parkway
Seattle, WA 98195
206-543-2100
Admissions phone: 206-543-9686
Application deadline: February 1

UNIVERSITY OF WEST
FLORIDA
11000 University Parkway
Pensacola, FL 32514
904-474-2000
Application deadline: June 1

UNIVERSITY OF WISCONSIN
A.W. Peterson Office Building
750 University Avenue
Madison, WI 53706
608-262-1234
Application deadline: February 1

UNIVERSITY OF WISCONSIN,
EAU CLAIRE
105 Garfield Avenue
Eau Claire, WI 54701
715-836-5415

UNIVERSITY OF WISCONSIN,
GREEN BAY
2420 Nicolet Drive
Green Bay, WI 54311
414-465-2000
Application deadline: August 15

UNIVERSITY OF WISCONSIN,
LA CROSSE
1725 State Street,
La Crosse, WI 54601
608-785-8000
Application deadline: Open

UNIVERSITY OF WISCONSIN,
MILWAUKEE
Milwaukee, WI 53201
414-229-1122
Admissions phone: 414-229-3800
Application deadline: None (suggest June 30)

UNIVERSITY OF WISCONSIN,
OSHKOSH
800 Algoma Boulevard
Oshkosh, WI 54901
414-424-0202

UNIVERSITY OF WISCONSIN,
PARKSIDE
Box 2000
Kenosha, WI 53141
414-553-2000

UNIVERSITY OF WISCONSIN,
RIVER FALLS
River Falls, WI 54022
715-426-3500
Application deadline: February 1

INDEX

UNIVERSITY OF WISCONSIN, STEVENS POINT
Main Street
Stevens Point, WI 54481
715-346-0123
Application deadline: Open

UNIVERSITY OF WISCONSIN, WHITEWATER
800 West Main Street
Whitewater, WI 53190
414-472-1234
Application deadline: Rolling

UNIVERSITY OF WYOMING
Admissions Office, Box 3435
Laramie, WY 82071
307-766-1121
Admissions phone: 307-766-5160 or 800-DIAL-WYO 342-5996-in WY and border states
Application deadline: August 10

UPSALA COLLEGE
Prospect Street
East Orange, NJ 07019
201-266-7000
Application deadline: Open

URSINUS COLLEGE
Collegeville, PA 19426
215-489-4111
Application deadline: March 1

UTAH STATE UNIVERSITY
Logan, UT 84322-1600
801-750-1107
Application deadline: One month prior to entrance

VALPARAISO UNIVERSITY
Valparaiso, IN 46383
219-464-5011
Admissions phone: 219-464-5011
Application deadline: August 15

VANDERBILT UNIVERSITY
Nashville, TN 37240
615-322-7311
Admissions phone: 615-322-2561
Application deadline: January 15

VASSAR COLLEGE
Poughkeepsie, NY 12601
914-437-7000
Admissions phone: 914-437-7300
Application deadline: January 15

VILLANOVA UNIVERSITY
Villanova, PA 19085-1672
215-645-4500
Admissions phone: 215-645-4000
Application deadline: January 15

VIRGINIA COMMONWEALTH UNIVERSITY
914 W. Franklin Street
Richmond, VA 23284
804-367-0100
Application deadline: February 1

VIRGINIA MILITARY INSTITUTE
Lexington, VA 24450
703-464-7000
Admissions phone: 703-464-7211
Application deadline: March 1

VIRGINIA POLYTECHNIC INSTITUTE AND STATE UNIVERSITY
Blacksburg, VA 24061-0202
703-231-6000
Admissions phone: 703-961-6267
Application deadline: February 1

WABASH COLLEGE
PO Box 352
Crawfordsville, IN 47933
317-362-1400
Application deadline: Open

WAKE FOREST UNIVERSITY
Winston-Salem, NC 27109
919-759-5000
Admissions phone: 919-759-5201
Application deadline: January 15

WALLA WALLA COLLEGE
204 S. College Avenue
College Place, WA 99324
509-527-2615
Application deadline: Open

INDEX

WALSH COLLEGE
Canton, OH 44720
216-499-7090
Application deadline: Open

WARTBURG COLLEGE
222 9th Street, NW
Waverly, IA 50677
319-352-8200
Application deadline: June 1

WASHBURN UNIVERSITY
1700 College
Topeka, KS 66621
913-295-6300
Application deadline: July 1

WASHINGTON AND JEFFERSON COLLEGE
Washington, PA 15301
412-223-6107
Admissions phone: 412-223-6025
Application deadline: March 1

WASHINGTON AND LEE UNIVERSITY
Lexington, VA 24450
703-463-8400
Admissions phone: 703-463-8710
Application deadline: February 1

WASHINGTON COLLEGE
Washington Avenue
Chestertown, MD 21620
301-778-2800
Application deadline: March 1

WASHINGTON STATE UNIVERSITY
Pullman, WA 99164
509-335-3564
Admissions phone: 509-335-5586
Application deadline: May 1

WASHINGTON UNIVERSITY
Campus Box 1089, Brookings Drive
St. Louis, MO 63130
314-935-6000 or 800-638-0700
Application deadline: February 1

WAYNE STATE UNIVERSITY
5980 Cass Avenue
3E HNJ Student Services
Detroit, MI 48202
313-577-2424
Application deadline: August 1

WEBB INSTITUTE OF NAVAL ARCHITECTURE
Glen Cove, NY 11542
516-671-2213
Admissions phone: 516-671-2213
Application deadline: February 15

WEBER STATE UNIVERSITY
Odgen, UT 84408
801-626-6000

WELLESLEY COLLEGE
Wellesley, MA 02181
617-235-0320
Admissions phone: 617-235-0320
Application deadline: February 1

WELLS COLLEGE
Aurora, NY 13026
315-364-3264
Admissions phone: 315-364-3264
Application deadline: March 1

WESLEYAN COLLEGE
4760 Forsyth Road
Macon, GA 31297
912-477-1110
Application deadline: March 15

WESLEYAN UNIVERSITY
Wyllis Avenue
Middletown, CT 06459
203-347-9411
Admissions phone: 203-344-7900
Application deadline: January 15

WEST CHESTER UNIVERSITY
West Chester, PA 19383
215-436-1000
Application deadline: Rolling

WEST TEXAS STATE UNIVERSITY
Canyon, TX 79016
806-656-2020
Application deadline: open

INDEX

WEST VIRGINIA UNIVERSITY
Morgantown, WV 26506-6001
304-293-0111
Admissions phone: 800-344-WVU1 (in state)
Application deadline: March 1

WESTERN CAROLINA UNIVERSITY
Cullowhee, NC 28723
704-227-7211
Application deadline: June 1

WESTERN KENTUCKY UNIVERSITY
Bowling, Green, KY 42101
502-745-0111
Application deadline: August 1

WESTERN MARYLAND COLLEGE
Westminster, MD 21157
301-848-7000
Application deadline: March 15

WESTERN MICHIGAN UNIVERSITY
Kalamazoo, MI 49008
616-387-1000
Admissions phone: 616-387-2000
Application deadline: August 15

WESTERN NEW ENGLAND COLLEGE
Springfield, MA 01119
413-782-3111
Application deadline: open

WESTERN OREGON STATE COLLEGE
345 N. Monmouth Avenue
Monmouth, OR 97361
503-838-8000
Application deadline: April 15

WESTERN STATE COLLEGE OF COLORADO
Gunnison, CO 81231
303-943-2119

WESTERN WASHINGTON UNIVERSITY
Old Main 200
Bellingham, WA 98225
206-676-3000
Application deadline: March 1

WESTFIELD STATE COLLEGE
Western Avenue
Westfield, MA 01086
413-568-3311
Application deadline: March 1

WESTMINSTER COLLEGE
New Wilmington, PA 16172
412-946-8761
Application deadline: Open

WESTMONT COLLEGE
955 La Paz Road
Santa Barbara, CA 93108
805-565-6000
Application deadline: June 1

WHEATON COLLEGE
501 East College Avenue
Wheaton, IL 60187-5593
708-752-5000
Admissions phone: 312-682-5005
Application deadline: February 15

WHEATON COLLEGE
Norton, MA 02766
508-285-7722
Admissions phone: 508-285-7722 x251
Application deadline: February 1

WHITMAN COLLEGE
Walla Walla, WA 99362
509-527-5111
Admissions phone: 509-527-5176
Application deadline: February 15

WHITTIER COLLEGE
13406 E. Philadelphia St.
Whittier, CA 90608
310-907-4200213-693-0771
Admissions phone: 310-907-4238
Application deadline: February 14 (priority date)

WHITWORTH COLLEGE
Spokane, WA 99251
509-466-3212
Application deadline: March 1

INDEX

WICHITA STATE UNIVERSITY
1845 Fairmount
Wichita, KS 67208
316-689-3456
Application deadline: Open

WIDENER UNIVERSITY
Chester, PA 19013
215-499-4000
Admissions phone: 215-499-4125
Application deadline: March 1

WILLAMETTE UNIVERSITY
900 State Street
Salem, OR 97301
503-370-6300
Admissions phone: 503-370-6303
Application deadline: February 15

WILLIAM JENNINGS BRYAN COLLEGE
PO Box 7000
Dayton, TN 37321
615-775-2041
Application deadline: Rolling

WILLIAM PATERSON COLLEGE OF NEW JERSEY
300 Pompton Road
Wayne, NJ 07470
201-595-2000
Application deadline: June 30

WILLIAM PENN COLLEGE
201 Trueblood Avenue
Oskaloosa, IA 52577
515-673-1001
Application deadline: Open

WILLIAM SMITH COLLEGE
(see Hobart)

WILLIAMS COLLEGE
Williamstown, MA 01276
413-597-3131
Admissions phone: 413-597-2211
Application deadline: January 1

WILMINGTON COLLEGE
320 Dupont Highway
New Castle, DE 19720
302-328-9401
Application deadline: June 30

WINTHROP COLLEGE
701 Oakland Avenue
Rock Hill, SC 29733
803-323-2211
Application deadline: May 1

WISCONSIN LUTHERAN
Milwaukee, WI 53226
414-774-8620
Application deadline: Open

WITTENBERG UNIVERSITY
PO Box 720
Springfield, OH 45501
513-327-6231
Application deadline: March 15

WOFFORD COLLEGE
429 North Church Street
Spartanburg, SC 29303
803-597-4000
Application deadline: February 1

WORCESTER POLYTECHNIC INSTITUTE
100 Institute Road
Worcester, MA 01609
508-831-5000
Admissions phone: 508-831-5286
Application deadline: February 15

WRIGHT STATE UNIVERSITY
Dayton, OH 45435-0001
513-873-3333
Application deadline: Open

XAVIER UNIVERSITY
3800 Victory Parkway
Cincinnati, OH 45207
(513) 745-3000
Application deadline: August 1

YALE UNIVERSITY
149 Elm Street, 1502A Yale Station
New Haven, CT 06520
203-432-4771
Admissions phone: 203-432-1900
Application deadline: December 31

YESHIVA UNIVERSITY
New York, NY 10033-3299
212-960-5400
Admissions phone: 212-960-5277
Application deadline: April 15

YOUNGSTOWN STATE UNIVERSITY
Youngstown, OH 44555
216- 742-3150
Application deadline: August 15

NOTES

NOTES

NOTES

NOTES

NOTES

NOTES

NOTES